MEETING THE "IS"

MEETING THE "IS"

Memories and Cogitations

Miriam Hope

Celo Valley Books
Burnsville NC 28714

This book can be ordered by sending $12.95 plus $2.00 shipping and handling to: Ms. Miriam Hope, Route 2, Box 574, Lake Park GA 31636.

Library of Congress Catalog Card Number 92-71976
ISBN 0-923687-21-1.

CONTENTS

LIST OF ILLUSTRATIONS

ACKNOWLEDGEMENTS

Publication of this book was made possible by a bequest from an uncle and aunt of mine, Charles and Blanche Collier. I owe them thanks not only for the money, but also for some lovely hospitality they gave me and my children when the kids were growing up.

I must say, too, that this book has been greatly improved by the good work of my publisher, Diana Donovan. It is no easy task to suggest to an opinionated writer like me that an idea may not be as clear as it should be, or that there's a *non sequitur* in the text. Diana managed this with tact, clear perceptions and a real sensitivity to the integrity of what I'm trying to say. Beyond that, she has used her expertise to set up what had been a rather hodge-podge manuscript with different styles juxtaposed, into what we hope is now a manageable expression of my lifetime of experiences and ideas. I am deeply grateful to her.

The world's a mess, and so's the human heart,
But God does find a home within
        and sends us out to try again.
                                from *Thoughts at Christmas*
                                by Miriam Hope

PREFACE

When my son Forrest, my first-born, left home, I gave him a hand-sized stone that I had picked up along the Sacramento River. It was much worn, smooth, and seemed to me to have grown by the grinding into a lovely and satisfying shape.

I tried to tell him the meanings I had come to find in the stone, how it gave solid form to an idea I had that human beings are ground down by life bit by bit, day by day, struggle by struggle, until the grinding gives us a meaning beyond our original intent. When we are young, each decision seems sharp and positive, made forever, a thing of great import. It is only gradually we find that the same decisions have to be made again and again and again, in different ways, in different times, against the changing realities of our living.

Some twelve year later, I checked with Forrest as to whether or not he'd understood what I was trying to get across with the stone. He hadn't. The idea seemed new to him, but by now worth considering. He thought, though, that the grinding usually made people ugly, splintered them, distorted them. We do in fact have basic differences in outlook.

Now, as I'm coming into my seventies, I begin to think that the major buffetings of life may well be over for me. Has my life attained some unity of form, some quiet grace of meaning?

Throughout my adult life there have been times when an experience or an insight gripped my attention and called on me to form it into words that I could put down on paper. Once in a while, if the writing was recognizably a poem or a story, I sent it off with a self-addressed envelope, but the envelope always came back with a polite rejection. Aside from a brief disappointment, those rejections didn't discourage me much. I've delighted in my writings because they seem to capture a central truth about my being at that particular time and circumstance.

Now that I've edged out of the main field of active work and am looking back over my life, these writings have served as live reference points for what was really going on at one period and another. Rather like the numbered dots that children can connect to make a picture of something.

I do think I see a picture appearing out of the years of my past living, a central theme that holds the whole thing together. I call it "Meeting the IS". I know that's an awkward phrase grammatically: the IS has to come into the idea at an offset angle, never quite on the same plane as the rest of the phrase. But that's part of the reality of my experience. There has entered into my living a Being which remains outside me and my experience, which has its own central spring of living reality and which enters my life always at its own unexpected angle.

In the Bible story of God's relationships with the people of Israel, God's revelation to Moses in the burning bush remains important. In that revelation, God tells Moses "I am who I am", and further instructs him that "Yahweh" is the name by which He wants to be known for all generations to come. The Jerusalem Bible supplies a scholarly discussion* of the name "Yahweh". As a conclusion to the etymological consideration it says: "There seems little doubt that it (Yahweh) is an archaic form of the verb 'to be'." I hope I can claim, then, a precedent beyond reproach for my use of the verb/noun IS as an expression for the Being who has entered into my consciousness time and time again in many variations of form.

But there's also a less transcendent connotation for my "Meeting the IS". It means meeting each part of the reality that comes at me — the small child on the swing who calls for my attention, the woman on the bus who wants to talk to me, the angry response from my fellow worker — as fully as possible on its own terms, with its own complexities and style of being. I want to take it into my consciousness with its own full integrity of being, not smoothed over and pre-digested by how I might want to see it.

Finally, let me note that the "meeting" indicates that I at least

---

*Exodus 3:14, footnote *h*

try to meet whatever-it-is that comes along with my fullest awareness and response. I do not want to just let things flow by me or carry me along in a least-resistance type of passivity.

What I am offering the reader here is a chance to share in the parts of my past living that strike me as being significant.

Along with my current memories and thoughts I have inserted the earlier writings. I have tried to form a setting for them so that the transitions are not too abrupt and that relationships are apparent. I may not always be successful, but it is more important to me to keep the fullest possible flavor and integrity of the original expression than to strive for one consistent level or mode. As a bit of help for the reader, pieces of writing that have been thus transported from their original time and place are set in san serif type.

Beyond that, I am inviting you, the reader, to "ride loose in the saddle" as you come with me through this story of my living. Feel free to pick up whatever you can find that has any promise of interest or worth for your own living.

IN THE MOUNTAINS

The summer before I was fifteen, my family took a hiking, back-packing trip up into the Oregon Cascades. By the second night out, sleeping under the stars and the trees, I found myself feeling at home as I had never done before, and when we came in our final days into the magnificent alpine country at the foot of Mt. Jefferson, I was given an unforgettable experience of the presence of God.

As we walked along the trail, lightly marked through carpets of small flowers, with the dark fir trees and snow patches standing separate but fully combined in the total scene, I was filled with an intensity of response to the beauty around me. At some point I found myself aware in a new way of a living reality in each of the separate, multitudinous realities around me — each tree and branch and needle, each stone, each swell of the water in the small creek. Each was living from within; all simultaneous and real, making a harmony and standing together in relation to each other. I was a part of that, too. I felt my own inner living reality come alive in response to those others around me, so that I was caught up in something beyond the limits of the self that I was used to. My consciousness, still rooted firmly in my body and in who I was, reached out in a great surge of glory to gather in all the other pieces of reality around me, to feel as much as I could each different, separate way of being, and to respond to an all-encompassing, nameless Spirit that gave each one of us our reality, and that held us all, vibrant with life, in this total harmony of meaning.

My sister, inveterate biologist that she was, had picked two little flowers to observe and classify, and before she threw them into our campfire she handed them to me. As I looked at them, lying there in my hand, I saw not only the small petals and asymmetric leaves, but became aware of infinitely tiny parts flowing through them and in them, giving them the life that was theirs, making the solid reality of their being, and it came to my mind that they were perfect, just as they were. Each of them had been pushed back, intruded upon by other life around them; the leaves were flawed, irregular. But they were in themselves (and also as part of the total harmony) absolutely where they should be in time and space, totally, in every part. They were "living" — even in their forms now cut off from the roots that gave them life — in a spirit of such immensity and splendor that every piece took part, and I myself was swept up into a glorious joy that felt as though it would make my spirit burst.

I don't think I felt the Spirit as a person, but I certainly responded as a person, and I felt myself responded to. It occurred to me that no matter what griefs, miseries, sorrows I might run into during the rest of my life, there would be no weight which could outweigh this gift of joy, even for this one time of sensing.

I had in my mind some images gained from church and Sunday school, and it surprised and puzzled me that in the Spirit I could feel no trace of the Jesus I had tried to reach toward. The Spirit was fiercer, more terrible, more immense, more intensely alive in itself than anything I had learned or thought of Jesus. And yet, as I say, there was soul-filling joy and a feeling of being finally, eternally "at home" — where I was known utterly in every recess of my being, where all falsehood and phony defense fell away, no longer needed, no longer desired.

I tried to find a name for the Spirit, but there was none. There was only the reality of its being, without beginning, without end, without bounds or explanation. The word that came to my mind was IS.

* * *

It was an experience that has formed a kind of baseline for my life, an experience so entire that if it is false, then I am also false. I have not always been able to integrate it into my living, and there are still times when it seems somehow to be separate from and in contrast to the Christian insights that have come to be more and more valuable to me.

Maybe if I'd been having a more successful life as a teenager, the experience might have been filed away and at least partially forgotten. Or if I'd been part of a satisfying church group where I was in touch with people who had live contact with deep spiritual things, someone might have been able to help me translate it into more orthodox terms that could have been shared with other people's religious experiences. As it was, it remained like a live coal in my own heart, an infinitely precious thing which warmed me and stirred my heart, but I couldn't seem to find any way to act on it.

The self which I'd built up from babyhood in response to the bombardments of life around me was not really the same self which had sprung to life in response to my meeting with the IS. They weren't altogether foreign to each other, but the new one was far out and away the strong, true, sure one. It felt whole and right, whereas the old one was all hung up with self-consciousness and self-derision, and a whole mess of petty entanglements. But it was the old one that had all the habits and the accepted place in my world of family and school and friends and acquaintances. After I met that IS up in the mountains I knew that that was where I belonged, that I should be striving to get closer to it. At that time the only way I knew to get to it was out in the woods, and I didn't have the guts to find a way to go out into the woods to live.

I didn't have the guts even to tell anyone about it. My mother was a clear-headed and vigorous person who wanted to help all her children be independent and grow in their own ways. But she was also a strong personality with very definite ideas about how things should be done. She wasn't really good at easing her way into how someone else might be feeling about things. She tended to charge directly at a problem presented to her, putting herself mentally in the same position that she understood the other person to be facing and then using her own critical intellect and her sure competence to solve the problem. She seemed to have almost no understanding of people who weren't at all sure of themselves, who might be trying to operate from an uncertain, groping position in which rather fragile values were trying to develop roots. The thought of laying out my experience and my feelings and desires about it, all inarticulate as they were at that time, was more than I could face. And it seems that for one reason or another she was the dominant personality in my life. It was to her that I looked for approval. It was her values that I had accepted to judge myself and my living.

So for some eight years (until my twenty-third year) I lived a double life. Most of the time I was Miriam Collier, hard-working and highly approved student, first at high school and then at college. I was great in the classroom; I understood what the teachers and textbooks were trying to get across, I got it, and I could return it on demand. I wasn't just a grind, though. I could deliver the goods with humor and beyond the point of normal expectation. I really understood the stuff and could use it fairly creatively. It was quite exhilarating and fun, and I did absorb things that turned out to be very useful in my later life.

But my social life was miserable. I almost always chose some unsuspecting boy whom I carried in my heart with terrible sensitivity and unworldly passion, but I never did anything about it, not even talk to other girls about what I was feeling. I developed a few friendships which are still important to me, but at the time I didn't push them into the areas of deeper meaning where I needed someone to talk with.

My other self, the one I had found in the woods, stayed alive in pieces and patches. When I was by myself I could find it again in the sight of a tree or the green grass growing. I used to have a blade of grass in my Latin book as a bookmark, and it let me remember the live beauty out there. Whenever one blade got too old and dried up I'd replace it with a new, green one. But the real tie I kept was that each night, before I went to bed, I'd sit down by my open window and look out over our yard and the trees and the night sky. I'd let my spirit go out there into the dark and the calm, along with the growing things. God was always there still. S/he* never abandoned me. S/he

---

*I've found it necessary to develop a set of ambisexual pronouns. This subjective form, which I pronounce "see", appeared in something I read and struck

always received again that bit of life that was me, cleaned off the mess and the ugliness and the faulty fears, and let me just be there with Hirm. I made no special effort to ask for forgiveness. Just by entering the space where life and beauty were, everything which was not of God dropped off. Forgiveness and cleansing were given to me every night for some eight years.

I don't know whether just by myself I would ever have managed to make the step to choosing integrity in my living. But I got a great shot of vigor and spirit from reading the stories of William Saroyan. The godliness and grace he reported finding in plain people all over San Francisco and Fresno and the world felt to me like the same living reality as the IS I'd met in the mountains. I guess the identity isn't obvious or unavoidable, but it certainly struck me as real. It felt like the same home grounds. So here was someone else to give me confirmation about what I'd been feeling. Here was someone else who had met the same God I had, who wasn't afraid to talk about Hirm, and who seemed to be living among people with a style based on that Spirit. I knew Saroyan might be just a writer writing — most of the critics took his religious message very lightly, just as a kind of too-simple optimism that pleased the readers — but I finally figured out that that part of it didn't matter. Even if he didn't really believe what he was writing about, I did, and it was time, and past time, that I got around to living that way. I resigned my teaching job, spent some months with odd jobs in my home town, spent one week by myself up in the mountains again,

---

me as being simple and useful. The other forms are, so far as I know, my own invention: objective, hirm; reflexive, hirmself; possessive, hirs; predicate adjective, hirs. I'll be using these throughout the book when I'm referring to an individual person who may be either masculine or feminine. In the case of God, I want to imply both genders at the same time (insofar as there is gender), leaving space for manifestations which may seem at times more definitely masculine or definitely feminine in our human understandings. The universal IS does retain for me an almost impersonal reality, too, so that I would be tempted to consider a form like "s/he/it", except that that has disastrous effects in contemporary usage. At any rate I feel that ambisexual pronouns actually enrich the meanings of God, and in general usage they help me be "inclusive" without the endless detours of thought that occur if I insert an "or she", "or herself" and so on.

visited my sister at the University of Missouri and then, at the age of twenty-three, took off for San Francisco, seeking the kingdom of God.

TRIP BY BUS

I

Night Travel

Snow rushes at the broad window of the bus.
I am leaving, I am leaving the city of my youth —
the house where I have lived, the dishes in the kitchen,
the eyes of my mother.

So much, so much I leave behind me
of despair and unfulfillment;
so much, so much that cries within me for amending;

So much which never can be changed,
never set right,
never made whole —

never, in all the wide world's wandering.

II

Dawn Beside the Pacific

O God! Thou Life! Thou Never-to-be-forgotten!
How can I be sad, how can I sorrow
even for evil done,
when beauty sings so sweet, so clear
throughout this ocean sunrise?

III

The Journey Finished

Stir not the blind embers of despair,
call not shame back, nor defeat.
Sing in the time of the singing,
rejoice in the joy of present strength!

Gladly do I come to Thee, God —
gladly, with the joy of singing on my lips.
The tangled error and despair no more about me,
swept away in the sweet flood of beauty known,
again do I behold Thee, God.
With rejoicing is my heart full.

Photo by P.M. Collier.

Miriam in the mountains, 1934.
On the Oregon Skyline Trail. The South Sister in the background.

SECTION TWO
IN SAN FRANCISCO

ADVENTURES IN LIVING

I stood on a sidewalk on Clayton St., part way up Twin Peaks, and looked out over the city of San Francisco with a sudden fierce increase of consciousness. Fog lay over the city, the spires of Golden Gate Bridge rising up through it, grayly. The beauty of it, the strange, tangled beauty of it, the reality of the parts — this, and this, and this and that other, each clear and distinct, real, living — came together in a sudden synthesis so that I found myself again in that strange ecstasy of feeling so keen as to be almost painful. The wire mesh fence beside me, and the winter-old brown bush down the hill below it, fell into their places in the living pattern, and I reached out my spirit eagerly, like a searching tree root, to bring this living reality entire into my own being.

I had started down again, in the great freedom of my almost unbudgeted time, toward the little waitress job in the city which gave me enough money to buy food and pay for the small room in which I lived. Two miles down into the city, this way and that, along the sidewalks, by the stores and eating places, filled with men, women, and children, each separate but combining into endless variations on the theme of human life on the earth. There had been the old Italian who came into the same little lunch counter each morning for his breakfast glass of red wine, commenting upon some pretty girl just leaving the place, and bringing down upon himself the jovial comments of the proprietor about being eighty-three ("Yes, eighty-three years

"Down to the sea in ships," he said;
Down to the city, I —
To the dead walls, and the hearts within them,
To the tired shopgirls and the mannequins' stares,
To the ten-cent* hamburger joints!

———————
*This was 1941–1942.

* * *

Moment to moment flying,
sweetly singing o'er the earth,
my heart's blood is buying;

my heart knows its worth.

* * *

The city is a city that I love, and the streets are full of life. I walk
along, toward my dwelling place and a number of small errands
on the way, and I try to take and hold within my consciousness
the rhythms, the complete mode of being of this many-faced,
ever-shifting thing which is the city, lying not separately by itself,
but also having a clear, bright star over it, and the evening sky.

* * *

A little dog who barks on the
street at night, on the dark and
lighted street, under the stars;
speaking to the earth and the
solid things of it, stating his
presence with a sure and
native voice.

old!") and still having both his little glass of morning wine, and his eye for the pretty girls all right.

There had been the thin little boy, struggling on new roller skates, who had accepted wordlessly my offered hand and had left a black smudge on my wrist, which I discovered later with the greatest delight when I was using the washroom in the public library.

There was never any telling what small adventure would unroll before me, or around me, or with me, or what strange truth would flick a tiny portion of itself into my searching vision, so that I would have to stand still for a while in the sun, staring at the dirty brick wall or the beach pebble, or the blade of grass, following the child farther up the street to try to enlarge the sudden suggestion of meaning, engraving it on my memory, absorbing it into my expanding consciousness.

There was a fierce exhilaration in this way of life, this search. I felt as though, bumping along with a bare four cylinders, I had discovered under the hood of my spirit a magnificent roaring sixteen cylinders of power. I lived freely, and on my own terms, walking through the earth with deep involvement — if you looked at things from the position of the Infinite. And yet if you looked at things from the usual three-meals-a-day, the "and how are you today, Mrs. Olsen?" position, I was almost totally unentangled in the usual cares of living.

The two hours a day I put in at the lunchroom at the Medico-Dental Building supplied me with money enough for my food and room. My real work, and my recreation, and my passion was this search for Truth, this hunting for God and for meaning in the world of humankind. I had no long-range plan of attack. I simply walked out into the world with my consciousness as fully alive as possible and followed whatever bit of meaning turned up as long as I could, or as long as it provided spiritual nourishment.

I had not especially intended to start writing. But it had not been long after I began this search in San Francisco that I had wanted the little typewriter I had used in college, and found myself first simply talking on it, and then as some idea or another would come to form within me, making small poems upon it. The typewriter and the writing were very dear to me

SIMPLE SONGS OF A SIMPLE SPIRIT

Simply as the rain falls
I would sing to God;

simple as clear rain drops
I would have my songs.

* * *

So much I do not know,
so easily think myself with knowledge,
and see before me suddenly the gaping lack,
and know myself a fool,
and laugh.

* * *

How strange that we should all be blind
and have no eyes nor ears;
how strange that we should know no peace
and weep such sad, salt tears!

* * *

Life?
I will believe the sun
before I believe a man of learning.
Life? Life is good!

Death, do you say?
Death — and fruitfulness.
For they are lovely inseparables;
they are beautiful siblings,*
one and the same.

* * *

The one word, God,
is all that's really true —
and the rest but little melodies
played upon the single string.

*For the sake of contemporary usage, I have changed the original "brothers" to "siblings." It seems to work all right.

now, but I had not chosen them; they seemed to have happened as part of the way of living.

The amazing thing about my new lifestyle was the response. People seemed eager to talk to me. There was the middle-aged woman standing next to me on Market St. to watch the Columbus Day parade who had urged me to come along up for a cup of coffee at her daughter's apartment just around the corner. There was the deaf-mute I had met at the zoo, who had got out his pad and pencil and begun an extensive conversation as we sat together on a bench and then moved along from one area to another.

I would not have been at all surprised to have met hostility, or suspicion, or "What makes you think I'd want to talk to the likes of you?". But when I walked out in openness and love, and spoke to people just as one anonymous human wayfarer sharing this particular moment and place, there was invariably a response of friendliness and warmth, a kind of eagerness to take part in communication.

Most miraculous of all had been the encounter with Sgt. Seffert, sitting on the sidewalk of Market St., back leaned against the wall, with a little cup beside him. It had been fairly soon after I came to San Francisco and I was still feeling timid and uncertain, so I had at first simply walked on by him, a white-haired man with a beard, begging on the street. There had been something in my new spirit, though, which had insisted that I meet this piece of life head on, so I had turned back to where he sat, said "How are you?", and extended my hand to him.

He had looked up, direct and clear-eyed, and taken my hand in his. We had talked for a while at the two levels, and then I had settled myself on the pavement next to him for further conversation. He told me he'd just got back from picking hops in Oregon, but that work was slowing down now and it would be getting cold soon up there. Besides he'd got too old to do the kind of fast picking that used to give him a fair nest egg of money for the winter. He told me about having been a sergeant in World War I, and philosophized a bit about human life in general and his own in particular. "It's really been pretty good," he said. "Even like this." And he waved his hand from our place on the pavement up toward the crowds of unseeing people coming on past us.

To have a woman's body
and not bear children
is a sorrow;

but one has life
(a single life, which ends)
and in the living is much richness.

* * *

How delightful and ridiculous it is
after dwelling in the infinite,
to find oneself still foolish-finite;
To walk in almost selfless consciousness
and stumble over the curb,
sprawling on the unastounded pavement,
and scraping to the red
two knuckles on the left hand!

* * *

They go down in the morning, making the city run, filling the offices and buildings, standing behind counters, sending out lists and filing away forms, and then come home at night on the streetcars jammed to the doors and beyond, tight-packed and weary. It is quite a sight to watch the city of commerce being built in the morning and struggling back to its multiform home in the evening. It is a city built each day, dispersed each night, and its inhabitants are its lifeblood. They do not feel like cogs in a meaningless machine — nor should they. Each has hirs living circle of faces and duties, each hirs home to receive hirm at night, and even viewed from the unentangled distance of impersonal consciousness, the city is less a machine than an infinitely complex organism, living stuff, functioning with inevitable coordination like the pulsing ebb and flow of blood in one living body.

At some point the main sharing seemed to be ended and I asked him what I could do for him. He said that fifty cents would give him a bed at the Salvation Army that night. I gave him the fifty cents from my purse without any embarrassment on either side, and stood up. As I said good-bye, he said, "I'll see you again." And I was sure he meant me to know he was speaking of a meeting in heaven.

As I walked on down Market St. again with the whole crowd of humdrum pedestrians, I felt that my body could easily have soared up into the air if I'd had some kind of wings. I had been given a role to play in a human encounter in which fellow feeling and sibling love had been expressed fully and cleanly, without flaws or confusions, exactly as they should have been for their particular time and place. It had been a jewel-like piece of shared living that had about it the same kind of perfection that I had seen earlier in the little mountain flower. For that brief meeting, Sgt. Seffert and I had been moving in the full harmony of God.

(It is probably an important part of the story to say that I met him again several days later. This time he was being supported and moved along by a younger man with him. He was red-eyed and rumpled, unsteady on his feet. I did greet him, and he started in recognition and said to his companion "That's the girl I was talking about!" I pressed another fifty-cent piece on him, but this time it had become all corrupt and ugly; there was shame and guilt and trouble in it.

Oddly enough, the later encounter did not at all change for me the reality and perfection of the first meeting. That had been complete in itself, and the later flawed meeting between the same two persons had no power to corrupt the earlier one. I hoped and prayed that he would not feel any guilt or shame that would muddy for him the reality of the first meeting.)

There had been other beggars, too. I had struck up minor acquaintances with a number of them, managing to give away small change without disturbing a basic equality of human existence with each of them. But one evening I had met the legless man who propelled himself on a square board with wheels at a time when he was fuddled with drink and unnaturally expansive. I had thrust a five dollar bill on him, which he had accepted gratefully enough at the time. The next time I saw

There was a man who loved the sun
Who loved to see it rise,
And every morning without fail
He watched it with his eyes.

There came a day when he was blind
(As all who live will be)
And though he could not see his sun
His soul was now so free

That without any thought or wish
Or striving so to gain
He rose up to the thing he loved
And rode right in its train.

CASSANDRA

The visions whirl within her troubled brain,
the shrill words called, and the cry of terror;
Before her eyes no sight of kinsfolk, unbelieving,
but the burning chaos of a mighty city.

Against the crowd of joyful Trojans
she throws the fierce, the maddened words,
and strikes with futile fists
against the rolling horse of Greece.

Vain effort, knowledge without use.
Before the night is over the many slain
shall scald your eyes with never-ending tears,
and your faint voice fall on ears which can no longer hear.

* * *

Upon the streets where I have walked
is still my image, but only because
the image was with God.

him, though, sober, he would not speak to me and in fact looked at me reproachfully as he went by. I understood then that I had demeaned him by giving too much. The casual passing of small change could take place without anyone giving it any importance one way or the other; one could maintain the mutuality of respect and acceptance. With the five dollar bill he had been forced into a position of obvious need and had become an object of pity. He would never have let me give him that much if he had been himself. I had taken wrongful advantage of his vulnerability.

On another occasion I had just come out of MacFarlane's candy store, where I had happily indulged myself by buying a bag of their chocolate creams, advertised at a good sale price. Slightly ahead of me, up the sidewalk, a middle-aged man in a business suit was walking along briskly, shaking off from his elbow the attentions of another man who seemed to be pleading with him about something. The pleader gave up and slowed his pace. I caught up with him and asked simply "Do you need money?" A very slight pause and then, "Oh no. That's a man I've known. I was talking to him about something else." "Oh well", I said, "How about having a chocolate cream with me anyway?" and I opened the bag for him. "Thanks," he said, smiled, took the candy, nodded at me, and went along.

The closest I had come to disaster had been with a soldier I had "picked up" on the street. By some progression or another I had invited him to come up to my room for tea with me. He had seemed pleased and had stopped along the way to add a small bottle of whiskey to the occasion. I should have known better, but didn't. It was not until we were in my room and he tried to pull me down into his lap and fondle me that I had pulled free and told him that wasn't at all what I had in mind. He was indeed angry and told me I shouldn't ever try to pull that kind of stunt on anyone else. But the long and the short of it was that he had left peaceably enough, even abandoning the whiskey with me. It had stayed on my closet shelf for quite a long while, giving me a number of occasions to think about the whole thing.

They were all of them brief, temporary encounters. I was not going to have to deal with these same people day after day, every morning when I woke up. I would not have to work out

DANIEL

Daniel in the lions' den
Looked to right and then to left,
Saw the lions round about,
Heard the teeth gnash viciously.

Daniel in the lions' den
Prayed to God with all his might,
Knew the beasts were things of God,
Knew they would not shame their Lord.

Daniel in the lions' den
Saw those big cats drawing back,
Watched the lashing of their tails
Slowly quiet down and die.

Daniel called out to the king
That he still lived down below
Daniel went back forth to men
Again to try their teeth and claws.

* * *

I walked along the streets, with the houses close, and saw the sun, bright red, going down beyond the sea. Long, long walking on the pavement and the sun's fiery glow cut across by telephone poles and streetcar lines. A long walk home from the K streetcar line, after I had ridden out to talk to a woman in a brown coat and had remembered too late that I had only two cents in my pocketbook. The boys rasslin' in the street. Standing under the great cross on the hill, and up by the trees.

with them the compromises of living. But yet there was some kind of amazing consistency and truth about the responses. There seemed to be in each human spirit I met a living warmth which sprang to life when I reached toward it in open friendliness and without any of the usual traffic in gain and loss, in "what can I get you to do for me?" or "what ways might you be able to harm me?". It became quite obvious to me that Saroyan had not needed to invent any of the characters who moved through his stories with such appealing simplicity and humble, unselfconscious individuality. The streets, the shops, the parks were brimming over with vivid, unique personalities, eager to consider with me the vagaries of human life, and to tell me about their own situations and compromises. All it needed was the "Open, sesame" of an inquiring, loving spirit, unhampered by any need to achieve personal gain, and a magnificent rich tapestry of multitudinous human life would unfold before me.

I could not, however, rest simply in the delight of my beautiful discovery. Glorious and inspiring as was the vitality of human hopefulness, humility and generosity which I found around me, it could not change at all the power of the other side of human existence — the waste, the stifling of that spirit in all kinds of miserable shackles, the despair generated by human relationships bogged down in petty resentments and bickerings where once there had been joy and trust. The full range of the "slings and arrows of outrageous fortune" — probably even with additional modern frustrations and confusions that Shakespeare wouldn't have known — were obviously still bombarding humankind with full accuracy and deadly destruction. The grace and beauty of those human spirits who responded to me were somehow embedded in a great shambles of ugliness and misdirection. It was a kind of miracle, and an indication of just how strong that grace and beauty must really be, that they could rise up through such muck to shine in unselfconscious splendor before my amazed and thankful eyes.

In the evening the city stands quiet, and the mood of twilight throws a holy and melancholy stillness over the streets and the people still moving toward streetcars and home, or toward this evening's amusement at the movies. The air begins

I walk through the city, laughing,
and it seems a strange thing that I should laugh
in this time of war and desolation;
it seems that maybe I do not know these things,
or have forgotten.

I walk through the city, laughing,
but my laughter is not heedless.
It does not forget.
My laughter knows all sorrow I have known,
and I am not — as Whitman said —
"contained between my hat and shoes."

Within my laughter lives
the desolate lump on hard, cold pavement
which was a living man, begging for coins.
Within my laughter you may hear
the stricken hate and anguish
of the young sailor remembering Pearl Harbor.

* * *

I am ashamed and weary of myself;
My feet are heavy with the weight of guilt.
Slowly, through mired long ways,
I drag my wounded footsteps
To the foot of the cross.

Christ, will you look down and see?
Will you look down through tears of agony
To feel my longing?
Christ, will you smile,
        (O slow sweet smile — though bleeding)
And grant one beggar alms,
And grant one beggar place
To hang beside you on the cross?

to cool and in the clear light which comes after the sun, one feels the wholeness, the pattern, the strange paradoxes bound together into one thing which is human life.

I stood on the corner, waiting for my bus, but could not wait there, going back to the four walls of the house. I must walk about the city and see again — must walk and see this time of the city. There is nothing to see — the faces have become lost in a general humanity, the streets stretch endlessly and without their daytime sharp special meanings. The whole of the city is merged into the one darkening being.

The faces are relaxed, unstrung, drifting toward the undemanding rest of evening. The figures on the streets take the shape of deep-rooted symbols. The man standing next to the empty market, still holding up The Watchtower, is no longer really trying to sell to the wandering ones. He stares at me almost unseeing, alone and silent on the empty pavement. The movie-house lights, dimmed for wartime, still light the faces of movie heroes and heroines, and of the couples who hand over their tickets to the doorman and who go on in to the darkness. There is much here and I feel it humming to me with the pulse of human blood, but it is more a mood and an intangible rhythm than anything else; it is not a meaning one can fit into words and sentences. It is a part and a whole, and a thing of little and of great meaning. And finally I get on my bus and move smoothly along these quieted streets, away from the central core of the city to one of its placid outskirts.

* * *

I have heard the city singing. I have looked across the many homes to a flushed sky of early morning, and heard the symphony of many men singing as one. It was a multitudinous song, with many parts, with many interwoven comings and goings, but it was finally a prayer and a hallelujah, a striving upward and a song to God, full-bodied, nothing missing, neither the ugliness nor the despair nor the confusion, but all mingling into one strain of many meanings and yet one, striving upward to the light.

CLIMAX IN MADNESS

I do not know. Just how the search I was on and how the limits of my mind brought me to madness I have never understood. I may have had some feeling that I was getting into too-deep waters when I wrote a little verse:

> "Young lady, you are mad!
> Poor girl, you walk in lunacy!"
> If this be madness and upon me proved —
> still let me walk in the light of the moon.

I didn't really feel in any danger at the time, but it *was* madness — or was becoming madness — and it was upon me proved.

I have lost track of the sequence of events and don't really know the timespan of the last piece of high-pitched living before I broke connections with myself and with reality and was cared for at San Francisco General Hospital and then at two private sanitariums.

There was a spirit, personal rather than universal, and definitely masculine, male to my female. He responded to my spirit at a time when I was reaching out with love toward all creation, and he joined me in my little room and out walking around the city. He led me through some hurdles of learning; I remember there being a succession which involved my giving myself up totally to him in a kind of death, and then finding myself restored to my own consciousness again for the next step of instruction. He had me write a long poem in which I partly participated, but in which often I knew the words only as I was writing them down on the typewriter.

I suspect that there are ways to explain what I experienced within the framework of abnormal psychology. As I said, I don't know. There was, however, one area of insight that struck deep chords within me at the time, and that has proved useful for me since in pulling together my understandings of life. I have taken it to be true. I've never felt there was any authority for offering it to other people as true revelation; it was too closely tied to what became obvious insanity. But I'm going to lay it out here as best I can, for whatever it's worth.

It was a vision of Christ on the cross.

I had in my room a phonograph, the ancient kind one

winds up for each playing, and a selection of records, mostly slightly cracked or scratched or with a chip knocked out. I had bought the whole works from a second-hand store for ten dollars. One of the records was "Eli, Eli", the Jewish song using Psalm 22, that fiercely despairing one beginning "My God, My God, why have you forsaken me?" that Jesus used from the cross. I wound up my phonograph and the urgent, tearing chords of "Eli, Eli" filled my room.

I found myself standing at the foot of the cross, with Jesus hanging up above me there, in agony. I knew that I was really supposed to have been up there with him, crucified also, but I was not. Partly it had been fear and smallness of spirit, partly it had been that I clung to the beauty of the earth and its life, and could not accept death as he did. He looked down at me, and even through his suffering, smiled in forgiveness and love.

All the bits and pieces of the puzzle I had been working at — the innocent, loving responses from this person and from that, tangled irrevocably with flaws, incompleteness, despair and ugliness; the whole thing set in the vibrating disaster of our world at war, but paradoxically shot through with glimpses of the full glory of God — all these pieces came together with utter cohesion and unity into the single figure on the cross. This was not just the death of one man. There was gathered into the form and spirit of Jesus, that living glory, all the bits and pieces of our human love and grace, all the bits and pieces of our vileness and cruelty. He was accepting them totally, the sweetness with the evil, into his own spirit, gathering them in through love, as the roots of a tree gather moisture from the earth, and carrying them with him up onto the cataclysmic agony of the cross. From there they could be finally offered to God. Held in that love and suffering they could be received into the wholeness and the glory of the IS.

I cried to the full capacity of my body to feel grief. When the record came to its end, I was freed from that intensity I felt I could not bear much longer and sat back, emptied of all feeling. Fortunately I had also a record of the Easter Hymn from *Cavalleria Rusticana*, and when I played that it came across my spirit with great healing. Not so immediate or graphic though, as the crucifixion experience. No specifics, no person of Jesus there. It was more like a release, a necessary follow-up from the depths of the crucifixion. It let me see again the city out beyond my window, and the continuing life with its constant renewal.

I'm going to deal later with the fuller meanings I've developed over the years from that one immediate experience. Right now I think I'd better plow on through the story of my insanity.

As I've said, the connections of events there are lost. At some point I took off all my clothes, went downstairs, and jumped through the glass of the front door out onto the street. Sitting on the front walk with the shattered glass around me, I seized a jagged piece of glass and began gashing my legs, feeling a kind of fierce relief that I was finally bringing myself to justice. But after cutting two or three long gashes (after almost forty years I still see the scars), I gazed at the streaks of blood down my legs, and there came an enlightenment that stopped me. I knew suddenly, without question, that there was no way my small frame, my limited spirit, could contain the punishment that would really be appropriate for what I had done during those eight long years of cowardice, the kind of punishment that would really counterweigh on a scale of strict justice my refusal of a God who had offered Hirmself to me. What I needed to do was simply accept the mercy of God and rejoice in Hirs goodness. And so I laughed wholeheartedly up to the sun, and stopped my self-mutilation.

The police came and picked me up. I think there was some kind of stopover in a cell at the station, and then they took me to the General Hospital. Someone sent a telegram to my poor parents, and my mother came down to try to pull the pieces together. She found the best psychiatrist she could, who apparently was unable to unscramble anything for me, but he had me transferred to a private sanitarium. It was not until my mother heard somewhere about an insulin shock treatment and found a doctor willing to try it on me that I began to make any progress back to sanity.

For me there are disconnected images of faces, the ceilings of hospital rooms, a foul-tasting medicine someone made me take, being wrapped tightly in a wet sheet, going somewhere in an ambulance, and a surging whirl of confusion with hitherto-unknown personalities sharing my body with me, a feeling that I was responsible for a universe running madly out of control, and a kind of shrill terror from which I feared that not even death could release me.

I have a dim memory of complaining to a number of people about how devastating the insulin shocks were physically. But they did work. There came an early evening when I was myself again. Washed out like some kind of limp, shredded rag, but wholly contained again in who I was used to being. There was a leather cuff on my ankle holding me to the bed, but I hauled the bed along with me so I could get to the window in the room to look out again at grass and trees and the evening sky.

An attendant came pretty soon at the sound of the bed scraping, and put the bed back and me in it, but I think my progress was fairly steadily upward from that point on. They took the cuffs off and I began to have more regular days, which I spent with the other patients in activities. Later they let me go for walks beyond the sanitarium, first with an attendant, then by myself.

It had been about three months that I'd lost completely, and then a couple more weeks before they felt I was ready to go back to my family in Portland. My sister, on her trip home from Missouri, came south to California and we rode home together on the bus.

RECOVERY

The psychotic break was a fierce blow, and left me with great ragged questions. Did the fact that I had run into such a devastating brick wall mean that my whole approach was wrong? Was there a basic flaw in my perception of the IS and in my efforts to tune myself to it?

I had struggled so long trying to pull together the courage to live by the truths I had been given, and had finally arrived at a point where I felt I was meeting each day in ways that were true to my light. Now the whole thing had been knocked out from under me. Was I going to have to give up what had seemed so true and right, and start hunting for an altogether different foundation for my living? I was in a limbo of helpless uncertainty.

As I searched for some way to give meaning to what had happened, I found myself remembering an experience from my earlier days in the Oregon mountains. Here finally was a context in which I could view my catastrophe as being analogous to an earlier set-back which had shaken some of my cherished beliefs without forcing me to abandon them.

Camp Bountiful
(a side trip into analogy)

On one of the succession of backpack trips that my original family took in the summer before my San Francisco experience, my father, sister, brother and I went up around the south side of Mt. Jefferson. We started out in high spirits and good weather. We had a couple of days of getting used to the high air again, and of getting our legs and backs into shape. Then, on about the third day, we completed our mileage for the day and came upon the campsite we had chosen on the map.

A small, crystal-clear spring ran down beside the campsite into a lovely lake. The campfire area was neatly contained in an orderly and useful arrangement of rocks. There was a sound, simple table. There was an abundance of thick evergreen trees to provide a good browse bed. A perfect place! Not only beautiful but also ready to provide for our comfort and delight. When my father sighted a couple fish already rising in the early evening, the total magnificence became too much for him not to memorialize in some way, so he announced that he was christening the place "Camp Bountiful."

We constructed an absolute masterpiece of a browse bed with ample use of the evergreen boughs. While my sister and I got going on a hearty supper, my brother scouted around and my father tried out a couple of likely fishing spots as a promise for more good fishing in the morning. After a leisurely campfire we went to bed with a deep sense of comfortable satisfaction and anticipation for the morning.

It must have been about three o'clock the next morning that the rain started lightly. By four o'clock we were all awake, guessing at just how wet our sleeping bags were getting and how long it would be sensible to stay inside their relative warmth before climbing out to start the day.

My father got a fire going and my sister and I struggled with breakfast. It was hard cooking pancakes with the rain making a damp layer in the bottom of the pan all the time, but we managed it. My father and brother constructed a small lean-to of boughs near the fire and we consolidated our belongings carefully under it. At least they wouldn't be getting any wetter than they were already. We decided to tough it out and hope that the rain would stop sometime that day.

My father got his fishing gear together and went down to the lake to work at those fish he'd seen jumping. For a while I changed into my swimming suit with the idea that since I was going to get wet anyway, I might as well join in with things that way. This was, however, high mountain country and really cold. I could not overcome it by vigorous exercise and hopefulness, so I admitted defeat, put on all the clothes I had, and stayed close to the fire, leaving it just to share in the duties of gathering wood that was still dry and of keeping the fire alive.

We had one bit of exciting distraction when my father shouted out to us from the lake and we finally deciphered the fact that he'd got stuck in some quicksand and needed my brother to come help him out. No serious problem. It wasn't a big or a deep patch, and the two of them proved quite able to handle it. But no more fish, and Pop's socks and boots were wet and sticky with mud. The rain went on raining, just a kind of steady drizzle through the trees.

That night we put our sleeping bags as close together as they'd go under the lean-to, right next the fire. We transferred some of the evergreen boughs from our good bed of the first night, but it wasn't the same. It scarcely disguised the hardness of the ground, and there were roots of the tree behind us sticking up here and there. Besides, we were so close to the fire that we had to keep our feet curled up in a crouch position. At first the lean-to had kept out the water altogether, but sometime into the night it developed a special capacity for consolidating drops which then ran down the loose boughs hanging above us and fell with what seemed to be deadly accuracy and malice aforethought on an exposed neck or shoulder. The icy shock would startle each one of us again out of whatever thin layer of fitful sleep s/he had managed to gain. My father had taken for granted his role of parental responsibility and assured us that it was better that only one of us should be getting really wet by climbing in and out of a sleeping bag to put wood on the fire, so he did that faithfully.

It was a long and miserable night. In the morning, with no sign of the rain letting up, we packed up our soggy things and took off for a campsite lower down the mountain, where the map promised a sheltered cabin.

Camp Bountiful had given me my first real failure of spirit since I'd started thinking of the wilderness as my home. Before, the cold nights, the hard ground, the mosquitoes, the primitive living had been easy prices to pay for the freedom, the beauty, and the harmony of nature and myself. Even when I was grousing about blisters or a sore back, or shivering from a cold wind through my light sleeping bag, I knew that I was thoroughly glad to be there, that I was enjoying it, maybe even a bit more for the discomforts which gave my relationship to the woods more bodily reality.

This time was different. I had been thoroughly cold and miserable, aware that I was not enjoying it in any way, shape, or form, that I wished to be somewhere else. I had run up against a hard reality that was more than I could handle, that was foreign and hostile, that I could not in any way cajole into being part of my feeling of joyful, loving relatedness.

It did not change for me the beauty and reality of what I had felt earlier. The beauty and welcoming quality of the first sight of Camp Bountiful remained true along with the sodden leave-taking. My awareness of a soul-filling IS which came at me with glory and relatedness from the life of the wilderness remained real and vitally important, but there had been added to it another element — grim, intransigent — which claimed its own life and reality. The two different realities would somehow have to be juggled together, simultaneously, if I were to achieve any kind of truth in my living.

* * *

To get back onto the main track, my catastrophe of insanity acted like the rain experience at Camp Bountiful. Bigger, fiercer, and more devastating, but the same kind of message. I didn't have to give up what had been true and beautiful. I didn't have to slip back into a phony kind of living and put a cover of worldly conformity on things. But I did have to recognize that there were some great chunks of difficult reality that I did not understand and that I was not strong enough to cope with.

It wasn't easy recovering. I doubt that it ever is for anyone, from any kind of psychotic break. Insanity is no easy out from the difficulties and confusions of living. It can seem to a patient's family and friends that the central character in the fearful drama is drifting along free and easy and without any responsibility, while the family (or friends) are left to tear themselves to pieces trying to find a way to help. But the jangled consciousness and total insecurity inside the troubled one are devastating and fearful, and the psychic strength required just to hold oneself together through the bombardments of a single day are quite impossible to convey. God alone knows the kinds of heroism and gallantry under fire some mental patients may be displaying when they simply make it through a "normal" day.

But I was blessed in many ways. I was young and vigorous. My parents provided me with a safe place to live day after day, and managed not to push me too hard. My father was always the most accepting and easy-going of men, and my mother's efforts to help were domineering only in my view of them at the time, not in her intentions.

Having more recently watched patients in our mental health system struggling against the array of drugs that are now so often used, I suspect I was very lucky not to have been subjected to anything but the insulin. Neither I nor my parents felt a need for me to have psychological counseling, so I just survived wanly by myself, gradually gathering my feet under me once again.

I have kept some of the things I wrote during that time of convalescence, and some of them seem to have enough form to be given here.

Sunlight and warmth — despair and agony. Walking through this fairness of the earth, seeing with blank eyes the greenness and the growing joy once so dearly loved, seeing without feeling, with utter blankness, with half-desire to feel, but no capacity. Dead, and the scenes which brought this death ever seen, though no more consciously, lying like dead weight of fog through every particle of the mind. It is this incapacity to feel, this death known dully which brings the sudden urge to slash the wrist, to stop the breath with violence, a dull ache ever present, which seems too heavy a weight ever to throw off.

Live, breathe, pass formless through sunrise and sunset and soft fall of evening, and finally form returns and the bounds of individuality. Again the heart can leap to caress the beauty of a flower moved by the wind, again the spirit can stretch out to the sun, but it is not quite the same again — or maybe I have not passed yet through enough days and nights, the slow rebuilding of the spirit. Tears may start for petty things, for the self turned back, discouraged, but they cannot continue long; the mind knows too well other griefs far deeper, beyond the reach of tears, and will not weep for these things. And one may give the heart's love, but somehow not completely. There is some part of the heart which remains staring at the wild wheels of the universe, tangled in the urge for order, and cannot find completeness or rest in another's being.

* * *

When there is no form and the mind is troubled, when the feelings are torn between peace and weeping, energy being too far gone for laughter, unless it be the sad, almost bitter kind — and yet not, for at the thought my mind is ready for the laughter of delight, though I feel I could not laugh so long, but would break to tears — as I was saying, when the mind is troubled, without form, it is a good thing to go out and see the order and sufficiency of nature, to try to absorb into one's own disorder that endless "being" — unless, however, one feels urged to report to hirs typewriter and to try to say something burdened in the mind. Which is at present the case with me.

If I were to tell you, who read this, that I am lost, would you know what I mean? I do not think so. I think that you would certainly need more than that in the telling. I myself need more than that. It is not enough. It does not say how I am at this moment or during this evening. I know only that my strength is mired, that I cannot really call for help with a full voice, nor can I feel at peace. I am at wrong here; I am not behaving in accordance with what I feel I should be doing. I am following the path of expedience at present — as nearly as I can analyze — and it likes me not.

I would be free and clean and strong, and feel that I have perhaps lost those early joyous qualities forever. I do not know as yet what other things may be mine to replace what I have had at some favored moments. I feel myself old and "hopeless" and as though my truth were no more to be wholly trusted — as though I have lost my soul and my life's anchor in a futile shambles. It is time, and past, that I try to straighten out those things I have, that I try to marshal them forth into the open light and see them. My life has been strange — as perhaps are more people's than I would realize. At any rate, I seem to have lived a great part of my life in a sort of unconsciousness, a fog in which I did not see my way. An attempt, perhaps, to translate everything into intellectual terms when my natural way was otherwise, so that the conscious could have little to do with the perceived (ach no, lady, ach no — words, mumblings without substance)

I have been soiled and put upon, trampled and disgraced. And how it has been done I do not know. There is no life here in the sorrow. There is no meaning in the troubling over things past. Is there any profit in marshaling things into camps and following reasons? I am as one dead.

* * *

God, how is it one becomes something different from what one has been — the childhood falling away, the sharpness of feeling muddled, the wonder lost? The falling off of remorse, the increasing lack of apology (this an advantage). How much acceptance of things as they are is truly part of maturity, and how much is simply a commodious means for sliding unalive through life?

* * *

There is no need to be aloof when the Ides of March have struck. There is no need to hide the head carefully in sand after disaster. Speak as though you are still whole, face the world with a calm eye that says such things have been done before, and are not fatal, and oddly enough the world will often accept you more naturally than you would suppose. If you seem to know what you are doing and why, the world will tend to think you do, too.

* * *

Most recently, as I have been breaking up my household so that I can move into some kind of less-cluttered-by-things manner of life, I have done considerable reading of old letters I had squirreled away because I felt they were too valuable one way or another to be just thrown away. I'm glad I saved them. I'm glad they were there to be saved. (I sometimes wonder how much we are losing nowadays with the greater immediacy and interchange of phone calls.)

At any rate, there were a number of them that family and friends had sent to me during the times of my high adventures in San Francisco and after, when I was working to rebuild myself after the psychotic break. There is in them much love, openness, and understandings about the world and God that were really not that far from mine. It was more the degree of intensity in which we differed.

Why was it that I felt I had to keep my vision to myself? Why did I feel so terribly alone in needing to do what I had to do, in the way in which I had to do it?

R.D. Laing, English psychiatrist, has written about the way "so-called schizophrenics" often protect a "real self" from all contact with the working world of activities and interchange with others, turning their worldly work over to a "false self" whom they do not accept as being themselves and often, in fact, despise. I think that was partly what I did in the eight years before I burned bridges behind me and set off for San Francisco. But with the new style in San Francisco, I did successfully bring my "real self" up into the driver's seat and sloughed off the old "person"

The strange thing, though, is that people who knew me didn't seem to see that much difference in me. The changes were really nothing tremendous or earth-shaking, at least on the outside; maybe there hadn't been really as much difference as I felt between the old and the new. But was I just utterly blind and self-centered not to have seen that I could safely have been myself in the setting of my old life?

I'm not at all sure. I remember one time telling a new-found friend of mine at Reed College about my experiences of God and what they meant to me, and she exclaimed "How amazing that you've developed all these deep ideas!" She took it all as something that had come from my own mind and thought, not at all as an experience of reality which had been given to me. I realized I had been talking "about" God instead of talking about life or the world from the vantage point of being "with" God. The talk had carried me away from God instead of to Hirm. I think I've developed ways by now to speak of my beliefs and my experiences without falsifying them, ways that are a result of working at it for a long while through trial and error. But in those days I didn't have the know-how.

Maybe the transcendent would have remained vital for me even with some of its sharpest edges rounded off so that it could fit smoothly into ongoing patterns of moderate religious feeling. Maybe if I'd gone further into other people's experiences, I'd have found that they had kept within themselves a keener response than they showed to the world. I still don't know. But somehow the IS stirred in me a feeling of urgency, of the need for uncompromising purity of response, and any time I tried to deal with it as just one of many experiences or as only one piece of life, I felt I was betraying something precious.

So I did just coast along, day after day, taking it as it came, trying to look as though I knew what I was doing. For several years there would be times of nightmares, dreams that carried me back to the hospital or to the confusions of the sanitarium. And there would be waking times when I felt the possibility of recurrence (the doctor had in fact warned my mother that recurrences were common). But a recurrence never came and gradually I began to feel again that my own mind and feelings were to be trusted.

A lasting benefit has been a special sort of enforced humility; if I cannot claim solidity even in my essential consciousness, in my who-I-am, how can I lay claim to certainty in any of the ideas I form about life or even about myself? How can I be absolutely sure of anything? At least I won't ever fall into the pride of Henley's *Invictus:* "I am the master of my fate; I am the captain of my soul."

The reckless, total commitment of my search in San Francisco was gone, but the IS remained real and present for me. That light which had burned fierce and central dimmed — or more likely it was that I turned my eyes partly away. But still when I had a pause of quietness in my living, or when I reached out for help in need, God was there, always the same but always somehow new and different.

That has been for me one of the continuing amazements of my meetings with the IS: that each one has been partly the same, as familiar and comforting as the repetition of each morning's daylight, and yet that each one has been particular to its own time and place, always new and essentially unpredictable. I live along, taking it as it comes, earning my living, trying to occupy my time in productive, good ways, and there will come upon me, there in my path, some bit of human generosity that shines far beyond any reasonable expectation and I will find my heart singing in thanksgiving. Or there will be a sudden searching question put to me by a particular incident or maybe directly by another human being, from hirs own consciousness, and I will find a probing light cast upon my activities and my motives. Even as structured, and apparently repetitious, a meeting as the Lord's Prayer keeps renewing itself in unexpected ways, partly from the other people who may be saying it with me, partly just from the different meanings it picks up as my life situation changes.

My daily life itself, however mundane and apparently stuck in materialistic details it may be, still has within it the vitality of the IS, still provides me meetings with God.

SECTION THREE

IN DAILY LIVING

ACTIVE LIFE WITH CHILDREN

I had known for a long time that I wanted to have children. It was really not part of my mother's influence. It may have been even contrary to it, as I felt it at that time.

My mother had been very much a part of the first wave of feminism that brought women the vote, and it was a natural style for her. She had been captain of a girls' basketball team for which the townspeople of Williamsport, Pennsylvania had actually turned out to cheer, and when she moved to Oregon with my father, she was able to report her first voting before any of her sisters or her mother in Pennsylvania had been able to. Jane, I, and Rox (christened name Robert) had grown up sharing chores without distinction as to girls and boy, (well, my father did put more effort into wood splitting instructions for Rox than for us, but Rox had to take his turn at dishes and clearing off the table). My mother had never liked the dolls people showered on her when she was small, so we all equally had teddy bears. And my mother often mentioned that she hadn't really planned to get married when she was a girl, and made sure that Jane and I recognized that marriage was only an option.

But there was in me (though usually hidden from view) a gut-level desire for children, a response to mothering situations. I remember a party for the college chorus at which a girlfriend and I happened to find the beautiful young children of our music director and spent the evening playing with them instead of mingling with our peers.

But there does need to be a father (hopefully husband), and I was sadly lacking in the graces that attract boys or men. Shy, too intense, trapped in an image as a single-minded top student with flat-heeled shoes and glasses, I had gone through high school and college without any dates at all, with no experience in the give and take of girls and boys finding their ways toward the mating experience. When I finally married at age twenty-seven, it seemed like a sort of miracle, and I did not have the softening, trustful ways that might have made possible the development of a real, cohesive bond between me and Champion Nixon. Nick was then thirty-five years old, never married before, and had his own set of protective armor and fears and insecurities.

When we got to talking about marriage he was sure we should consult carefully with a psychologist friend of his. The man talked to us briefly together, then for quite a while with Nick, and finally at some length with me. He recommended against marriage, suggesting that it would be better for us just to go on living together. It is one of my tender memories of Nick that when the psychologist and I returned to the waiting room, he was obviously very tense, even frightened-looking, and when I told him that I wanted to marry him in spite of the recommendation, his face did leap into joy.

We didn't really achieve a good marriage, but we had enough affection between us for almost ten years of interesting living, and we had the three children. Not a bad score really. I'm afraid that he came to feel that I had married him primarily for the chance to raise children. I don't think I was quite that cold-blooded really, but it is true that when there was a choice between my relationship with the children and my relationship with him, I normally chose the children. (Let me say in my own defense that the choice didn't often arise; the points for potential close relationship with him were few and far between — or was I blind?)

I had met him while volunteering my services as a ceramist at Letterman Hospital, where he was teaching ceramics to soldiers just returning from the battlefields and camps of World War II. At the end of the war and after we were married we set up a private pottery studio in an old warehouse on the San Francisco waterfront.

It was on the second floor of Harry Kidd's potato and onion warehouse just up from Pier 5 — 551 Davis St. There was one huge room with flues and things where there'd once been a big restaurant stove. We figured it as a natural place to set up our kiln. And then there were three rooms along the side which could serve as living quarters. Their most recent use had been for storing smoked salami, so there were still crude 2×4s nailed into the walls, but up above were the remains of decorative painted flowers and leaves and the outlets of pipes for gas lights. Several old-timers who visited told us we were occupying what had been Sanguinetti's Restaurant, which went back to pre-earthquake days. The three rooms we lived in had been fancy private dining rooms.

There was a lot of hard, dirty work getting it ready: windows to replace, plaster to patch, shelves to build. Our first heat was the trash burner section of an old gas stove we bought and installed and it was months before I had a counter area to connect that stove with the sink standing on its own set of 2 ×4 framework. It was fun, though. Everything we did improved it by great steps on which we could congratulate ourselves. It never reached a state of polished completion which might have called for high-level housekeeping. It was always more like camping out, and kept us at a primitive level of appreciating the simple comforts we did have.

It was just about seven months after our marriage — with the studio and our living quarters at least under control — that I checked with a doctor and found out that I was indeed pregnant.

My body responded beautifully to pregnancy. Mostly I felt extra healthy and vigorous. I figured out pretty early that it was just nine months of my time, but that what I did could make a difference to the baby for all of hirs life. So I took good care of myself, and although I kept right on working in our ceramic studio, I had a good excuse not to get stirred up about any of the sometimes hectic schemes that Nick tended to generate. The only real problem I had was varicose veins. A few months into the first pregnancy, the veins in my legs started bulging out, so it became a standard routine during pregnancy for me to sit up in bed first thing each morning and wrap an ace bandage up each leg and then pull on elastic stockings. No pain, though; just the nuisance of it. A small price to pay.

There is something special about carrying a baby. A feeling of real significance in your living, no matter what else you may be doing. At first the sort of glow one gets from being in charge of a joyful, important secret. Then when the baby starts to make hirs own movements inside you, you become aware of the beginnings of one of the most intimate of human relationships. The little erratic bulges or rolling turns that push out against you are definitely not your own, closely integrated though they are. The rhythms do not have to do with your digestion, your movements or gas in the intestines, your moments of sleepiness. They are the result of a new creature there inside you, and the baby becomes real long before s/he makes the perilous passage to the outer world and to the state of doing hirs own breathing and eating and sleeping. I, at any rate, was at enough leisure and peace with the world that I savored fully the miracle of growth taking place inside me.

The first birth was a long and difficult one, and I was anesthetized into unconsciousness for most of it. My first sight of the tiny baby, my son — after all those months of knowing him as a moving reality inside me — was utterly wonderful. How exquisite the tiny parts — fingers, wrists, curve of nostrils, ears against the head — each functioning entity articulated minutely into the next! How beautiful the living breathing whole! How miraculous the transformed features of his father (who was also still beautiful to me)!

We had been having a very jolly get-together, waiting for the birth. This was my parents' second grandchild, but the first from a daughter. There were a number of other family birthdays in July so it had been added fun to speculate as to what day the baby would actually choose. There had been time, too, for my father to help build a small "sun porch" right outside the studio window, creating a properly floored play area over the sloping, graveled roof of the warehouse we lived in. They were days of special common feeling between my mother and me, a mutuality that had been sometimes badly broken during my late adolescence. The triumphal trip home from the hospital with the beautiful baby was, of course, glorious, and the amazing days of adjusting to absolutely undreamed-of new demands were certainly made better — or even possible at all — by support from all the family, but especially from my mother. At one time, when little Forrest was crying, she commented about how newborn babies sometimes get cold, and reached down into the bassinet to hold his two feet in her warm hands. Sure enough, he did stop crying. (Years later, when I was doing the honors with my own first grandchild, I was able to duplicate this grandmotherly feat. A great feeling of competence and even wisdom!)

I had had almost no experience with babies, so the first days were rather fearsome, and even beyond the initiation period I might suddenly be aware that I was handling Forrest more like a sack of cornmeal than like a proper baby, but he was tougher and more resilient than he looked at first, and we both survived. That was the amazing thing: the increasing responsiveness, the way he fit himself to my styles of handling him, even while I was fitting myself to his ways.

What a mixture of earthy reality and unhindered clarity of spirit it is! Here is this totally new, utterly unknown being in your charge, to be fed, changed, and kept from crying, and to be fit somehow into the life you've been living, and into all of the clothes and diapers and gadgets and bits of advice that you've accumulated in preparation. As s/he does take hold of life, and uncurl the tight fists, and sleep and wake and grow more solid in your arms, there comes back to you, bit by bit, uncertainly at first, the gropings of response, the ease of tension when you hold hirm warm against your body, the curving in to fit your body and your breast, the start of smiles, the waiting while you change a diaper, the expectation of the next step in a simple common ritual. More and more this tiny body, helpless, totally dependent on you, becomes a person with hirs own center of volition, a being answering your ministrations and your hopeful efforts to make happy, a being looking out upon the world with hirs own eyes and with who knows what deep considerations of the life of Man! And all of this, of course, in the midst of messy diapers and milk spit up at any kind of moment, and crying that interrupts the most urgent other business, and interrupted sleep, and overall the total destruction of your accustomed freedom to call your life your own.

While we lived there on Davis St. the city's produce exchange went on all around us, and the big produce trucks used to wheel into the alley under our bedroom window by about 4:00 or 4:30 each weekday morning. It was no wonder that Forrest tended to wake bright and early. I found it easier just to get up when he wanted to rather than trying to find entertainments or threats to keep him in the crib after he was already up, or to turn him loose on his own. Aside from that restlessness and energy that kept us both on the move, he was an agreeable baby to care for. Mostly he'd have a smile for me when he roused me from sleep or took me away from something I might rather have been doing.

It was always a pleasure to nurse him, a meaningful interval of calm and comfort for both of us. For me the warmth of a small body and the gentle suckling were always physically pleasant and satisfying. It was moreover a satisfying thing in the mind and feelings to share that complex but simple cooperation for life and growth.

Forrest did mostly enjoy his food and didn't have any real problems with any of it. By the time he was sitting in a high chair his feeding times were quite companionable. In other areas, too, we developed little games around things like my folding the dry diapers on top of him on the bed. By and large I was able to work him and his needs into a total living pattern that included him naturally but that didn't put him in center stage.

That, I think, was one of the great gifts of living right in the midst of our family work, the pottery studio. It was of necessity not a spic-and-span place, so it allowed for informal inclusion of the youngest member of the family more easily than would many another home industry. The work to be done was seldom of the right-now, quick-precision type, so I could sling Forrest under my arm, or later let him toddle around without any real problems.

The demands of students or of customers coming in to buy glazes or to pick up firing took precedence over the baby's minor needs. If the bell rang while I was feeding Forrest, I stopped, picked him up out of the high chair, and took him along while I retrieved someone's firing and made change. After that we'd come back and go on with the feeding. He didn't seem to mind at all. He wasn't ever shoved off in an isolated corner by himself while I took care of business, and most of the time the activities were kind of interesting.

That was the other great thing about the Nixon Craft Studio: all the cheery, friendly people who came in and out. After an early attempt at private classes, we'd found we really drew in more lively, interesting students (and a more secure salary) when we operated as part of the adult education system of San Francisco. Nick continued teaching for the Army in occupational therapy at Letterman General Hospital, and then we started having evening classes (and later, afternoon ones) for the adult education people right in our own studio. The students were mostly people who came to the studio for recreation, to get their hands in clay and try some creative things that would be fun. No strain, no pressure, no competition, and it is the nature of clay that almost everyone can find a level of skill that s/he can master, from the simplest building of an ashtray by pressing clay into a bowl, to the creation of a piece of fine art. Nick at his best was a really talented teacher, able to develop confidence and enthusiasm, to stir people up and beyond where they thought they could accomplish things. It made for a good and lively atmosphere.

Forrest was part of this. Some people made a point of greeting him each time they came. He could carry things for them, or bring something over to me. Some few felt themselves especially rewarded by his remembering them, knowing their names, keeping watch for them. But he wasn't on display, didn't have to respond to them in some expected form. Many of them came and went without interacting with him at all. It was open on both sides, a bonus for anyone who happened to enjoy it, no obligation for anyone who didn't feel like taking time for him. And for him there was always something else to see or do, some other person to "talk" with.

Besides our studio, too, there was a smaller one sub-leased by two weavers. They used to let him come in and play on the treadles of the looms and greet *their* students. One time when I went over to fetch him back for lunch, I found him sitting happily on the floor next to their open china cupboard, exploring their collection of really good cups, saucers, and other pieces. They calmed me, at least partly, by assuring me that they often let him play there, and that he'd never broken anything yet.

Even before my second pregnancy I had been reading Dr. Dick Grantly Read's book, *Childbirth Without Fear*. It seemed a shame to me that I had not been able to experience such an important event in my life as the birth of my first child. I talked to my obstetrician, Dr. Faisal, about it, and she seemed to be in full accord with the idea of helping me have this second baby without anesthetic. When the labor pains seemed to be starting in earnest, Nick and I put our plans for Forrest's care into effect and Nick drove me to the hospital. Then I went through one of those ridiculous and frustrating things that can happen to pregnant women. The pains stopped completely before morning and I hung around the hospital all morning waiting to see if they might pick up again.

Fortunately they did, and I was into it fully by early evening. The contractions *were* painful, even in spite of my best efforts to relax, and they finally reached such a pitch that I asked for an injection of anesthetic. But there were only two contractions after that before the second stage of labor began, and I found my body taken over by powerful, coordinated pushing efforts which felt elemental and irresistible, but not really painful. They felt, in fact, good, somewhat like an effective bowel movement on an intense and mammoth scale. However Dr. Faisal came in belatedly at that point, had me wheeled hurriedly into the delivery room, and plunged me into unconsciousness with an anesthetic.

So I missed out again, at least on the last part of the birth. With my third and final child, down in Palo Alto, I finally made it. Again the attendants had miscalculated about how far along I'd gotten and hadn't alerted the doctor in time. He didn't arrive until the baby's head was already partly out, but the nurse had been very effective at helping me slow down the full-tilt push of delivery by doing a kind of forced panting, so there was only a minimal tear, which the doctor stitched without more than a pin-prick sensation. It was certainly the most satisfying of the three births I experienced.

It is, however, my considered opinion that birth is really not an easy thing, even probably for the other mammals. Those women who give birth quickly and without damage and apparently with almost no pain are, I believe, the exception. Certainly there can be unnecessary difficulties thrown in the way by our artificial ways of living, by fear, and by ignorant techniques, whether simple or sophisticated. But maybe we should not expect a natural process — even when most naturally and healthfully undertaken — to proceed without difficulty, stress, or sometimes pain. The biblical story which condemns Woman to bringing forth her children in pain — and the customs and expectations of many primitive tribes — are based, I think, on a good deal more than superstition. The whole thing is definitely worth it. The joy of the child safely started on hirs own road to independent life certainly overbalances the pain of the birth, so that the mother quickly forgets just how fierce the trial may have been, but it's really not "a breeze".

Later in my life, with a Bible Study group composed chiefly of older black women, I had a good opportunity to ask some real experts. Two of the women there had each gone through more than ten births of live children. They had each started young, and most the deliveries had been made at home, assisted by family members or a midwife. We'd got on a discussion of childbirth from some point in that book which covers so many vital aspects of life, and I asked them if birth had ever been easy for them. No, they agreed, there remained a kind of dread of the actual time of delivery. Each birth had been slightly different, in timing, in location and in style of pains. Neither woman had been able to know for sure just how this particular birth was going to proceed or complete itself. They were fully accepting of the necessity of going through the delivery, glad to do it for the joys of the child brought forth, but the delivery itself was not pleasant or easy.

Ruthie was a fine large baby (10 lbs. 1 oz.), healthy, beautifully formed. She turned out to have not only an amiable temperament but a metabolism that functioned more slowly and deeply than Forrest's. She should have been no problem at all, but in fact she provided me with my worst experience in caring for a baby. My mother had been unable to come help this time, and we had arranged for Miss Wilcox, a private nurse who specialized in newborn infants, to come work for us. My sister Jane and her husband John, who were just 2½ months into caring for their first child, had known "Cox" for some years. She was an old hand, with many testimonials about sickly babies she had pulled through grave difficulties. Maybe she was too expert in difficult cases, and too far away from just normal, run-of-the-mill ones. She immediately spotted a case of "thrush" in Ruthie's mouth, and we had to go through a periodic several-times-a-day application of potassium permanganate to control the fungus. (I was told afterwards that thrush is quite common and that it is often left untreated without ill effects). She worried about the dirty cracks and nooks of our crude apartment, and made strenuous cleaning efforts. But it was in the area of my breast-feeding that Cox really caused havoc. She always weighed the baby after I'd nursed her, and reported to me the increase — or lack of it — in the baby's weight. She constantly referred to my really gigantic baby as a "poor little mite" and fed me horror stories of mothers who had been so insistent on holding onto their pride over nursing their babies that they had starved them. The long and the short of it, what with my psychic energy at a low ebb anyway, was that she worked her way into beginning supplemental bottles of formula for Ruth; and I was lying awake at night, knowing I needed sleep more than anything else to restore a decent milk supply. I was unable to get out of the endless track of trying to figure out how I'd gotten into this awful mess.

Finally Nick realized that something had to be done and he phoned Jane and John, who told him emphatically that he should just fire Cox immediately and they'd come up from Palo Alto and give us a hand over the hump. How amazingly everything straightened out after that! There *are* some times when changing the circumstances will really solve a problem.

Jane did double duty for a while, nursing both our little girls, while I was working up my own capacity again. Then they were able to go back home and we sailed along peaceful and easy after that. Ruthie was the kind of baby who would manage to sleep double time if there was a crisis demanding my attention at one of her regular feeding times. She managed to stay fat and vigorous on my milk supply, which hadn't been able to satisfy Forrest's more active needs after the first five months. All in all a model baby. Too bad she came after Forrest, who continued to wake me early and keep me running!

Forrest had some rough times while I was in the hospital with the new baby, and busy with the complications of things when we came home again. There was one particularly ugly incident in which I and Nick miscalculated badly (and at cross-purposes) how to respond to his emotional needs of us. I shall probably always regret it. Not too long ago I recounted that incident in some detail to Forrest and his wife in a kind of hope that if he knew about it he might better be able to straighten out whatever psychological kinks it could have left. Probably a ridiculous hope; whatever damage was done had undoubtedly been already woven into his psyche long since. But I continue to be sure that in every living thing there is an active principle which struggles mightily for wholeness, for the fulfillment and growth to perfection of whatever unique qualities and character- istics lie in the central seed-core of that being. If all the bruises and traumas and disasters that afflicted us when we were children, or that we inflict in turn on our children, attained their full potential for damage, we would hardly any of us survive even to the state of health and normalcy we now enjoy. "There is a divinity that shapes our ends, rough-hew them how we will." That line doesn't really express what I'm talking about and I'm sure it wasn't the major direction of Shakespeare's thought, but maybe it applies in a kind of way. A tree, growing upward toward the sun, may be twisted and distorted and bent by other things that buffet it and beat it down, but it will go on strug- gling to reach its style of balanced symmetry, against all kinds of odds. I think human beings have that same inborn urge toward health and fullness of growth. Without it, it would be almost impossible to face the responsibilities of parenthood.

Shortly after Ruthie was born, Nick and I decided that we'd rather raise our family in a more rural type of place, and we found an interesting acre in Mountain View down the Peninsula just below Palo Alto. It had a huge, basically sound building accessible to the road and suitable for the studio and glaze making. It also had one good little house we could live in, another smaller unit rented out to a young couple, a kind of shack at the back that had potential as another rental, and a whole row of old chicken coops extending the length of the crude roadway that connected the back of our house to the shack at the back. We moved me and the two children to Mountain View in May of the year Ruthie was born, and Nick finally completed transferring all our goods and belongings from San Francisco and moved in permanently in about October.

At the time, we had a happy confluence of my family in the

Palo Alto area. My sister Jane and her husband John, with their baby daughter Sibyl, lived at the edge of the Stanford campus, where John was completing a doctorate in physiology. They had helped my brother Rox and his wife Connie with their first two children locate quarters right around the corner, so Rox could work on a doctorate in economics (the GI Bill was providing money for education, and my family tended to be strong academically). Sibyl, as I mentioned earlier, put in her appearance just 2½ months ahead of Ruthie, and Connie's third child, Charlie, was born just about six weeks after Ruthie. It was a great time for comparisons and sharing and taking pictures of the three babies together. It didn't last long; Jane's family moved to Illinois that fall; Rox and Connie, with their brood, moved a year or two later to Washington state, then down to Southern California for several years, and on to Utah. Even while we all lived within a few miles of each other, each family was very

Champion and Miriam Nixon with Forrest, Meredith and Ruth, 1953.

busy with its own affairs, but there were many chances for good family get-togethers and mutual cheerings-on.

My brother, who has five grown children now and five grandchildren, had a neat way of describing the stages of development in family life. "First," he said, "you're a couple. With the birth of the first child you're a couple with a baby. After the second child's born, you become a family, and when you've got three you begin to wonder who's running the show!"

Forrest turned out to be a good older brother. He was interested and patient about what Ruthie did. Especially I remember the first time I spanked the little girl. She was already walking — I hadn't been as edgy with her as I had with Forrest about the need to avoid "spoiling", and she was anyhow, as I said, a model child. But there came up something that seemed to be best answered with a direct, intentional swat. She was much shocked, and cried rather desperately. She looked at me first, and then went on over to Forrest, who put out his arms for her and took her in for comforting. Everything seemed to be okay again. She had learned that I might hit her to stop her from doing something I didn't want, but at the same time she knew she wasn't being cast out of the sphere of human warmth and comfort.

The two of them made a pair of it for some four years before Meredith was born. Ruth seems always to have been unusually aware of other people's desires and needs, and responsive to them. She was an apparently happy follower for Forrest's ventures. I remember one Halloween when Forrest decided she should go around with him as a witch, and dressed her up accordingly. He got her one of my old dresses and a broom to carry out behind, and a couple of pillows (for some reason he was thinking of a fat witch). Mrs. Skinner, our good neighbor on the corner who always made up popcorn balls for the wandering children, told me afterwards it had been the high point of her evening to see little Ruthie, all uncomplaining, struggling to keep the pillows under control at the same time she steadied the broom and tried to see out of the overall face mask she had on. It would have been the Halloween after Meredi was born, when the baby was just seven months old and I'd stayed home with her. Most years I had the fun of going out with the kids for early evenings. Our neighborhood was a

When I was a girl, I very much admired my mother's hands. They were strong, active, unmanicured hands, and they had fascinating veins which stood out on them all the time.

I wanted to have hands like that myself, and I would be very pleased with the way my own hands would look when I'd let them hang down next me as I was riding to school on the bus. True enough, when I held them up again, they'd be smooth and without character, but I could see there was real hope that someday I would myself have beautifully corded hands like hers.

I have just now come back to the kitchen from checking my two little children, finally asleep. It was as I turned out their plastic merry-go-round lamp — with the zebra and the lion and the bear and the elephant silently moving round and round — that I looked down at my hand, and saw the veins on a strong, unmanicured hand, and remembered suddenly my mother's hands and the way they looked to a child.

* * *

I think it is in the Iliad that old Priam, Hector's father, speaks of the terrible thing it is for a son to die before his father. I suspect that it takes a parent to get the full impact of this. It is true somehow that the center of one's life shifts to the welfare of the child; that it becomes nothing more than obvious and natural to sacrifice personal comforts and desires for what seems to be the best interest of the children. My child is me, though s/he is also wholly hirmself and without binding strings. The individual is not really separate, not really whole within hirmself. S/he lives also in what s/he loves, and when s/he has broken down hirs walls of separateness, s/he is also more whole. "I am not contained between my hat and shoes." This opening out of spirit seems more inevitable and natural between parent and child than anywhere else. Flesh from my own flesh; also spirit of my spirit, even when the expression of that spirit may not be understood or feel comfortable, person-to-person.

mixed, nondescript sort, but it was safe enough and it was just the local kids who roamed around in it. When kids in the wider area wanted to hit the big-time with their trick-or-treat bags, they went to the wealthier, more concentrated tract homes.

Meredith was named, rather cunningly, after my father who had never wanted any boy to have to carry his first name, Percy. I don't think I even consulted him about using his second name, but he seemed to enjoy the fait accompli. Meredi says she's always liked the name, so that all came out fine. Meredith turned out to be a well-knit, compact person, certainly with the best muscular coordination of any of my three and, I suspect, with the sturdiest ego. She was not at all a natural follower. I still enjoy the memory of hearing her and Ruth negotiating a play agreement. Ruthie wanted her to play "school" with some of the dolls and assorted animals, but Meredi insisted she wouldn't do it unless she could be principal!

Another incident when Meredi was already school age is more flattering to her, and probably even more typical. She had gone with Kathy Marquez, who lived across the street, to our corner grocery store. When she came back she reported, still under the impetus of a righteous indignation, that a boy they knew (who certainly was within their general age range) had purposely run into them with his bike. In fury at such transgression, Meredi had charged him without hesitation, made him get off the bike, wrested it away from him, and refused to let him go off again until she had told him off thoroughly.

While she was going to our local seventh and eighth grade school and then to our high school, both of which had acquired more and more of a "tough" reputation, she found it quite useful to trade on her dark complexion (her father is part Native American) and her friendship with a number of chicana girls, to keep most the student body in the dark as to whether she was chicana herself. It put her in a good position to resist any possible aggression.

I know it's hard to be sure what's innate in a child and what may have been developed in response to a particular position in the family and to the expectations that the family and other people may have of hirm. A human being is fearfully and wonderfully made. But I continue to think that there's a lot of basic temperament and "style" in the child right from the beginning — whenever that is.

In the one house
strangers,
not knowing —
each in hirs own silence kept.

The ties bind and bruise in strange patterns,
small movements made important.

Many the years together,
many the days shared,
and yet each is separate,
strong in the power to harm,
helpless to make again whole.

Words are not good when tears
already fill another's eyes.
One stands helpless, troubled and remorseful,
the real things too deep for speech.

* * *

In cases of divorce, I've thought it's easier on kids when there's more than one child so that they can share the problems. I know my kids seemed always to get a lot from each other, both in their childhoods, and in later years. And I think it was much easier on me, too, to have enough of us so that we remained for sure a family. Really, the main share of dealing with the kids had always been mine. The summer before I actually started divorce proceedings, Nick had spent the whole time in Mexico, and life on our acre had been almost unchanged (we had a great assistant, Ernie Kim, who had picked up most the responsibility for the studio). At any rate, it didn't seem to me that the divorce made that much of a disruption right at first. It was later on that the inevitable sad gaps caused by there not being some kind of working model of a man and a woman functioning together made it harder for the kids than I realized at the time.

There was one period when Nick remarried, a woman named Gloria who had three glamorous almost-grown children of her own and a fine spread of land — with horses — up in the Santa Cruz mountains. They invited my three youngsters to spend a weekend with them, and I was faced with the problem of just how to send them off. I still feel good about the way I finally did it.

I got the three of them together and told them that it was always a good thing to have someone who wanted to love you and care for you the way a mother did, and that it didn't make it any less good if there were two mothers instead of just one, that it wouldn't take away at all from my being their mother if they found out that they could have Gloria as a mother, too. So they were to go along with free hearts and open spirits, to join in the best way they knew how with whatever their father and Gloria were doing, and to give both of them as much love as they could.

I don't know. If their marriage had lasted longer, or if Gloria hadn't been as good a woman as she was, I might have been in for a long, tough session, but I think it was the right way to do it, in any event — for the kids, for me, and for everyone involved.

When my three kids came home again, they all seemed to

have had a great good time, and showed no signs of potential psychological trauma. The only problem was that Meredi had overdone herself by riding and riding and riding "her" horse to such a state of exhaustion that I had to keep her in bed one day. At any rate, Nick and Gloria were divorced after about a year, and some time after that Gloria invited me to have dinner with her. We had a very good time together. It was somehow reassuring to me to find that the second woman who had married Nick was a person I could honestly like and admire. She turned out, too, to have a good sensitive appreciation of my children, and a real affection for them. For many years they each got special, tasteful Christmas presents from her. O the strange bonuses that can come from trying circumstances!

It was not easy raising three children by myself (at the time of the divorce Forrest was close to ten, Ruth seven, and Meredith three). But I doubt if it was really that much harder than it would have been trying to raise them in any one of the ten thousand other ways that children have to be raised. It is never easy raising children. Even under what may seem to be ideal circumstances, there lie hidden strange pitfalls, and dangers recognized only too late.

As to financial security, I have known many families fighting constantly against worse economic straits than our little foursome had to contend with. And, of course, wealth provides its own hazards. (The horrors of slick vacuum that John Cheever records, for instance, were clear out of our ken.) The worst flaw, of course, was the lack of husband and father. But there are ways this lack can develop even without the definite break of divorce, and there are certainly marital situations which bruise and tear the parents — and the children — in violent ways that make a steady nurturing of growing beings close to impossible. For me really, it was easier to be alone in my parenting, and to know I was alone, than it would have been to go on meeting the confusions of a partner who was there but not there, and who could create erratic cross-currents in ways that I had finally given up trying to understand. I did not have enough confidence in my own capacities as an attractive woman to consider seriously looking for a second mate, and so I accepted the single parent role and we went on with our living.

While Gloria was with Nick, they sent us a steady $100 per

month, which certainly did help, but after that there was no regular money from that source. My family, however, were all solidly established in their various locations and willing and able to help if needed. I had a college degree that I could write down on job applications (turned out to be a bit less than helpful for unskilled-type jobs, but anyway). After we'd been in a rented house for about a year, I began looking seriously for a home to buy; and Forrest, who was riding around on a paper route, spotted a really nice three-bedroom house on a big lot, already planted with attractive bushes and flowers and ten top-quality fruit trees. With money borrowed from my parents and $2,000 from Nick, I was able to make a down payment which took us right up to the FHA loan. Total price $11,500 — and the payments never went over $93 per month! I stayed in that house for almost exactly twenty-three years, and then sold it to a young couple who were happy to have it for $75,000. It is currently furnishing me with a large piece of my income.

Years later, when Meredith was the only one still living with me, and she a self-reliant fifteen-year-old, I began working as a caseworker in the Aid to Families with Dependent Children (AFDC — Welfare) program in South San Mateo County. It gave me good reasons to think about how many advantages I'd had when I was functioning as a single parent with young children. It was not only the safety net of the family, the college education, and an inexpensive home of our own. The four of us had gone into our ordeal all heathy and vigorous, with years behind us of relatively successful experiences of meeting life's problems. Even Meredi had had some time to work up confidence in herself as a person who could handle things. It was not until I'd been in the Welfare office for a while that I realized what a heavy weight of sickness and physical disabilities of one kind and another most of the poor are carrying, and furthermore how deadly can be the many debilitating fears and uncertainties about their own abilities and about the abilities — and even loyalties — of the people of their own families on whom they have to depend. Privilege — or the lack of it — is a far-reaching, pervasive thing, affecting almost all areas of life, and it must not be discounted.

When I realized I was going to have to earn our living, I looked first to school teaching. I had a secondary teaching certificate from college, and the superintendent of our local Whisman School District had enough confidence in me because of the way my children functioned (Forrest had put in five years there and Ruthie two) that he offered to hire me with a temporary credential if I'd get in some observation with a bit of practice teaching and go to a summer session in elementary education. I did, and started out with high hopes and only a little trepidation at one of our elementary schools (not where my own children were). I could well have had more trepidation. I did not have what it took to keep a fourth grade classroom in order. In spite of good support and consideration from everyone else on the staff, and special, really great help from two top-notch teachers (who had each worked out quite different methods by which they could honestly be themselves and still keep a classroom full of kids learning at a reasonable rate in decent order), I decided — with the principal's concurrence — that it was not a task I was cut out for, and they let me resign at the Christmas holidays. Ah, what a relief, what an easing of pressure and frustration! But it did leave me with some uneasy, panicky feelings.

The Department of Employment figured I'd be a possible for electronic assembly and sent me out to Sylvania, who had an opening. They gave me a most careful general interview, with worry about whether as a college graduate I might become dissatisfied with the work. The man explained to me about how Sylvania tried to develop a trusting "family" of its workers, and took time to find people who could stay with them loyally. He had me meet and talk with two foremen, and then made an appointment for a physical exam. The exam was as thorough as anything I'd ever had. The doctor did ask about any history of previous mental problems, and I admitted to a nervous break-down back there in '42. It was a few days later that I got a regretful letter stating that the opening for which they had been considering me had been eliminated, and from that time on I kept my mouth shut about anything to do with mental problems.

I went out to Hewlett-Packard, who gave me their test for general dexterity, which they told me I'd passed handsomely, but my friendly guide showed me a whole file-drawer full of job applications for the same jobs I was applying for, and sure enough I didn't hear from them. I talked to a company who needed a receptionist who could do also a small amount of typing. It seemed as though my primitive typing system would have actually done the work, but they felt that it just wouldn't be the right image to have me typing with four fingers in the front office.

Then the Ampex Corporation put in a request to the Employment Office for assembly workers, and I was one of those told to report to work. They hired 93 of us all at once, and after a brief general instruction put us right out on the assembly lines with our respective crew leaders. They counted on a 30-day trial period to eliminate impossible workers. It was a closed union shop for all us production workers, so on Friday when they announced that there would be work that Saturday, at time and a half, they had to invite us raw recruits, too. I took them up on it. The money was most welcome.

The pay at Ampex was considerably higher than I'd been getting as a beginning teacher, and it came in every week. But the best part was that when my work time was over, I walked out the door a free woman. I didn't need to plan for the next day, or to try to figure out where I'd made the misstep with little Arthur and Ronnie, and how I might be able to do better tomorrow. And I wasn't carrying any burden of responsibility for valuable, vulnerable human spirits.

It was interesting to me to find that many acquaintances wanted to commiserate with me when they found out that I had resigned from teaching and was working on the electronic assembly line. They commented about how sad it was that I was really having to go to work now. They seemed to feel that teaching would have been so admirably suited to my needs as a mother — the hours, the summer vacations — that it could hardly be counted as burdensome work. I tried to put them straight, but I guess some myths die hard.

It was not just the better pay and the freedom from responsibility, but the fact that it didn't drain from me those very qualities of patience and interest in a young one's discoveries that I needed for my own children. The work at Ampex was mostly interesting and I enjoyed the people.

With the kind of assembly I was doing, most jobs were no more than just six or seven stations in a row, and some of them

(at Ampex)

    It arches overhead, not as the Gothic cathedral arches, but in white, drab, functioning swell, housing the products and the efforts of the human ants, walking here and there, checking the numbers, wheeling the boxes. Within, too, the long workbenches brightly lighted, where the women loop and bend and solder the colored wires, talking of dresses and children and men and Saturday dances.

    Red checked shirt. These are Americans, individual gripers, casual grapplers with confusion and the tanglements of orders from above. There is a knowledge to this state of being, a form of grace and propriety beneath this arched dome. Only so much speed and no more — only so far is the job important and no farther.

* * *

    "Moon", in a purple jacket, rides around in the yellow truck with the two steel prongs in front, moving platforms of loaded boxes from one place to another. Moon, with vigorous gray curly hair, a man who long since has accepted meaninglessness in eight-hour parcels. Corrupt but hardy, living for the pleasures he can get from whiskey and women.

just two. The jobs were laid out in notebooks that every crew leader had. They were on blueprints that many of the more alert older hands were perfectly capable of reading themselves, but which union regulations kept them from being required to read. The books of jobs were about four inches thick, and the longest I was ever on any one task was three days. When you first started on a new job it took your full attention until you'd learned it. After that you could turn at least part of it over to your hands, and think about other things or chat with your neighbors. There were some cliques of people all tied into parties they'd been to the night before, and who was going with whom, and which workers were making a play for which crew leaders or foremen or even upper echelon. But there were also plenty of people pleased enough to talk about their kids or to recount experiences from earlier times and other places and to indulge in a bit of consideration of human life and its strange ways.

I especially liked Carmen Moreno. She had a direct, quick-moving way, and was somehow well-centered in herself. She was really still young and good looking, with a trim figure, but she never flirted at all. She was just matter-of-fact and friendly with the men she wanted to speak to, and they all seemed to accept her style. She was supporting four children by herself (with no well-off family to back her up), the oldest being a boy about seventeen years old. He was the one she worried about most. One day she told a few of us that he'd not come home the night before until after midnight, and when he did show up he was miserably drunk and sick. She'd lit into him, trying to get him to understand things better, and then had put him to bed, big as he was, and cleaned up after him. Her third son was just a bit older than my Forrest, and then there was a gap before her little daughter. She told me her son had outgrown a jacket that was still good and asked if I thought Forrest could use it. When I said yes she brought it in and gave it to me. She'd had it dry-cleaned first!

Before I continue on into other areas, let me complete a bit of my employment history. We had a strike the next summer after I started working at Ampex. A large, impersonal affair between a coalition of electronics companies and our section of the Machinists' Union. I'd been really impressed by the effectiveness of the union shop stewards in controlling potential conflicts not only between workers and management, but also between individual workers. I had been much interested in the union meetings. It was my impression that anyone who really wanted to find out what was going on and put in hirs oar, could very well have done it, but that most the workers didn't really care, and just paid their dues and attended the compulsory meetings because that was how things were. Before we took the strike vote there was a mammoth meeting at the San Francisco Cow Palace, and the leaders presented the history of our current conflict — the original demands and the offer of the companies, which we had now either to accept or reject. No question that the presentation was aimed toward rejecting the offer, but microphones were freely available to anyone who wanted to speak, and the balloting was secret. I myself voted to accept, and there was no one who saw what I was writing, but the overwhelming vote was to reject the offer.

Very soon after that the public address system at work called all us workers together. Management had thoughtfully prepared our final paychecks for us, told us that we were to consider ourselves still Ampex employees until things could be settled, but that from this time on we would be locked out. We went to the Employment Office and applied for unemployment insurance and then went off to our respective homes to wait it out. It lasted for the full month of July (1957). One small incident seems to me worth reporting. A number of us had signed up to give our blood to the Bloodmobile at its periodic visit to Ampex. They told us to come ahead anyway, and we did. The great barn-like place was all quiet and dark and empty, except for our former crew leaders, who chatted with us quite amicably while we took our turns with the Bloodmobile. Certainly a calm strike, seemingly not really involving any of us little people in a personal way.

At the end of the strike, the women assembly workers went back to work at $2.05 per hour, magnificent wages for those days. But by that time I had already been at work for one week with the Spinco Division of Beckman Instruments, and finally decided to stay with them instead.

The job description on which the Department of Employment had sent me out was simply for a production worker with good manual dexterity and some mathematics. Spinco did not yet have a personnel office, so I had just talked with Fred Williams who would be my immediate supervisor, and to Dr. Durrum, the head of the research department. What they were really prepared to pay was $250 per month, but when I told them I just couldn't survive on that, they raised it to $270, with the proviso I'd have to wait a full six months for any raise, and told me to come in the next day.

What I was going to be doing was making tiny pipettes out of polyethylene tubing. Beckman had contracted with a Swiss doctor to manufacture and market a system he'd developed for analyzing blood serum samples in very tiny quantities. The whole thing depended on measuring small amounts very accurately, and what he had been using were pipettes he made by hand from plastic tubing. The polyethylene was very malleable with heat, inert, and so water-resistant that no drops clung to it. Up to now Dr. Sanz had just made himself a set of pipettes for each determination. Whatever size the pipettes turned out to be after he'd pulled both ends of the tubing, he could use them. But now it would be necessary to manufacture closely identical pipettes in a series of precise, standard capacities. Eventually they'd be making them with some kind of machine, but they needed to make enough of them by hand for a prototype system and for sets that they could distribute to friendly clinicians for testing.

Fred Williams had already figured out the basic techniques for making them, and which gauges of tubing seemed most appropriate for which sizes. He also had the system for calibrating them and had determined how much variation in volume the system could tolerate. But there was still a lot of pioneering both in perfecting the techniques so they were repeatable, and in spotting (and hopefully) improving difficulties that showed up in handling the pipettes. Even in the week before the strike at Ampex ended, I could see that work at Beckman/Spinco offered all kinds of challenges, and that the research department was eager to help me learn anything I wanted to ask about, and would be glad to use any abilities I showed. So I stayed at Beckman, and worked there almost eleven years. Fruitful, interesting years they were, and they provided the financial foundation for the main period of my responsibility for the growing children.

Now let me jump back again to the days at Ampex.

After I got acquainted at Ampex I'd found that there were some other women from my area, so I became one of a car pool who drove in together each morning. The rides turned out to be a special entertainment of their own. One of the riders was a woman who'd been around a lot, working as a cocktail waitress and the like, and she often regaled us with a series of really funny stories whose humor turned on one aspect or another of sex. None of the sneaky, sniggering, looking-for-dirt style I've avoided at other times. Hers was a direct head-on approach, with no hesitation over the blunt names for things. A great deal about sex really *is* funny, and she had a talent and the timing for highlighting those crazy impasses. The twenty minutes of our ride were just about the right time to be involved in it. I used to look forward to her and her stories.

I usually walked a couple blocks from our rented house to one of the thoroughfares where it was easier for them to pick me up, and then back again in the evening. One evening I had a sudden sight of grim reality. Some time later I wrote it down.

> Beside the road there was a dead cat, striped orange fur over the once-warm body of flesh. I watched him day by day as he lay there, muddied by rain, slowly sinking into the weeds and dirt around him, head flung to the side and paws up, helplessly.
>
> In the morning I would hear the birds sing, and the grass would be green and beautiful in spite of the weeds and the old beer cans and rumpled papers. In the evening though, walking home along the other side of the road, I would be tired and the tender spring green of the one tree lovely against the clean sky would not be quite enough. I would see grief and ugliness, "unmeaning", would feel a groan of lonely bleakness in my life, and the cat would lie there pitiful to my sight, flung without dignity or honor, muddy statement of a sad reality.
>
> Turning down my home street, I suddenly saw my rented house as the sordid, unkempt place it is — the old mud-ruts in front of the teetering mailbox, the foxtails and crab grass sprouting in the browning "lawn", the hideous faded pink of the door, and it seemed that I had descended myself — and had led my children with me — into a stupid and beaten level of existence, into a dank and ugly cellar of life.

That was in its own way a true enough picture of life at that time, the kind of realization that it is better to hold at bay, away from one's central awareness. But it seems to be the case that often several apparently quite different things can be true at the same time, and the major tenor of our life was not really bleak.

The day that we moved from our rented home at Leghorn Street to our purchased home at Wyandotte was a Saturday of some confusions. I had forgotten about Pacific Gas & Electric not working on Saturdays, so that neither lights nor gas were available. The worst thing, though, was that Ruthie had been stricken with a bad ear infection, but I'd been lucky enough to get the younger doctor of our pediatrician's office to agree to come out to see her and probably give her penicillin, which usually cleared everything up quickly. Fortunately one of the beds had come with the rented house, so Ruthie was in that, while we worked around her with our boxes and things. Then the doctor did come, radiating competence and good cheer, gave her the penicillin — which showed effects quite rapidly — and we bundled her up and moved her over last of all into one of the newly established beds.

That night, after the helpful friends and neighbors had left, Forrest and I started a good fire in the fireplace, we gathered our small family together in front of it, with candles set around us, and had a good supper from a casserole one good neighbor had thoughtfully given us.

There is a great satisfaction in getting successfully through an obstacle course like that. True enough I had fumbled badly from lack of planning about P.G.&E., but through the various crises of the day I had been able to steer a workable course and to maintain the role of capable helmsman, the calm leader to be trusted, the solid foundation for the children. But it was not only that I was pleased and relieved to find my own capabilities sufficient for the need; the children had all risen to the occasion just beautifully. No whining, no panic, no frantic questioning of Mama. Forrest had pitched in effectively wherever he could, Ruthie had been her usual patient, uncomplaining, not-wanting-to-bother-anybody self, and by the end of the day was not really having to fake it because she'd begun to feel better. Meredi just took everything in stride, counting on the rest of us to handle

what needed handling. They'd proved themselves good companions under trial, and I could be proud of the motherly input that
showed, but also delighted and somewhat amazed at the
resources they each brought forth from internal areas of their
own, areas altogether beyond and separate from anything I'd
given them. It was a night when I went off to sleep with relief
and a swelling gratitude to God.

The hardest part of those early days, naturally enough, was
finding someone to take care of Meredith while I worked. While
I was doing the part-time observation and practice teaching, she
stayed very happily with our next-door neighbor, who had five
children of her own, including the youngest, Freddie. He was
just enough older than Meredi that their play ideas still fit
together well, but that he naturally assumed a gentle lead. As a
matter of fact, Meredi somewhat adored him. Ruth always —
and Forrest sometimes — came home after school to the
Sanchez's too, so Meredi didn't feel strange or abandoned. But
then the Sanchezes were offered more money for their house
and lot than they felt they could refuse, and moved off to San
Francisco where Mr. Sanchez worked. We were left with: first,
their empty house; next, a totally vacant lot, with everything
swept to the back indiscriminately by a bulldozer; and finally, a
huge concrete building which offered no hope nor comfort.

The summer while I was in school, my parents took care of
all three children down at their beach place. At the time I
certainly appreciated it and, I hope, thanked them adequately,
but I didn't really grasp just how much of a noble offer and a
task completed that summer really was. As I count up the years
now, I realize that my mother was slightly older than I am now
— and I get pretty tired just from a one-day stint with my little
granddaughter.

Anyway, when we all came back to Mountain View in the
fall, I tried another neighbor farther up the street, again with
children whom Ruth and Meredi were used to playing with. It
worked for a while, but there were signs of things going less
than well, and one evening when I came for them, Meredi was
looking disconsolate and there was a chill in the atmosphere.
Ruth corroborated for me the story Meredi told about what had
happened between her and the woman. I have totally forgotten
details, but it was anyhow a clear sample of a kind of careless

emotional cruelty that I knew I didn't want to have Meredi facing day after day. Next morning, which luckily was a Saturday, I went over to talk to Frances Bastidas, yet another neighbor and mother of an only child, a girl who played very well with Meredi. Mrs. Bastidas welcomed me cordially and gave me plenty of time and attention to lay out my problem. Then she asked if I'd like to join her in prayer about it. I'd known she was a serious Christian — she'd been a missionary when she met George Bastidas in his native Ecuador, but it was actually the first time I'd run into a Christian who used the tools of her Christian faith unabashedly in public and for everyday occasions. It seemed like just what I needed, so I said yes. She spoke to God simply and directly, and did indeed carry me along with her fully in her petition for help and guidance. She didn't seem to be treating it as just my problem, but joined her own involvement along with it in a very natural way that made me feel that I had found a human friend as well as the divine assurance. The prayer all in itself was a good strength and comfort, smoothing off the panicky edge of aloneness that I had been feeling.

Mrs. Bastidas was not able to take care of Meredith on a steady basis, but she did take care of her for several days until I was able to scout around and locate a licensed day-care center that I liked the looks of. (Incidentally, Frances Bastidas was the good neighbor who cooked us the casserole which served our needs so well on moving day.)

The child-care center was located in a big old home in Palo Alto, and run by a relaxed, competent couple named Castleberry, who managed their own four children right along with a modest-sized brood of outsiders. Every weekday morning I delivered Meredi over there, and picked her up again in the evening. I remained confident that she was safe and well cared for, but it wasn't all easy. Meredi really didn't want to cry about it in the mornings, but try as she might, with whatever encouraging talk she gave herself and me beforehand, she always seemed to have to break down into crying when we got really close to Castleberry's. Leila Castleberry assured me that she recovered very quickly after I left, and for sure she always seemed pleasantly occupied and full of the day's activities by the time I came for her in the evening, but it was definitely wearing emotionally for both of us to go through the morning's delivery. I'm sure she stopped crying sometime during the period that she stayed with the Castleberries. Maybe it was, in fact, only a week or two that she had to struggle with her tears, but it does stick in the mind.

When it was time to enroll her in kindergarten, I decided it was much better to have her going to our own Powell School, and so brought her back again into our own neighborhood. This time I worked out an arrangement with Marie Palesi, several blocks away, whose only daughter Beatrice was a friend of Ruthie's. I'd drop both my girls off at Palesi's in the morning, and from there on Marie Palesi would organize the comings and goings of the two older girls and Meredi's shorter trip over and back to the school.

By the time Meredith was in first grade, my mother had come to live next door to us, and provided Meredi with a home base to come to after school, and someone also for special things like getting our cat and her kittens in adequate order so that she could "share" them with her classmates right after lunch one time.

Through all the time of changing babysitters — and also in later negotiations with Grandma — Ruth had been acting as a kind of second mother. The two sisters had always got on well together, and when my absence at work made the gap in our family structure, good little Ruthie had moved into it as best she could. When she was around, she'd act as translator for Meredith's utterances, which weren't always crystal clear, the child being likely to weave into her current comments all kinds of earlier family happenings that no one around could possibly know about. Ruth was always steady, calm, and reassuring, so that just having her there — or soon to arrive again — seemed to keep Meredith feeling secure.

Which summer was it, anyhow, when we'd been visiting my folks at their beach place in Washington, and my sister and her family were there, too, and talked us into letting Ruthie stay on longer to keep Sibyl company and then come home to California with them? At any rate, we began to miss Ruthie in strange ways. It wasn't just that her own special reactions to things weren't with us any more, but I began to notice that I was running into sharp edges on Forrest, and on Meredi, and they seemed to be running up against me, too, with more than usual friction. I finally figured out that Ruth had been supplying our family group with the grease between the gears, the yielding buffers that helped us adjust to each other without our stark selfishnesses banging each other directly. It was good to have her back again. I think Ruth has carried a special kind of blessing with her into every group of people she's been with — but it has sometimes been pretty hard on her.

For all the years we lived on Wyandotte St., the Marquezes were an important part of our lives. I never involved Mrs. Marquez directly in any of my official arrangements about child care, but she and her family acted as a continuing source of family-type support for both Ruth and Meredith. John and Bessie Marquez, with Joey and Rachel and Lupe and Carmen and Rosalie and Kathy and Jenny, were either already living in the house across the street from us or moved in very shortly after we came. Rachel was in Ruth's class at school and Kathy was a bit older than Meredi, and started school a year ahead of her. Mrs. Marquez was at home most the time, except that in the summer she usually worked in the cannery, with the older girls in charge and strict orders about staying in and around the house.

Mrs. Marquez told me once about their early days when she and John had both been working and they had three little kids at home. They'd pretty much seen each other only in passing — one of them working night shift so they could cover. She remarked it was a serious strain on their marriage not only the lack of time together, but that it was almost unavoidable that each one of them would have hoped for some particular household task to have been finished off by the partner, and to be kind of irritated when they found it hadn't been.

Anyhow they were a solid, active family when we knew them, with relatives visiting and barbecues and guitar playing periodically to enliven things. The Marquez girls came back and forth to our house pretty freely, and the Nixon girls went over to Marquez's also pretty freely. There was probably more time spent at Marquez's — even when I was home — because they had a television and we didn't. It had been an active decision on my part (with Forrest definitely concurring), but there was a tendency to gravitate toward TV. Also there was the weight of numbers, and possibly that my girls were free of primary responsibility for household tasks over there. At least when the whole group, or different sections of it, came over to Nixon's they'd be prepared to generate their own play ideas. Really, even when the TV was on at Marquez's there was a lot of side-play, too, so it wasn't pure and simple sitting in front of the "boob tube."

There was one day I came home and found out that there'd been a false alarm at Powell School with their nuclear attack warning system. There'd been no really good way to check, so the authorities had actually sent the kids home as planned. Ruth and Meredith went right along to Marquez's, and Mrs. Marquez assembled all the brood and calmed them down, and held things steady until she could get reliable word on what was going on. I was very grateful just for that one episode, but it started me to thinking further. And I knew that if that had been in fact a real attack, Mrs. Marquez would have been protecting Ruth and Meredith just as fiercely as she would her own youngsters. Top-notch neighbors!

It was after my children had all left home that I lost the Marquezes in the same kind of way we'd lost the Sanchezes earlier. A trucking firm offered them too big a price for their house and they moved to San Jose. The house was vacant for a while, and then one day I came home to find a thick layer of dust all over everything at my house. I looked across the street, and sure enough, a bulldozer had pushed their house, and the fence, and all the bushes, clear off to the back. A sudden shock of loss, with all the memories of the Marquezes crowding into my mind.

There were some cheery birthday parties we had at our place. A midsummer one that Forrest put together for his friends — just boys, with Ruth and Meredith and me consigned to the sidelines. There was a great battery of home-designed games, climaxed with each boy being issued a plastic water pistol, with two buckets of water available as ammunition. When the girls were in charge a usual feature was that the early arrivals were allowed to help with decorations — balloons, crêpe paper streamers, etc. — and also with deciding on games and how the refreshments were to be served. The extemporaneous style always seemed to bring everyone together with special enjoyment.

Christmas had its own proper progression. The first Christmas after the divorce Forrest announced that he would provide us with the tree. We waited until the last evening before the big day and all trooped down to the lot Forrest had chosen and picked out a decent-looking tree from those left unsold. Forrest paid the man the modest sum that was being asked in those last hours, and we took it home quite grandly. Our other decorations were already up, so it was just the final climax to get the tree set up and the balls and the lights on it. It was always a fight for me to get everyone to clean up the house before we started setting out our Christmas decorations. The kids always wanted just to pile into our red cardboard box and start putting things around, in spite of clutter, dust, and dirt (the house tended to get pretty bad).

It was standard practice just before the kids went to bed Christmas Eve for all of them to bring out the presents they'd prepared and set them under the tree. I usually waited to lay mine out until they'd gone to bed. Christmas morning everyone got to choose only one present and open it and the stocking presents before breakfast. After breakfast all rules were off, and of course it always went too fast and we'd each come too quickly to that point when all the goodies were laid open before us, with no more hidden surprises to be found under the tree. There were usually a couple of good new records, though, which we'd listen to together at least once, and some games to try out, and each thing to savor as fully as possible. I remember the Christmas I gave the game "Gettysburg" to Forrest. By afternoon he'd got Reed Klatt from across the street to try it out with him. Reed turned out to be as eager a tactician/ historian as Forrest himself, and for weekends after that the two of them, or a succession of other boys, would be spending 3- or 4-hour sessions at our living-room table, asking what time it was, and just how soon General Hooker was due to come over the hill with his cavalry.

Our camping trips were special times, out of the context of our usual days. Very enjoyable for me, and I am pleased to see that all three of my now-grown offspring continue camping experiences with their new families. I had taken the kids on the simple, near-at-home, comfortable kind of camping trips that are made easy by the good state parks in California. Meredi was just about 3½ when we first tried out a new 5' × 5' green tent at

Portola State Park, the closest one to Mountain View. She seemed to feel quite at home in our campsite with its redwood needles, and spoke with considerable authority both to and about the Stellar Jays that abounded, calling them by a name that sounded like nothing else than "tea pot". Almost every summer, too, we visited my parents at Long Beach, Washington by traveling up the coast along Highway 101. We took about three days for the trip and stopped overnight first in the California Redwoods and then in one of the good Oregon State Parks. We had become fairly seasoned hands at camping.

But I wanted to let my children have a chance at the wilderness experiences that had meant so much to me, and I could tell that I was moving toward a time when I wouldn't have the stamina for backpacking. After gauging minimum and maximum, I picked on the summer that Meredith was 9 (Ruth 13½ and Forrest 16) and I was 43 to try our first backpack camping. Cultus Lake in Southern Oregon had been a place where my brother Rox and I had spent ten delightful days of easy-access wilderness camping. There had been a mountain road that touched only one corner of the lake, and the rest of it was untouched except for crude trails. We had driven in in Rox's hardy Model A, hauling behind us the rowboat he and my father had built in our basement. We'd left the Ford parked next the road, loaded our things into the rowboat, and rowed across to a good spot on the other side of the lake. We'd chosen an undeveloped site and built our own table. Everything had been so untouched by other human life that we'd notched the table as each day passed to keep track of the time.

The up-to-date map that I got showed still only one dirt road into the lake, so we embarked. Remarkably it hadn't really changed that much, but we did get the full impact of the changes on the first night we arrived. We'd come in on a Saturday, and the place was crowded for the weekend with water skiers and other motorboat fans. Since all other sites were taken, we had to hunch our campsite into a bare bit of ground right next the road. In the morning we broke camp, loaded up, and hiked along the trail at the side of the lake. It took us just about a mile and a half before we were safely away from the crowd. We had our choice of a number of good lakeside campsites and settled into one.

The weekend boaters had almost all loaded up and left by the next night anyway, so the population explosion hadn't been really that bad a problem. What was a problem, though, was a lively thunderstorm that came up during the night and pelted down on us. The high mountains are always cold at night, so this was not easy to take. "Camp Bountiful" over again for me, but this time considerably worse because I had my children with me, whom I'd freely brought in, in the folly of my heart. I remember watching the branches above me whipped back and forth by the wind, absolutely black in the dense clouds, and thinking that if that had been snow instead of rain coming down on us I wouldn't have been any more effective with my prayers than I was for the rain, and we could die there in the bosom of Nature without waking any response in the living universe. Finally the sky did clear, and I shall always remember the blessed look of those bright, reassuring stars shining on us again. I don't know. I don't seem to have the stuff for a faith that moves mountains, and in some ways I seem to feel more natural with a fierce universe which follows its own physical rules unremittingly and does not yield to my small entreaties.

By the light of morning, things didn't look too bad. We renewed the fire, and there was even a bit of sunshine to provide a dim warmth. We proceeded with our plans to hike on to Muskrat Lake, which showed on the map as being only a bit over three miles on a trail that took off from Cultus. The pack loads we'd assigned to Ruth and Meredith seemed to be just about right for them (Meredi's included her favorite teddy bear, strapped on the last thing so that he was watching the trail behind her). Forrest carried his pack along at a good pace and came back to relieve me of mine after he'd already left his at our new campsite.

There was an old cabin on Muskrat Lake, and the lake itself had a fairly wide clean beach, not many tree branches or reeds. There was also a simple log raft beached on it. We set up housekeeping in the cabin — after our recent dousing from the storm a shelter had real appeal. That evening we had a pleasant campfire out front where we could watch the stars come out, and crawled into our separate sleeping bags early, before all light had left the sky.

Sometime the next morning we noticed that there was a

small dog huddled at the side of the trail we'd come in on. No sign of any owner, no person around at all. If one of us tried to approach her, even talking gently in an effort to reassure, she'd get up and retreat, watching intently. I saved some pancakes from our breakfast, and set them out on a metal plate about two-thirds of the way to where she settled down. They disappeared. I think I had to refill the plate once again before she came on up to eat from the plate set at my feet. She was starved, weak and bony, a small, tan short-haired terrier-type. The only thing we could guess was that she must have been with a group of fishermen or a horseback expedition and got lost some way. What experiences had made her afraid of us human beings we didn't like to speculate about. It wasn't very easy, feeding her. We'd come in with a bare-bones minimum of food, trying to cut to a minimum for weight in our packs. Someone had left in the cabin a small bag of carrots, now limp and unappetizing, and a few potatoes — not the sort of thing that one would bring home from the supermarket. When I prepared them to add to our rice and dried onions and Canadian bacon, I saved all the peelings and cooked them, too. When Forrest caught a couple small trout out of the lake, I saved the heads and guts and fins and cooked them up in a kind of broth. We all gave "Girl" the bones and tails we disentangled from our servings, plus whatever free-will offerings we felt we could sacrifice. She ate everything, gratefully. She'd sit there, quietly but tense, watching us eat our food, smelling it but not moving to make a snatch. There was just one time she transgressed her self-imposed discipline. A piece of bacon came too temptingly close to her nose, and it was gone! We were all eager enough about our food portions by that time that she heard quite an outcry, but she knew she was guilty and looked utterly miserable, so no one stayed angry long.

The second day she was with us we decided to spend the day at Teddy Lake, not that far away. We'd just walk freely without having to carry anything but our lunch and Forrest's fishing gear. We kind of expected Girl to stay put. She was pretty weak and hadn't been doing that much walking around. But when we all got up and started walking down the trail, she pulled herself up and followed along behind us. She'd adopted us for sure!

One evening at our campfire we heard a strange noise off across the lake. Beast-like in effect but I certainly didn't recognize it. Not really close by the sound, but not far enough distant to leave us untroubled. Girl, who'd been lying behind me, got up growling in her throat, went out away from us toward the noise, made two sharp challenging barks, and finally came back. No real protection, of course, but it was the right idea and maybe let some animal know there was some style of human encampment where we were. At any rate it made us all feel better.

As the time came for us to pack up and go home, we began to wonder what to do with Girl. We had left a good, faithful little black and white dog named Butch at home. It had seemed kind of mean not to give him a chance at this family outing, but he had never gone camping with us before. The state parks frowned on animals, and we'd always left him at home when we made our camping/travel trips to Washington. (Grandma and Grandpop had a dog and cat of their own and it didn't seem right to add too much confusion.) Anyhow, it seemed as though it would be adding insult to injury to go back with another dog — even though she was female. When we got her in our car, any indecision was satisfied. About every two or three miles she'd get so restless and troubled that we'd have to stop the car and take her out to see if she needed to do something. She never did, but it was obvious she wasn't going to travel at all well. Fortunately the first U.S. Forest Station we tried had a friendly man in charge who had his wife and a couple of small children with him. They didn't have a domestic pet, and when we told them the story of the little dog they were glad to take her in. They lived year-round in one of the nearby small towns and would be able to take Girl right along with them at the end of the summer. As we drove off down the road, we watched her straining after us, but she was held securely in the arms of the Forest Guard, while the two children waited impatiently below to get acquainted with their new dog. Mortal life does seem to be filled with many small deaths of one kind or another — and many small births, too!

But there were deaths of the big, final kind that touched our lives, too. Way back there when we'd first come to Mountain View from San Francisco, Forrest and I had walked around, looking at things and meeting new neighbors. It was quite a rural section still. People kept rabbits and chickens, and sometimes bought a calf to raise and kill later for the meat. Forrest had a lot of questions and I'd just answered them as simply and directly as I could. One day he startled me by asking "Mama, do people ever raise children to eat?" He didn't seem to have made the emotional connections, any imagining of real flesh and blood action along those lines, but he'd been turning it over in his head, putting two and two together intellectually. When I said "No they don't", it seemed to satisfy him. He took my word for it.

With Ruth, I remember her dealing rather with an experience of loss. There'd been a little bird that stunned hirmself against one of our windows. I picked hirm up in my hand, and with that warmth, s/he began to revive a bit and stir. I passed hirm over into Ruthie's carefully held small hands, and she watched hirm closely and in a great wonder of delight. The small warm body lying all yielding in her hand, the exquisitely soft feathers, the small scratching of the feet, the tiny eyes moving in the sleek head. Moment to moment the bird gathered strength and vibrancy again, then took off right from her hands into the freedom of hirs own movement in the air. Ruthie watched the wings carrying hirm away, looked down at her two empty hands, still cupped, reached them out toward the bird again as if asking hirm to return, and then began to cry. I did not even try to distract her with a toy. There seemed to be a truth and rightness about her grief of loss that should not be disturbed, that she should be helped to go through whole. I put my arms around her and just kind of murmured something or other until the crest of her crying had passed, and then I did indeed pick up the thread of what other things there were to do, and we went off about our work.

The fiercest death occurred before the children were old enough to grasp it in any personal way. It was, in fact, even before Meredith was born. There had been a small family of Russian people who moved in next door to our Mountain View studio. My first sight of Marthe Riabyh had been when Forrest and Ruthie (in the buggy) and I were setting out for our evening stroll. Marthe was moving vigorously down the length of a garden patch some 14 × 40 feet long, turning the soil over deeply with a spade. She was already about a quarter of the way through it, moving methodically and without pause — in with the spade, shove it down deeply with the foot, up and over, down deeply again. We swung over to the fence to say hello. She looked up, smiled expansively and came over to greet us. It was obvious quickly that she didn't understand much English, but she was perfectly clear with her gestures and body language. She was delighted to see little children, and full of warm neighborliness toward me.

They were peasant, farmer people. Their son, in his early twenties, had come to the United States first, learned enough of the language and the ways to make his own way, and had then arranged for his parents to join him. They had had an older son, too, but he had completely disappeared and been lost to them during the confusions of the war. The younger son here had a job with a tree surgeon company, and was able to get his father some work there, too. They worked at developing their one-acre lot into a small farm — Marthe by herself during the day, and all three of them together after the men came home. They had ducks and pigs and chickens as well as the big garden. Marthe would bring over fuzzy yellow ducklings for Forrest and "b-Roosie" to admire.

I had a foretaste of the big tragedy several weeks before it happened. Marthe came over to our house one evening very much upset, wanting me to go back with her about some disaster. When I got over there I found both Mikhail, the father, and George lying on beds. George explained to me that they'd run into another car on their way home from work. Fortunately, it was just at the intersection very close to home, and they'd been able to walk on home. He didn't think it was anything all that big. He thought it was just strains and bruises and he and his father would be okay again in the morning. They'd get the car going again. Thanks for coming over, but they were really all right. Marthe seemed to be taking Mikhail's injuries pretty much in stride, as though she figured he was tough and would get over it, but with George there was an edge of panic in her concern.

It was not too long after that there came the evening when I opened our evening paper and saw a brief news story on the front page about a young man, working high in a tree next to a power pole, who'd been electrocuted instantly and finally that morning. It was George Riabyh.

There was no way not to face it. I went across our lots to their back door and on into the kitchen. Women from the local Russian-American community were there, busy, doing what they could. Marthe, terribly distraught, frantic, came toward me and we hugged each other, so that her weeping had a resting place against me for a little while. There never is anything to say in any language anyhow.

There followed some terrifying days next door. At night you could hear Marthe outside calling to him: "Ge-or-da! Ge-or-da! Ge-or-da!" Piercing, heartbroken cries. The Russian-American friends came and went, and the Greek Orthodox priest, an imposing figure with his long black robes and a full gray beard. Before the funeral they had the casket over at the house and they asked Nick to come over with his camera and take photographs of it. Many pictures, it seemed, of the casket itself with the carefully-prepared corpse inside, and of the various guests and friends in their black suits and mourning dresses. We did not go to the funeral itself, but Nick and I did go over by turns for the funeral feast afterwards. A great lavish affair, on big tables, with vodka and wine ahead of time for the men, and great dishes of meat and sausage and vegetables and breads, and the hot tea served in glasses. At first it seemed like a cruel thing to put the old people through — they had to act as host and hostess — but I suspect that the necessity of having to prepare food and get out the dishes and plan for enough chairs available was probably the only thing that kept them going at all through the first shock of their grief.

The next Easter, our whole family went along to the cemetery where George was buried, for a special Greek Orthodox service. An impressive and somehow satisfying thing. The springtime sky was lovely, and the green, rich grass. We stood in a large circle with the headstone at one end, where Marthe and the other women had set around dishes of special Russian Easter breads and cheeses and desserts and some colored eggs. Each of us held a tall tapered candle, lighted, while the priest chanted a service, with responses now and again, also chanted, from the gathered circle. After the service we broke into talking, shared the food and went on home again.

I doubt if either Forrest or Ruth remembers much about that time, that ordeal of sudden death and partial healing, but it may have supplied a kind of background, an orientation to the way human life is put together.

My father died in the summer of 1958, before he'd had a chance to come see our new home. We flew north to Long Beach, Washington for the family gathering and the funeral. He was only sixty-nine, but he had been having trouble with his heart, and had been kind of preparing himself and us by a matter-of-fact attitude that showed in things like deciding not to put all his usual master-craftsman skills into the building of a new flower box because he didn't really care whether it lasted longer than he did or not.

It was a rather formal, traditional funeral in the little community church where my parents had been good solid pillars during the years of their retirement. I had asked Ruth to take care of Meredith and the other younger cousins while the rest of us went to the funeral. She did, very pleasantly and effectively, providing good cheer for the youngsters,

It was only years later that I discovered she'd been left with a feeling not only of incompletion, but even of personal guilt, because she'd been playing down on the sand while her grandfather was being buried. With Ruth, you had to watch out for her taking things *too* sensitively.

There were other deaths that came even closer to us, and with more sudden unexpected force, into our patterns of daily life. Cynthia and Janice Reyes had come to live on Wyandotte Street sometime in the earlier section of our long stay there. Cynthia was in Ruth's class at school and Janice in Meredi's. They had quickly joined the gaggle of girls who played together up and down the street. Meredi and Janice had hit it off especially well together and Meredi would often be up there with her. There were a couple little former chicken-coop buildings behind their rented house which lent themselves well to all styles of playing house.

It seems strange to me now that we had a couple pairs of roller skates, because our street wasn't paved and we didn't have sidewalks, and our back yard didn't have any concrete areas. There were, however, good areas over at Powell School (about three blocks away) and some of the neighbors' yards may have had concrete.

At any rate, we did have the roller skates and they were sometimes in demand. One weekend I felt the need to ask about them. It turned out that they were no longer in our possession. They had been carried off by Cynthia and Janice. No, they hadn't asked to borrow them — or rather, even worse, they had asked and been turned down, and then had just plain taken them off the porch. It didn't seem like the sort of thing that should be let go. As I remember it, I walked over with one or both of my girls to their small house on the big lot, and demanded the skates back, and got them. I thought about maybe some kind of a rule about not letting them come over to play for a while and not going over to play with them, as a kind of statement of disapproval, but decided against it finally — or maybe just let it go by default.

At any rate I was glad later on that I hadn't been tough, because several months later, I ran into their mother over at our corner grocery store and she told me that Janice had started getting sick and hadn't got any better, and the doctor was checking for all kinds of things and had put her in the hospital for a new kind of treatment that sometimes worked. Aplastic anemia was what they thought it was, and it had been tough times for all their family. Janice was in the hospital for several months and we'd hear about her once in a while from Cynthia. Then there was one day when Cynthia came down the street and told us that Janice had died. We asked Cynthia to join us for lunch and she did. We talked about Janice and remembered all kinds of things about her and all the things we'd done together with her, and then Cynthia went off again, to tell some of the other neighbors. We attended a Rosary (but didn't go to look in the casket).

It was for me a sad but lovely gift of life that years later, long after the Reyes family had moved away, we received from Cynthia the announcement of her wedding, and she followed it up for several years with Christmas cards.

I think every young mother must have had the experience of having an older woman stop to admire her children — in a grocery check-line, at a park — and say to her, as an important piece of advice, "Enjoy the children while they're small!" At the time it seems a bit stupid. You're so hung up with a bunch of never-ending, often frantic tasks that you don't really have the time and leisure to enjoy much of anything, and it's the children and their needs that put you in that bind. It is probably one of those paradoxical "no win" situations, but I understand pretty well by now what they mean. I may even find myself saying it to some young mother one of these days.

There is something about the childhood years — before the strugglings, the gropings, the frictions of adolescence begin to throw up blocks and disagreements — that is almost idyllic in its harmony. In spite of the difficulties that come at the family from outside — or almost because of them, if they're met successfully — there remains a harmony, a cohesiveness, a kind of closeness and loyal intimacy which provides the parent with a feeling of usefulness and fulfillment s/he's not likely to match ever again. The children make you part of a vigorous, growing life. The things they look at and enter into are new, bright, full of wonder, and so they become that way for you, too. The children respond to you, give you back love for love, give you a reason for working, for getting up in the morning, a direction and a feeling of progress. It is a time of surprises, of unexpected joys, of limitless possibilities. At their best, almost anyone's healthy children are, in fact, delightful people to have around. And the ones you know best, who seem to be so closely a part of you, are even more than that, a treasure beyond any valuing. But as I look back on it now, picking my way carefully toward the past from the realities of the three excellent people whom my children have become, I think that the harmony and cohesiveness as I felt them were more apparent to me than they were actual.

In our family the openness and exploring growth of childhood seemed to continue into the teen years without any noticeable break. Learning at school, both the classroom studies and the interactions with other students and teachers, became increasingly important. But I was still included in discussions about the meaning of one thing or another, and kept abreast of new incidents in a variety of continuing stories. The kids all seemed to be developing in ways that delighted me. I'm ashamed to have to admit it, but I guess I was even congratulating myself on being such an outstandingly sensitive and

understanding mother that I had avoided the pitfalls of parenting and was going to come through clean. I thought that my
offspring were going to continue to grow peacefully and
gradually into their own separate living, still looking to me as a
wise and loving companion in their growth.

No way! I was forced to realize, sometimes gradually but
often jolt by jolt, that my children were not the persons I had
thought them to be. The parts about each of them that I
cherished most were not the parts that they cherished about
themselves.

Sometimes gradually and sometimes by great stunning leaps,
they tore apart the fabric that had been woven through long
years of careful growth, and confronted me with new ways of
being that I thought I had never seen before.

I had thought they were each reaching their own good
maturities through impulses within themselves, building on
patterns I had watched for years, but suddenly there were no
patterns any more. What had looked to me like ingrained
patterns of character were really only modes of behavior that I
had forced upon them, false images to be discarded.

It's rough. I think it's extra rough on the single parent,
because there's no corroborating other witness to verify one's
memories of what was going on in the family household. There
were times when I found myself wondering whether I had
actually lived in the same house, or through the same years, as
my still familiar but now transformed offspring.

Let me run through the history of childhood as I now see
it. The parent feels as though s/he knows the child more
thoroughly and intimately than s/he has ever known another
human being. To turn around the lines from Psalm 139 (actually
this puts the parent in the role of God): "I know you through
and through from having watched your bones take shape when
you were being formed in secret, knitted together in the limbo
of the womb." S/he has watched every step of the way by which
the tiny baby grows from a strange, miraculous, helpless bit of
functioning body into a responding person, a full-fledged human
being. At the same time, I'm sure most parents find it impossible
to conceal themselves from the 24-hour-a-day scrutiny of childish
eyes, and give up any attempt at concealment. The warts and
the fumblings do show, and one is certainly better off to be
honest about them and let it all hang out.

So the parent feels that all is clear and honest and open between hirm and the child, and to some extent, so it is. But at the same time there are unavoidable differences between the parent's perceptions and experiences and the child's. One thing I discovered in later years was how different our memories were. I tended to have a great store of memories from times when the children were really small, when I had no work outside our home, when I included them in most my activities. Their effective memories, on the other hand, didn't begin until they were at least eight or nine years old, and had me always off at work, harried, piecemeal. Again, the focus of their minds was certainly often very different from mine. I'm sure everyone has heard some good story like the one about the little girl who comes in from playing to ask her mother: "Mama, where did I come from?" The mother, dutifully calling to mind all her own experience and all the advice from a child-development course, goes through a careful simplified description of conception and the birth of a baby. The little girl looks at her, slightly puzzled, and responds: "That's funny. Jeannie said *she* came from New Jersey."

I personally have always been subject to the fallacy of supposing that the person on whom I lay my carefully considered expressions of wisdom is really taking it in just as I've been laying it out. With adults I am sometimes warned by a certain look of blankness, of non-comprehension. And even with adults I often miscalculate. But with a child, how can the little one even know what comprehension would feel like, what understanding would be? So many things occur without any particular connection that the child can see; so many things that the adults do don't fit into any meaning that is the child's own. I think it's not a matter of conscious concealment, but just that the child responds in ways that seem to be expected of hirm. Agreement is so much easier than attempts to articulate formless questions or doubts. It is so much simpler to flow with a dominant adult's notions of style and direction than it would be to interpose other possible ways of doing things.

When the adolescent is struggling with the task of pulling hirs own separate being out of the pleasant (or unpleasant) security of hirs childhood family, s/he does not really start from ground zero. Behind the apparently open and thoroughly satisfied face of even the happy child there are, I am sure, internal questions, judgments made on hirs own, gropings in separate directions which will form the groundwork for the adolescent's search.

For the sake of other older parents, let me say that I found it helpful in healing my own wounds to organize in my mind almost a funeral for each of the children I had thought I knew. I consciously gathered together my most precious memories of each of them from babyhood through all the years they were part of my living family household, and said good-bye to them, putting them away carefully in my storehouse of past treasures. They *were* true in their own way. I can still draw richness from them. But I must not try to see them still growing in the adults I now know, nor expect those adults to recognize themselves in the pictures that I formed of their childhoods. Now I am free to see my son and daughters freshly, as new creatures with unknown potentials which I can explore from the happy vantage point of being, oddly enough related to them.

I have found an analogy that satisfies me as an overall history of my children and me. Suppose we were a four-piece ensemble, which I, as the original head of household, tried to hold together in harmony. The essential resonances in each of the other three instruments were really not tuned precisely to the key in which I had settled, and yet I had thought they were. I had been playing happily along, unintentionally forcing the other instruments to adjust themselves into my key. The more they developed the strength and purity of their own sounds, the more obvious became the disharmony, and they had to get clear of my sounds in order to develop their own.

However and whenever we managed it, I think we did all come through the rapids of disengagement successfully. The ensemble for which I was too much conductor is no more, but there are other good groups playing their own music, and they all manage to welcome me to join them from time to time with bit parts here and there.

I'm going to finish this section on my life as a mother with a set of Mother's Day poems written after I was already safely through the period of turmoil.

Mother's Day Poems

FOR MY MOTHER

You know our bob-tailed cat
and how she strikes at Panther,
seeing him just as foreign mass
of fur and yellow eyes.

Her mothering's done.
It's long ago she licked
the tall-browed kitten head
and helped blue eyes to open.

Memories come round her still sometimes
and she will lick his scarred
and battered tom-cat head,
then hiss and lash out once again.

We human beings hope for more,
more firmly tied to warmth
once felt like benediction,
to arms and voice that made
the boundaries of a world
and gave the energy for style and motion.

Times change, and with them hearts and
souls.
The new style must be made,
the boundaries extended out
to danger and the fierce unknown.

So each leaves home
(who has grown true and strong)
and mother-spirit welcomes it in part,
but still must hiss and spit a bit
at what she feels is foreign.

SOME COMMENTS FOR
RUTH HALDEMAN GRAYBILL COLLIER
ON MOTHER'S DAY 1968

In the world the generations come and go
("Talking of Michelangelo"? Well not really, of course,
but echoes of poor old Prufrock did creep in.)

and what is meted out to one
moves down the line, and comes out again
with variations of its own.

    Mothers are caught and beaten and battered,
    mothers are thrust with the struggling soul;
    mothers must make the meal after meal
    and wipe the small, runny nose.

    Mothers must stand with the probing spirit,
    reach out a steadying hand —
    and come to the place where they're no longer needed,
    where they're more of a drag than a home.

Crippled, all of us. The mixed inadequacy with what is good.
Only pray that what goes on from here has more of grace and
strength and beauty than what went before.

We cannot know, and must rest in some kind of strange paradox
of compassion, mingled with the poor herd of human creatures
who try, and try, and give up trying, and then weep — or
sometimes laugh — and try again.

So we women, one after the other,
we play the role as best we can,
and pass it down the line —
the long uncertain line,
moving out with the pulse of blood
and the lift of hopeful spirit.

Come take my hand, Mother Mine,
and do you reach back to that
warm, strong hand of your own dear mother,
and I'll reach on to Meredith and Sally
and we can give each other blessings
    and forgiveness,
and ask for strength,
and look in wonder at our motherhood.

FOR MY MOTHER

There is a peace in being only single once again,
      in seeing that the ties of childhood bind no more —
      on child, or mother either.
Within the network of those living veins
      that still bring back and forth
      the sustenance of love
      between us and all who form our human family,
      we move with more of freedom,
      being this time
      sister to our brother,
      wife to husband,
      teacher to our student,
      suppliant to a stronger,
      go-between for troubled disputants —
savoring the sweetest of our ties,
      beyond the needs of single time or pressing duties.
You talk and read with brother John,
      back within the family there in Williamsport.
You see "Chooser" in bright winter playsuit,
      even while you write to Sibyl of her wedding plans.
It is not single line or thin commitment that we have
      to all our loved,
      but strangely mingled consciousness that brings us all
each to hirs special, blessed place within the whole.

MOTHER'S DAY

We may not make it to success,
we mothers of this race of Man.
We mother, too, the shamed and flawed:
    the branded rapist strapped within a chair
    while newsmen watch;
    the man who sears a trail across the world
    and falls with bullets and the cheers of mobs;
    the blurred and weary girl
    with half-clothed babies and no man;
    the taut and fearful "bitch" in latest fashion
    but no love;
    the petty man who stands within
    the world's esteem, but fails his human meaning.

For every child, I think, we fail.
That early look of babyhood — the look that knows
beyond the scope of mortal things,
that untouched, boundless hope
of what this life can be —
fades as it grows, and mortal limits and disaster
crowd it out.

It isn't really all that good,
this "Mother's Day" affair,
the choice of "Mother of the Year"
and homage paid.

When Mary stood beneath the cross
and watched the soldiers strip her son,
I do not think she saw the Christ,
the risen glory at the side of God.

Madman or fool, enemy of the good and stable,
he stood with robbers and known criminals,
his ways proved wrong and shameful.

What honor had she then in being mother?
What choice except to bow in shame?

IN CHRISTIAN FELLOWSHIP

It was not until I was in my forties (and my three children ranging in age from fourteen down to seven) that I found myself meeting the IS again in still another mode.

My mother had moved to live near us, and invited us to come along on a weekend retreat of the Presbyterian church she had joined. We all had a good time there, and we began going to church services and discussion groups and the like. The minister, Rev. George Wilson, was strong on the values and richness of Christian fellowship and he began to open up for me a great new vista of meaningful living: communion with God broadened out so it was shared as fully as possible with other believers and seekers, with other human spirits also touched by God each in hirs own way. Nothing really new or revolutionary about that — the ideal of living fellowship is certainly as old as the church itself. But oddly enough the experience of it really was new for me.

In my youth I'd been terribly impatient with the fumbling mediocrity of the church, so I'd never got below the surface there, and even though I'd become pretty good at reaching out in love to other people and receiving their love back, it was almost always at the simple level of one human being to another. I'd be aware of God being in the encounter, but that knowledge didn't surface into mutual awareness. The God in me felt the God in them and there was a real response of unity and fellowship, but we didn't talk together about what that God meant, or try to figure out ways to make our common relationship in God deeper or more permanent. It was only rarely, if the other person happened to be consciously religious, that we could share together our knowledge of God.

No way would I try to pretend that the fellowship encounters in that church — or in any other I have known — were complete or perfect reflections of how the body of Christ should really be functioning through its members, but imperfect as they were, they did offer me a new dimension of the presence of God. I had already come to see God as being spread out in multitudinous spirits, simultaneously living each from hirs own center, but my response had remained single, only mine. Now I could take part in a whole network of response in which my own response was joined intimately with other people's praise and vision and searchings. Now I too was spread out, not dissipated or thinned down, but made more whole and richer by sharing other people's awareness of the presence of our God.

Have you ever watched young babies responding to the world they touch as their hands move about? They have felt the response of this thing or of that thing when it comes in contact with their fingers. But what happens when the fingers of one hand touch the fingers of the other hand? A double response, a strange reflexive experience. I think my progress from a single response to a shared response in fellowship was something like that.

It's a style of consciousness that's full of paradox. It does not lend itself well to descriptions by the logical, one-step-at-a-time forms which function so well for scientific exploration and discovery. But for anyone who has found it, it offers an infinitely rich field for growth. One cannot seize the glory all at once. The growing comprehension comes not just from thought or meditation but from the totality of one's actions and interactions in the world. A piece here and a piece there. A groping that reaches a dead end and has to turn around. An effort that fails, or one that looks successful but has soured. Each fellow being who gives you a piece of hirs own reality adds to your growth and to the comprehension of who God is.

Participation in the Christian church has become for me one of the richest and most meaningful ways I meet the IS. It strengthens the possibilities of a continuous living with God, an awareness of the IS that remains alive through all the pieces of daily life, no matter how mundane and earthy they may be. The sharpest, most heightened awareness of the IS may often be a single flash of insight that does indeed light up the whole scene for a moment, but it may not yield to me the kind of steady glow which I can bring into my home and cast into the corners where I store my potatoes and onions, my efforts toward subsistence, my ways of meeting the woman down the street. The presence of the Holy Spirit does not automatically result in knowing how to live a life of grace. One needs the conscious forms, the embodiments in daily life of the transcendent realities. The church has worked for centuries to provide believers with those forms and those embodiments. They are there for the discovery and they are great, rich treasures.

Unfortunately, though, many things can happen to forms and embodiments. Too often they become for those who use them a reality in themselves, a set of rigid supports and limitations which come to seem holy in themselves. Jesus had many pointed things to say to the Pharisees of his day about the evil effects of their concerns with small points of law and the proper keeping of the sabbath. The problem has not gone away. When forms are given life by a living spirit within them, they become organic wholes that can move effectively in the actual world of persons and things. When they lose the animating spirit, they become hard, unyielding shackles that bind into impotence the one who uses them, and act as obstacles even to an awareness of the spirit they were originally meant to serve.

It is indeed easy to condemn many churches as being shackled in forms that constrict even the human spirit, let alone the Holy Spirit. This is probably especially true when one looks at the simplifications and forms used to teach children.

It has been often my experience, though, that the members of a congregation may bring into a rote form their own living experiences of goodness and beauty, their own compassions and honest humilities and earnest searchings for the light. If they do, even seemingly outmoded forms retain their vitality. It is not just in the contemporary or antiquated style of language used in prayers or liturgy, or the spatial configurations of how the church serves its members communion that one can determine whether or not the ritual is indeed vital. Does the living spirit of God move in the hearts of the participants? Does the form rekindle for them an awareness of the presence of God? Those are the real questions, and there's no way anyone can answer them except for hirmself and for any others who wish to, and can express their feelings honestly.

In this section of the book I've collected ideas and experiences that are consciously and recognizably Christian. They've grown from my experiences within the Christian church and they use Christian imagery. For me the experienced reality of the Christian faith is something both simpler and more infinitely open-ended than theological thought. As the first expression, then, of my meetings with the IS in Christian fellowship, let me give you a glimpse into a Bible Study class that enriched me greatly.

The Bible Study Class

I no longer remember just how I began going to the East Palo Alto Senior Citizens Club, but go there I did each Wednesday noontime. It was potluck, and there always turned out to be something to eat, even if we ended up having a bucket from the Kentucky Fried Chicken place. Mostly black people, older folks or disabled, or just people with no place to go. And a few white, or Samoan, or Guamanian or something else. But great good cheer and human warmth, and acceptance of whoever the other person happened to be, and thankfulness for being alive and for having the food and friends, and always grace before our meal, and — greatest gift of all for me — the Bible Study Class.

Again, just how it began I have forgotten, but someone must have been talking about how Sister Riley used to have Bible Study and how nice it was, and a young seminarian from St. Patrick's agreed to meet with us, and we began the lovely process of sharing our Christian faith and experiences across our different ways of being.

It was a Catholic church we met in — St. Francis of Assisi — and our young man was certainly committed to the Catholic faith, but he was himself striving to learn, and open, and free of rigid interdictions, and we were not only Catholic but also Baptist and Holiness and Church of Christ and Methodist and Presbyterian and Seventh Day Adventist and United Church of Christ and I'm not sure what else. There was one interesting period when an avowed free thinker joined us to ask searching questions of a fundamental nature, but she gave up on us after several sessions, and for the rest of my experience with the group (some five or six years) we remained a group of "Bible buffs" who enjoyed being together, reading God's word with the guidance of the Holy Spirit, and sharing experiences we'd had in our living.

There were stories about struggles to raise children right, problems with husbands, problems on the streets they lived on, things learned from mothers, aunts or older church women, problems with members of their congregations and the mean squabbles that sometimes developed, shortcomings but also inspirations from ministers, prayers answered and unanswered, resentments and bitternesses overcome, sicknesses and other disasters survived. Two of the members had been blessed by feeling the healing power of the Lord administered directly through their own hands, and they gave us detailed but simple accounts of their experiences. On the other end of religious experience, one quiet Catholic woman told us about how she used to think there was something wrong with her faith because she'd never had any of the direct messages or the lightning fire of the Holy Spirit that her neighbors talked about, but she said that after she'd been praying about it she did feel one special complete assurance from God that he spoke to different people in different ways and that he was with her, too, so she'd quit fussing about it in her mind and was content.

We talked sometimes about the devil and how he was always after you, eager to catch you off-guard. I'd come to know these women, though, and how their faiths worked in their living, and I saw the concept of the devil finally become a useful one, related to the unending meannesses and perversities we all found in ourselves. The figure of a devil allowed us a kind of shorthand in communication.

In other ways, too, the words by themselves were often the same ones used by fundamentalists in their rigid, too-sure pronouncements, but the meaning was different. The insights from these women had been formed and tried and reformed and molded by struggles and hardships from day to day, humbly and with openness and searching. It was not critical research of theological concepts in which we were engaged; it was a sharing of hard-won experience in following the Lord.

I will always remember Leona Miles telling us about the time she and her husband had got all wrapped up and overly hopeful about a stand of corn. They were farming in South Carolina as sharecroppers and had planted the corn in front of their cabin. It grew extra well, and they got to looking at it first thing in the morning and then again at night, admiring the eagerness of the green leaves and the ears forming. They got to making plans about what they could do with the money they'd get from selling it. The way Mrs. Miles put it, they let themselves make a kind of God of that corn.

Well, the corn never made it to harvest. It began to turn brown and stopped its good growth and withered away so that they could hardly bear to look out the window at it any more.

Mrs. Miles felt that God had been giving her a lesson. The way she told it, it didn't sound like a God of vengeance who was punishing them; it was rather a God who was in everything that happened to her and who was offering this time an opportunity for understanding. She said she'd thought about it a good deal and had taken it into her heart as a lasting lesson not to put *anything* before God, so if she found herself giving glory to something less than God, or making plans that left God out of account, she'd remember the corn and put herself right again.

Her husband had died in South Carolina before she came out to California to live with some of her children, but it was clear from a number of stories that he had not held as strong or as church-oriented a faith as she had. Several times during the years our little group mulled over the question of men not being as religious or as interested in church doings as the women. I don't think we ever got a masculine viewpoint on it. After our seminarian left us we had a masculine presence now and then, but mostly it was all women. Anyhow, the consensus we usually came to was that just because men did have the physical strength and were used to being able to do something them-selves about most problems that came along, it was harder for them to put their trust in the Lord. Women knew they were weak, and they were often facing problems they couldn't possibly handle by themselves, so it was more natural for them to turn to the Lord, and then they found out about the strength and joy He gave, and they stayed with it.

It was very much the same basic idea we arrived at if we got started talking about wealthy people in contrast to the poor. If you got used to counting on money or a steady job, or any of the material things that made you feel secure in the world, then it was very hard to turn loose of that phony security and turn to God for the real, lasting security. I suppose I was usually the one who reminded the group about Jesus' words on it being harder for a rich man to enter the kingdom of heaven than for a camel to go through the eye of a needle. It was, after all, closer to my area of concern and responsibility.

I was, in the perspective of that group (and probably in basic fact) wealthy, had been secure most of my life by reason of material advantages, and counted as my friends many secure and advantaged people whom I knew as people of good will, and whom I cared about. But I had come to see Jesus' words as stating quite simply and accurately a fact of life: the bondage that goes along with material security. And, without any need for explanation, I could say that to this group of women who had lived through their tough ordeals of survival.

They couldn't help me really with my own dilemma of trying to find a place in the kingdom of God for those people I knew to be good and loving in their daily interpersonal relationships, but who were nevertheless blinded and made callous toward other sections of society by the walls of their security. That was my own struggle, not really theirs, but they were glad to have me bring into the whole group my experiences and thoughts and to give me whatever encouragement they could.

Hattie Kelley, a Church of Christ member who could find her way around in the Bible better than any of the rest of us, who could always give us the exact chapter and verse she was using, used to remind us time and again that to get the real meaning of Bible passages we must read "with the spiritual mind instead of the carnal mind." Once I got over the initial tendency to think of sexual sins and passions whenever she said "carnal," and realized she was simply wanting us to shift our perspective out of the usual literal material level and into an unconditional transcendent viewpoint, it became a very useful bit of advice. Especially for the parables, it helped us free ourselves from things like getting tangled with the talents and the marketplace and whether Jesus was encouraging us to go out and make money.

But the best illumination I got from a parable came again through Leona Miles. We'd been without an official leader for a while, and had adopted a plan of reading parables that we chose in turn. I had asked the group to work on the one about the workers in the vineyard. We read it, and I told them how it had always bothered me: how unfair it seemed that those who had been hired first and had worked in the Lord's vineyard through all the heat of the day were made to wait for their pay until everyone else had been taken care of, and then were given no more than the Johnny-come-latelies who'd breezed through the last hour's worth of work. I enlarged on my view to talk about how most of them had been carrying the burdens of church work most their lives — visiting the sick, taking food and clothes to the needy, struggling to help the drunks and the shiftless and the backsliders, living through grim days of poverty and crisis, working hard with the responsibility of heavy problems. Didn't it seem unfair, after all the long burden, that others should dance through without effort? There was a short pause while everyone thought it over, and then Leona Miles spoke up, with a kind of joyful lift in her voice: "But," she said, "you've been with the Lord all day!"

There it was. Absolutely on target, right there, the answer. Being with the Lord is just the best place to be, the most joyful, the most satisfying, and it really doesn't matter what else in the way of trouble and hard work and disappointments and disasters go along with that. So long as you're with the Lord, it's all right.

Poems for Christmas, Lent and Easter

AT CHRISTMAS TIME

Christ, how the idols leer at us these days!
The glossy ads for gorgeous raiment
on the perfect models, bright smiles agleam
on seamless faces!
The goods, the greed,
the need to make a show —
how have we come to this
in name of Christ-child in the manger?

Make no mistake,
the world has left the manger long ago
and gone awhoring after other gods.
Perhaps it's always been a remnant only
who stand beneath the stars on lonely hills
and hear the angels caroling.

No matter, here we are
amid the jumble of good will
and other things.
There's love and grace pop up amazed
even in our plastic jungle;
and children do retain some wonder,
and grown-ups still may catch their breaths
In sudden thanks for good things
thrust upon them,
treasured in the heart.

The Christ-child's always there,
the shepherds on the quiet hills,
the smile of Mary,
safe beyond the pain and struggle of the birth
to peace and joy and glorious hope
of new, beginning life.

Come quiet, as a child, to where
the living God breathes with us,
offering life.

The gaudy trappings of our plastic world
have nothing real to bind us.
Let them pass.

But let us live our mortal bodies with our souls
for all they're worth,
remembering that God can dwell in human flesh.

THOUGHTS AT CHRISTMAS

It seems a strange way for the God of glory
    to have come into our world —
The couple transient, young, arriving tardy
    in the crowded town, with no provision made.
Did neighbor women count the months
And look askance at Mary
    for the baby come too soon?

Our God's not fussy about "good taste",
Seems not to care about the polished elegance of things.
He welcomes all:
    the stink of shepherds with their sheep,
    the perfumed robes of wise men from afar.
He sees the heart —
    that unadorned and fragile,
    beating pulse of each one's life.

Christmas is the time when hopes are clothed in flesh,
When love looks 'round for gifts to give
    that can bring joy to other hearts,
    that can light up each well-loved face.

Our tinsel balls and smell of pine
Do not suffice — we never make it whole.
There's always still a piece of heart not spoken
    that gropes to find some other time, some other form.

There's always risk of grievous error,
Of word misunderstood, of hope that misses wide the mark
and even hurts where it was meant to heal.

There's greed creeps in, and selfish need —
The idol formed of something less than God.

The world's a mess, and so's the human heart,
But God does find a home within
and sends us out to try again.
And try we do, and try again
And partly still the message does come through of

"Peace on earth; good will to men."

FURTHER THOUGHTS AT CHRISTMAS

When there is no cure;

When the lost are truly lost;

When the starving refugees are dying day by day;

When the innocents
    are slaughtered once again,

Where is there then the peace of God,
    the joy of hope,
        the light of the Christmas star?

Christ Jesus, coming as a child into our world,
Opening once again the eyes of newborn innocence
    upon the place of this our being,
Reaching out again with love to mother and to father,
    to neighboring shepherds
        and the wise men from afar,

O Christ, be with us still!

We have not merited this Spirit born anew:
    The warmth of tiny body held secure against our own;
    The sudden act of grace from person
        where no grace could be expected,
        where all seemed dead
            and mired in disrepute;
    The struggling up of strength to fight once more
        for cause that seemed all beaten down
            in utter hopelessness.

We have not merited this Spirit born anew —

And yet it comes,

    the prodigal,

        the freely given,

The bursting glory of the God of love!

THE CHRIST CHILD

Into the dark winter,
Into the dark desert,
Into the dark night of the soul,
Comes the Christ Child.

Quiet radiance, clothed in helpless flesh,
Commanding by his need, not power,
He enters this our dark and blighted world,
He enters these our stained and weary hearts
And claims our joy and adoration.

Light that cannot be quenched,
Beauty that still will rise through sin and death,
We kneel before you, awkward in our wonder,
To catch soft, baby fingers in our own.

IMMANUEL

Death in the midst of life we have accepted.
We know the bareness of the ground in winter,
the trees all stark and lifeless.
We've found the ways to say good-bye
to one friend and another,
to face for each of us our own demise.

For winter's death is broken through by spring,
with buds that swell
along the dark, smooth branches;
and though the loss of one's dear fellows
is never quite made whole again,
there is the birth of new upcoming life
which speaks of infinite renewal,
of interchange for loss.

There is a comfort here, a sense of grace,
that what is good cannot be really lost,
that beauty changes forms, but lives.

But now we face a dreadful thing;
the blast that brings the death
of every living thing we know,
or — worse yet — mangles it to nightmare.

Christ child in the manger,
have you become too small
to bring us comfort now?
Is your sweet love enough
only for simple lives upon the earth?
Does it fall short
in times of automated buttons
and the unseen face
of hatred armed with violence?

What did we ever hope for from the Child?
A mighty power
to seize the troubles of the world
and set them right?
A burst of glory to banish every grief?

No, it was not that
which we were given.

Instead, a fragile and a tender gift,
a cry of need that trusts us still to answer;
soft, human flesh, all delicate, at hazard,
hungry and defenseless,
needing us for life.

Come, look into those Infant eyes
as you have looked into the eyes
of your own dear tender young.

There are no easy answers here,
no promises assured,
no guarantees;
but only hope and infinite potential,
a kinship
with the living heart of seeds.

We glimpse, in blessed wonder,
the endless Spirit of all life
moving here within our human flesh,
Infinite Love alight in tiny form.

God's with us still!

IN LENT

There is no easy way to live through Lent
(not really live)
for down the long way stands the cross,
fierce, jagged wood that tears the heart and hands.

Pain's real — and ugliness and terror.
Excedrin cannot cure,
nor hopefulness and common decency make real
a place where all is peace and affability.

The stricken cry. The innocent still suffer.
The innocent and guilty both, for who can say
where one leaves off and other starts,
where guilt is part of pain endured,
the heart's ache forced by madness of the world;
the young too young rushed out
to dangers past their coping;
the older spirit worn and worn and worn,
nibbled by rats of perfidy,
ground down at last
by the slow drip, drip of hopelessness.

Deep eyes look on this our pain,
and weep. Dark are the waters
and the blood that run throughout
the texture of our living.

O Christ, who still will see us whole,
who still will see
within the bruised and mangled spirit
that small glimmer of lost light
that marks us child of God,

How can you love and go on loving?
How can you spring again, new,
against all odds,
against all reasoned moderation?

HE WHO DIED AND ROSE

He will not yield
to meet the world on its own faulty terms.
He sees with eyes of God, not Man's,
and takes within himself the agony and grief,
hanging high above us on the cross.

He meets the world — does not deny —
but will not use the compromise and soft deceit
to enter in and merge with infamy.

There in the tomb,
behind strong rock pushed up to hold him safe,
he bursts out strong and living yet
in new and new and ever new upspringing life,
small pushing buds which will not stop
for blocking walls of poured concrete,
for leaden weight of apathy and hopelessness.

Within our tangled world, where mean complexity
makes action false and difficult,
he cuts divinely through our fetters,
setting each one free to live
as bodiment of grace, as flame of living fire.

The world can kill — and will — what's alien,
what will not play the game;
but yet there lives within the world,
deep rooted in the heart of things,
a wished-for, dreamed-of style of glory,
glowing with new light.
And each one seeing it and sensing "home"
cries out with longing from hirs bonded state,
and hopes that "if" and "were it not",
and struggles to be free to run
where love and glory blossom in the sun!

continued

HE WHO DIED AND ROSE (continued)

O we must live here on the earth.
There's no escape from dealing with reality,
or claiming we can move into a spirit realm
where poverty and violence do not reach.
We have to find a way to keep the glory live
while yet we stand here
in our rat-infested tenements
and in our own ignoble and much-muddied souls.

Christ Jesus, there is no way to resurrected life
save through the cross;
save willingness to bear
the snap-back enmity of worldly power,
to take within ourselves the evil that abounds
and face it straight, and see it clearly,
but refuse.

So help us, risen Lord,
to know there is a greater rule
than that of Caesar.
a higher way of being
that transcends our struggling modes;
and carry us along, like long-lost children,
into that realm which is eternal home.

Common Prayers and Other Liturgies

PRAYERS

We pray for the lost and the sorrowful:

For children to whom the world is strange and who lose their way in hopeless private troubles, who are not known to the people around them.

We pray for those who are crushed by fear, who would wish to be strong and clean and without flaw, but who have fear within their hearts for what the world can do, and so turn back to a familiar cowardice, weeping in the night sometimes for their lost strength.

Lord, hear our prayer.

We pray for those who have no work to do, who must sit idle in the midst of troubles.

We pray for those who work at barren things, running through the hours only to be through.

We pray for those who have no home, who seek in vain for a quiet place to be themselves simply and without effort.

Lord, hear our prayer.

We pray for parents who see their children going into danger and cannot stop them, nor give them any help, nor stand beside them.

We pray for sons and daughters building new patterns in the old, old world.

Lord, hear our prayer.

O strengthen us, and comfort us; let us see sometimes Your face, and the workings of Your hands.

* * *

Dear Loving God, help us here.

We have been stupid and blind to the needs of our brothers and sisters. We do not know — we still do not know. We are far from understanding this world of ours and its corners and its great areas where we move as strangers. Help us to open our hearts and our minds so that we may come to understand.

Help us to reach out our hands, so that even if we do so stupidly, it may be turned into some good thing. Help us to recognize our neighbor as s/he is, and to accept from hirm the riches s/he has to offer us. Oh God, beyond the confines of our own lives, beyond the borders of what we have known, guide us out into the great realms of your many-sided glory.

Bless us with the presence of Jesus Christ beside us.

Amen.

CALL TO WORSHIP

Liturgist: Come, let us worship the Lord!

We come together from our separate ways —

from daily work, the struggle and the tangle of our daily lives.

We have been torn; we have been bruised;
we have not been the best that we could be.

We seek healing —

Congregation:
from the hands and voice of God,
as we find them within the hands and voices of our neighbors.

Liturgist: We come together from lives not fully lived —
from routines that have lost their meaning,
from human faces seen only as the answers to our needs,
no longer seen as living relatives of God.

We seek new life —

Congregation:
from the heart of God,
as we find it within the hearts of our neighbors.

Liturgist: We come together knowing we are incomplete —
our understandings dim;
our wills unformed, distracted by each passing thing;
our hearts not grown, too small to feel what we could feel.

We seek growth —

Congregation:
from the spirit of God,
as we find it in the spirits of our neighbors.

LIGHTING CANDLES ON AN ADVENT WREATH

(Our family Advent wreath has holders for five candles. We use it on the four Sundays before Christmas, on Christmas Eve, and finally on New Year's Eve when we put it away.)

1. First Sunday

Leader: We light a candle for LOVE. We have known love here in our family and in our circle of friends. As we look forward to the coming of Christmas, to the time when Jesus first came into our world, we give thanks for all the love we have known in our lives, and we pray that love may go out beyond us into the world and all the people in it.

All: May love grow and send out its light around us.

2. Second Sunday

Leader: We light again the candle for love, and now another for PEACE. Where there is love, peace can grow, for each one cares for hirs neighbor's needs. There is no need to push and shove and grab the good thing, because each one yields gladly to make room for the other. As we look forward to the coming of Christmas, to the time when Jesus first came into our world, we give thanks for all the peace we have known in our lives, and we pray that peace may spread out into our neighborhood and our country and into the whole world.

All: May peace grow and send out its light around us.

3. Third Sunday

Leader: We light again the candle for love and the one for peace. Tonight we light the third for COURAGE. Even with love and peace we have troubles and hardships in our living. Each of us needs the strength to meet these troubles. As we look forward to the coming of Christmas, to the time when Jesus first came into our world, we give thanks for all the courage we have found in our own hearts and in our loved ones, and we pray that courage may spring up inside all people in the world and give them strength for all their good intentions.

All: May courage grow and send out its light around us.

4. Fourth Sunday

Leader: We light again our candles for love and for peace and for courage. Tonight we light a candle for HOPE. Even with love and peace and courage, the times can be hard and darkness can settle in around us. We need hope to show a way through darkness. As we look forward to the coming of Christmas, to the time when Jesus first came into our world, we give thanks for all the hope we have known in our lives, and we pray that hope may stay alive in our hearts and spread out through hearts around the world.

All: May hope grow and send out its light around us.

5. Christmas Eve

Leader: We light again our candles of love, and peace, and courage and hope. Tonight, on Christmas Eve, we light the candle for JOY, with all the good things gathered together. The waiting is almost over. Christmas Day comes in the morning.

All: Glorious! Glorious! Hip, hip, hurray! Alleluia!

6. New Year's Eve

Leader: Our holidays are over for this year. Before we put away our Advent Wreath, let us light once more our candles:

All: 1 for LOVE
2 for PEACE
3 for COURAGE
4 for HOPE
5 for JOY
Let us remember them throughout the new year.

On Language in Worship

AN EXCLAMATION*

If we must wait until we have the perfect word
    all fully molded on our tongues,
we'll never speak.

If we must name Thee with a name to call Thee forth,
Thou'lt never come.

So let's be bold — as Jesus said —
and plead with God in any terms that hold some meaning for us:

    "Our Father, who art in heaven"

    "Dear loving Mother-God, who feeds us at your breast"

    "Great Uncle of the universe"

    "You eager Maiden Aunt"

    "O helpless Grandchild, newly born, powerful in mystery"

There's not a tie of human kinship but can help some way
    to body forth an aspect of divinity,
an angle of the godhead that we know.

---

*(It was sometime in the 1970s that we had a troublesome confusion over the use of inclusive language in worship at the Palo Alto United Church of Christ (First Congregational). Some members wanted to substitute "Our God" for "Our Father" in the Lord's Prayer and we had finally developed a formula for anyone leading it to step back from the microphone at the crucial moment (before that, we'd gone for weeks without using it at all). Some members were upset when unexpected changes appeared in old familiar hymns. I remember a time when one of the members of a church committee had been asked to lead us in an opening prayer, and the poor man was absolutely tongue-tied with not knowing how to start the prayer to God. I wrote this poem as a response to my own frustration.)

How can we think to tie th'Eternal down to one fixed, stilted pose
   — like photograph that's caught forever still,
and never can reveal the play of movement 'cross a well-loved
   face?

O rich extravagance of whales and liver flukes, of grass and
   Matterhorn,
   of fleas, of dust upon the bookcase,
of the sweet strains of Mozart and the blaring clash of fire alarm!

How can we think to hem You in with petty, chosen words,
and hesitate to utter one — and draw back, all fastidious, lest we
   should trespass on some sacred prohibition of our own.

The speech is more important than the words,
   the reaching forth,
   the call from trust,
   the thankful answer to our God.

Reality's a greater dish than any of the verbal spoons we use
   to take a piece and set it on our plates —
and God's the central "Being" of it all!

GOING BEYOND WORDS

Dear God, we do not know you, who you are;
we only grope for you with words,
trusting you can hear our hearts
    beyond the foolish words we say.

We need you here;
we need your Word
    to speak within our hearts and lives,
to waken grace we did not know we had.

We sit, we stand, we speak together, sing together,
reach toward you with words we form out of
    the troubled textures of our living —
words muddied in the using, imperfect, incomplete,
bent within the confines of our own imperfect selves.

Come with your light
into our spirits gathered here.
Breathe truth within our words;
make new the meaning, purge the dross,
clear from our hearts the petty things that keep us bound,

that we may be, here in your being;
that we may live, within your living.

SECTION FOUR

ON ROADS
TOWARD SOCIAL JUSTICE

FINDING OUT ABOUT EAST BAYSHORE

It was in the very early 1960s, the time of the struggle to desegregate the schools in New Orleans. The kids and I had been watching the news stories. We'd been seeing pictures of white people lined up to curse and spit at two little black girls walking to their school under the protection of two white policemen. It was the ugliest kind of human hatred and violence. The kids were troubled about it. Wasn't there something we could do? It just wasn't right. I was not about to tell my good little old kids that there was nothing we could do, that it wasn't our concern.

We talked about it and we watched the one white family who came forward to brave the storm and bring their own children to the boycotted school. I wrote a letter of support, with a small check enclosed, put the best address I could devise on it and sent it off in the U.S. mail. It did find its way and we got a most gracious and informative letter in response.

So far very good, but it set me thinking more deeply. Why had I been so eager to cheer on the white family for their heroism, but hadn't really been feeling the courage and integrity of the young black girls? Was I somehow thinking of them as a race apart, just expected to be able to bear the troubles heaped on them with dignity and without bitterness?

It was obvious that I had some work of my own to do, and

that aiding and abetting good efforts in New Orleans was not enough. I had joined the NAACP a few years earlier and sent in my dues, but I'd never attended a meeting. I had been much stirred by the writings of James Baldwin.

I had first encountered him when I started reading in the *New Yorker* magazine "Letter From a Region in My Mind," which later became the main part of *The Fire Next Time*. By the time I got to the second paragraph, I realized I had been seized by an intense and vital human experience. He was not talking just about the outer oppressions that Afro-Americans experience in this country, but took me inside his own mind as he felt the humiliations and rejections, the fears and despairs of people forced to the bottom of the heap. But he did not give in to hatred or even bitterness. He was addressing me, the reader, as a fellow human being, capable of understanding and of sharing his own experience. Capable, too, of beginning to act for the bettering of conditions, for a deep transformation of our interrelated psyches and for the saving of our country, body and soul.

As I said, I was much stirred by James Baldwin's writings, but I had not yet set foot to pavement for any solid effort to change things. I began attending the meetings of our local NAACP.

We lived in Mountain View, south of San Francisco, down the Peninsula just south of Palo Alto. Palo Alto and the cities to the west of the Bayshore Freeway were not, however, the only components of our Mid-Peninsula area. On the east side of Bayshore Freeway lay East Palo Alto and East Menlo Park. At the time I first knew it, there was still one residential area which was predominantly white, but the whole area was low-income and social forces were driving it more and more toward being overwhelmingly black and cursed with impacted poverty.

Although Palo Alto and Mountain View could claim to be integrated communities, they were probably only about ten percent black, whereas East Bayshore ran more like eighty percent black at the time. Real estate practices and bank loan availability acted strongly to steer incoming white people to the west Bayshore communities and black people to the east Bayshore communities. Furthermore, the political divisions in the area worked against improvements in cooperation between east and west. The east Bayshore area was the southernmost, unincorporated part of San Mateo County, composed predominantly of affluent suburban communities where individual incomes ran very high. The west Bayshore area, including Palo Alto as its northernmost tip, was part of Santa Clara County.

Social programs and public agencies were set up on county lines, so that the greater social resources of Santa Clara County were not called on to spill over into the needy areas of East Bayshore.

Sometimes people of good will who had just moved into our area would notice the dark side of our community, the areas east of Bayshore. They would be startled that such inequities could be going on right next to Stanford University and the enlightened community surrounding it. At first they might try to stir up some useful action, but it usually wasn't long before the inertia of an accepted situation took over and they'd just not pay any attention any more to that part of our area, except to let newcomers know that it wasn't a good idea to be over there after dark.

Even the NAACP was divided in two parts: the Palo Alto/Stanford Branch and the South San Mateo County Branch. Fortunately for me and my understandings the two branches were holding joint meetings when I first started attending. They were getting together to launch a tutoring program for East Bayshore kids. That certainly sounded like an excellent idea to me and I said so. I was immediately signed up and invited to the next planning meeting at Rev. Gardner's C.M.E. (Christian Methodist Episcopal) church in East Menlo Park.

That was the start for me of being included in meetings which were black-run and black-oriented. The Palo Alto/Stanford Branch of the NAACP was somewhere near half black and half white, but the agenda and the meetings were oriented toward the dominant white society and its concerns. Was this particular incident a case of discrimination? If it was, what should be done? Was there an adequate representation of black people on the Palo Alto police force? They concerned themselves with problems in Palo Alto, on the Stanford campus, and in other close-lying west Bayshore communities like Mountain View. It was only occasionally that they seemed to feel responsibility for the problems of East Bayshore. The South San Mateo Branch of the NAACP, on the other hand, was almost completely black, and was overwhelmed with urgent, specific needs in a community struggling to survive.

When the two branches got together for the tutoring project, it brought a number of us white people who were eager to help into that particular work force, but the direction and the know-how for the project had to come from the people of the South San Mateo Branch. We white recruits were warmly welcomed, but the focus of meetings and discussions remained on problems in the predominantly black neighborhoods. No one was trying to impress anyone else, or to prove that discrimination existed. In these meetings, in fact, discrimination was simply accepted, without comment, as part of the way things were. The East Bayshore people were glad of our help and would explain things that we needed to know, but the group was focused on getting a job done as best we could, with limited resources.

There was lots of realism and the acceptance of nitty-gritty problems. Humor, too. I doubt if there was one meeting that didn't provide at least one good laugh for everybody. It was not bitter humor, or angry or vindictive. It arose from a common recognition of the absurd problems we were facing together. The meetings were always opened, too, with prayer, in a matter-of-fact way. There was a vitality and a feet-on-the-earth quality about those meetings. In spite of having to look at tough problems, I felt that I was involved in something that made sense in a way that many of the other things around me didn't. I was deeply grateful for the chance to be part of these actions, to be included as a co-worker with these knowledgeable, dedicated people. There were plenty of times when I didn't understand much at all of what they were talking about, especially when it got into the intricacies of San Mateo county politics. I just hung on and picked up whatever I could.

The disparity between the wealth and prestige of West Bayshore and the poverty and powerlessness of East Bayshore was a situation that called out for Christian action, especially from our wealthy side of the Bayshore Freeway. Soon after I'd started my own campaign to heal the breach, I heard that the regional jurisdiction of the Presbyterian Church, of which I was a member at that time, had also noticed the need for action, and instituted the Mid-Peninsula Christian Ministry. They had empowered a young minister, Rev. Carl Smith, to move his family into the East Palo Alto community and see what could be done. Three local churches in the West Bayshore communities were to provide his primary back-up and supervision.

The Menlo Park Presbyterian Church was the largest, the richest and the most conservative of the churches. Because Menlo Park was in San Mateo County, it also had the best chance to influence the agencies and governmental bodies that impacted the East Bayshore community. My own church, the First Presbyterian Church of Palo Alto, was more liberal in its approach to social issues and more modest in size and wealth. The third church, Covenant Presbyterian was definitely smaller than either of the other two and not noticeably political in either direction. Because I had already got my feet wet in the waters of East Bayshore I was chosen as the lay representative from the Palo Alto Presbyterian Church and served on the steering committee for a number of years. That was also a fascinating and informative experience, but it was more along the lines of what I was already used to, and did not challenge and stretch my spirit the way the experiences with the black community did.

It provided me with some interesting contrasts to see both sides of Bayshore in action. I remember a meeting of the Ministry Steering Committee at which it was decided that we could not, after all, expect people to give more than one night a month to the program. I found myself remembering a recent meeting of the youth council in East Palo Alto at which a member had assured us, "After all, it's *only* one night a week we're asking people to give." There was, too, the weekend in which two rummage sales were being conducted: one at Covenant Presbyterian Church, spearheaded by a pleasant, active woman in order to fund an integrated camping program, and one in East Palo Alto by members of the youth council for some of our ongoing needs. Our Covenant friends reported with great pleasure that their effort had raised over $2,000. The youth council women reported that they had raised $308 from their efforts. Was their planning not so good, their work more casual or slipshod? I doubt it. That was really just one expression of the resources available in the two communities.

The youth council was an outgrowth of the tutoring project

begun by the NAACP. We had managed to set up a regular weekly schedule for getting kids and volunteer adults together, and that bumped along with its own ups and downs. But the concern really went beyond just helping the kids with their homework. If there was one unifying goal in the black community it was the effort to help the kids — not just their own, but all the kids of their neighborhoods — to some kind of better life and opportunities. The core group of adults had obviously been working with kids around them for years. They knew the problems that led the kids off into blind alleys and wasted lives. They were glad to have a focused project and companionship for their efforts.

When we were first forming ourselves we had asked Bob Hoover to act as leader for the youth council, and he turned out to be a constant pillar of strength and understanding and unshakable purpose. He was an athletics teacher and had a deep and passionate concern for the well-being of all young people. I remember him once telling us about going out to talk to a service club about the urgent needs of our youth. They had become involved in a big discussion about the fact that white kids were having all the same kinds of problems, too, so it wasn't discrimination, and they seemed to feel that that made everything all right. "Dear God," he said, "it's no good for any kid — white or black — to have his life flushed down the drain because no one cares. It never has been a matter of discrimination; it's the kids' lives on the line."

For all his passion, he was unfailingly gentle and encouraging in our youth council meetings. He never gave up and he never got bitter. I remember another fund-raising effort. A beautician, a black woman, had developed a promotion scheme for her shop and came to us with a proposal to share profits if we'd help advertise and sell special tickets. We did, and I know several of the youth council people worked hard at it with their friends and neighbors. When the campaign was over we found she'd netted at least a couple hundred dollars, plus the publicity, but our share was only barely over $100. I was mad. I wanted to call her to account. I stewed over the injustice of it. How could anyone take advantage of a group like ours and the community we were trying to serve? If I'd taken the time to observe my inner spirit, I'd have found it shriveled and bitter.

At our next youth council meeting, though, Bob Hoover went over the specifics of the whole thing and then just said "I guess we learned something, didn't we?" and went on to our other plans ahead. I had a sudden flash of thinking, "to everyone who has will be given more, but to him who has not, even what he thinks he has will be taken away." Bob Hoover had somehow developed so strong and generous a spirit that an incident like that only added to his understandings, but it had practically derailed me. That was the first time I'd really gained a key to that parable.

The reason we were always trying to raise money was that everyone felt that if the community kids had a place to get together for good activities it would neutralize many of the problems we saw. Such was the poverty of East Bayshore that there really wasn't such a place for them.

That was the point at which my activities on the two sides of Bayshore came together beautifully. Our Presbyterian minister, Carl Smith, was no dummy. He was, in fact, a perceptive man and recognized as well as I did how much the whole community cared about their kids. He was able to locate an appropriate building and to finance it for youth (and other) activities. Furthermore, he got Bob Hoover to act as youth director. Community House, as it was christened, served as a live focal point for adults and kids working together in East Bayshore for many years.

It was at the gatherings of the Mid-Peninsula Christian Ministry at Carl Smith's home that I met the Rev. Ruth Lankford, an elderly, dignified black woman, widow of a presiding elder of the A.M.E. (African Methodist Episcopal) Zion church. Her mind and perceptions were keen and she had great reservoirs of experience within her, of the black community and also of the white, but above and beyond all that, deep experiences of the Christian faith. She did not seem greatly impressed by our efforts at Christian ministry, but she wanted to be helpful and she was gentle in her efforts to help us understand some of the realities of life in East Bayshore. She acted as a sort of quiet mentor and continuing resource for us.

She had been working to develop a small church in her own East Palo Alto home, encouraging the neighborhood kids to come in on a Sunday morning for songs and scripture readings. She was in the process of getting the approval and ordination in her own right of the broader A.M.E. Zion Church. When she invited me to come join them on a Sunday, I took her up on it, found it quite challenging and also spiritually nourishing, and began going to St. Mark's A.M.E. Zion Chapel on a more and more regular basis.

Ruth and Meredith were still living at home with me and they came along, too. Meredi began to play the piano for our hymns and it wasn't long before we were a real mainstay of the little church. I drank deep of Rev. Lankford's experiences and insights. Beyond that, too, she gave me opportunities for extra experiences I would never have had without her. One time I drove her up to visit a young man in the county jail. On another occasion she assigned me an active role in a funeral we held for a woman who had been an important member of our church. She was an especially vibrant, middle-aged woman who had been putting new life into our children's choir. She had had a massive stroke and died after a brief stay in the Palo Alto Hospital. All in all, St. Mark's A.M.E. Zion Chapel was for me an agent for broadening and deepening not only my distinctively Christian understandings, but also the circle of my human kinships and my knowledge of the world around me.

I had certainly been getting great benefits from the East Bayshore community. Was I giving them anything worthwhile? I think my main tangible contribution was as a secretary. My first effort in this role was for the Mid-Peninsula Coordinating Council on Human Relations (MCCHR). There had been some kind of fracas on a Saturday afternoon at the Varsity Theater in Palo Alto, and most of the young people involved had been from East Bayshore. The Palo Alto Times made quite an exciting story out of it. Some of the black ministers issued a call for a public meeting to talk about problems of racial tensions. When I went I expected to see all the members of the Palo Alto/ Stanford NAACP there, but it turned out to be only the black members who came. The only other white person in that fairly large assembly was a man whom I later came to know as Roswell Caulk, head of the local United Way. He was a highly knowledgeable and generally excellent fellow.

The meeting was a working session, not just talk. They moved right along and laid out the main groundwork for a public forum group which could air the main problems they saw, and hopefully get some common actions going on them, with participants from both sides of Bayshore. Rev. William Hunt of the Palo Alto A.M.E. Zion Church agreed to be president, and Zedolion Milton to be vice-president. They agreed to meet again in a week, but were unable to find anyone willing to serve as secretary. When we met again in the week's time, still with a good large group, no one had offered to be secretary, so I volunteered my services and began taking notes.

For several years we held monthly forums on a variety of problems that East Bayshore folks thought were important. I'd write up the notes in as lively a fashion as I could and take them in to "Roz" Caulk for his secretary to clean up my rough draft (at least it was always typed), mimeograph it and mail it out to a fairly large list of civic-minded people on both sides of Bayshore. Sometimes we'd have a topic and resource people that drew a large group, and then we'd also have good coverage the next day in the *Palo Alto Times*. Sometimes it was practically a dud with almost nobody in attendance, but at least the good information was getting out fairly widely.

I kept hoping people read those minutes. I remember one meeting when nobody at all showed up except us three officers. It wasn't lost time, at least for me. We had our steering committee considerations, and also a great swapping of personal experience stories. Rev. Hunt had worked in a wide variety of communities, and Zedo was doing clerical work in the South San Mateo station of the Sheriff's office, so he had some special inside knowledge of how that important department worked.

As I said, the MCCHR met monthly for several years, with ups and downs, but we were never able to get beyond the talking stage. It was that experience, though, which gave me the chance at a great ringside seat for watching the workings of President Johnson's War on Poverty when that began. Zedo Milton had been elected to the East Bayshore Community Action Commission and chosen as secretary. One night he called me, said that he had the flu and just couldn't make their meeting. Would I fill in for him? I did, and soon became their unofficial clerk.

Our chairman was Gertrude Wilks, as solid and competent a grassroots leader as I have ever experienced. The first time I met her, she seemed to be no more than a young Louisiana housewife transported to California, but she was powerfully radicalized by watching her older son destroy himself after graduating from the local high school without even the skills to fill out a job application. (They had brushed off her concerns during his school career by telling her he was "up to grade level" and so on.) She took on the educational system and other related apparatus of the powers-that-be. She had come to be recognized as one of the major movers and shakers of the community — not just in East Bayshore but in the more privileged sections of the Mid-Peninsula, too. She had been chosen as one of three local leaders to go to the nationwide training conference for War on Poverty leaders. As her own rock-solid foundation she remained an active member of her Baptist church, with unwavering perseverance and calm assurance.

She ran a really good meeting. It was not Roberts Rules of Order, but it was her own version of the same things. She'd go over briefly with the commissioners what things they'd have to cover in that meeting and then start in on the first proposal offered. She'd gather comments, questions and responses from the commissioners, making sure they all understood what was involved. Then she'd open the meeting to any questions or responses from visitors and work that into the whole consideration. Before the vote she'd ask, "Is everyone clear in their minds about this?" And then they'd vote to accept or reject the proposal, with any amendments they'd agreed were necessary for the proposal to work in their community.

I have heard of and also watched in action numerous other federally-mandated groups which were supposed to be providing input from the people served, but which were really a kind of manipulated rubber stamp for the particular authorities. The East Bayshore Community Action Commission really functioned as it was supposed to do. They were a good variety of active, knowledgeable folks, they had practical ideas about what might really work and what wouldn't, and they certainly were not intimidated by any of the powers-that-be. I can remember several occasions when I was asked to write a letter for them to some agency or another. My own style is usually conciliatory and diplomatic and I tried to use that style to deliver their message. They would have none of it. After I had read my version, one or another of them would object to the approach I had used and I'd have to rewrite it, getting back to the direct, uncompromising message they wanted to deliver. I have no idea whether my own butter-'em-up, diplomatic versions might have made better progress in some cases, but the commission did seem to be respected by the agencies who were trying to get War on Poverty money.

One fascinating episode was their confrontation with Stanford University itself. Stanford had sponsored an Upward Bound program for some of the East Bayshore teenagers one summer. It was written up in the *Palo Alto Times* in quite glowing terms. But East Bayshore parents did not lightly relinquish concern for their children. Some of them went to visit and discovered that their kids were being allowed to sleep in late and leave their rooms in a mess. They were being encouraged to play around with all kinds of seductive recreational opportunities, but there was very little solid academic work. The parents felt the kids were being "played around with", pampered, condescended to.

When Stanford asked for a renewal of the program they were given a solid "no", which occasioned many hurt feelings and expressions of disappointment, but which they made stick. I have forgotten just which one of Stanford's many departments or sub-groups stepped into the breach, worked closely with the Community Action Commission and other parents, and came up with a much smaller program which got approval for War on Poverty money, and which apparently functioned in a lower-profile, non-glamorous way for some real benefits for East Bayshore youth.

I'm afraid that almost always there has to be a trade-off for time spent. My evening meetings in East Bayshore meant that I did not spend that time with my children. For several of the early years my mother was living next door, and she used to come over to our place while I took off for meetings. After she moved into downtown Palo Alto, the kids fended for themselves. They seemed to be good at it. They were all doing well in school and they got along well with each other. It may even be that they were better off to have me somewhat out of their hair. But there is no way to know. I hope that I did not short-change any of them, or my mother, by putting so much of my time and passion into affairs in East Bayshore.

Toward the end of her life, my mother and I had several good opportunities to exchange our mutual forgiveness for the bruises and wounds we had dealt each other during our lives; and Forrest, Ruth and Meredith have been very gracious in these later years about forgiving my shortcomings as a parent. God grant that all things were well. For me, at any rate, those years when I was involved with East Bayshore were full of great richness, of discovery and of growth.

DECLARATION

(A second to James Baldwin's motion, now before the House*)

It is a time of terror and decay.
Like ghosts we rush through the days,
shutting from our waking thoughts the memory of bombs,
of starving Asian peoples,
of children mangled in their Sunday School.

Fearful of life,
bone-weary of the beings that we are,
we sink within the morass.

We know too much:
this problem here is huge;
it touches the emotional springs of millions of individuals,
each caught in hirs own necessity.
Employment ties to housing, housing to schools;
the economic "facts of life" dampen without a murmur
the desire to be decent.

What can I do? I am only one little cog.
It is not on my rental of an apartment
that the whole black question hangs.
How can I face responsibility for the great sweeping needs
that surge through the whole?

---

*James Baldwin's *The Fire Next Time* seemed to me to be so strong and essentially loving a call for our society to reform itself that I wanted to add my own voice to his appeal. As an ever-hopeful visionary, I was seeing our society as a vast body politic, capable of working as a whole on our common problems. Baldwin had stood up and issued his forceful statement and call for action. I felt the need to second his motion.

What has happened to that motion since he first made it? I'm afraid we'd have to say it has essentially failed, not because of lack of seconding, but because there has been no strong chairman to direct our resources steadily toward implementing his suggestions. Right now (1992, in the aftermath of the Rodney King verdict) it is obvious that the needs are still there. It's time we got busy working on them.

I say there must be a start.
I say we must start in somewhere
where it touches us.

We cannot begin at the beginning.
We begin where we are.
Now.
This moment.
In this place.
We stand like men and women once again.
We stand like living relatives of God
and face what is to be faced.

Honesty first.
There is no help in blinding our eyes
with what we wish to see.
There is no aid in clothing realities in words
to make them palatable,
to clothe our naked guilt in fig leaves of explanation.

The problems are huge,
but if I will not take responsibility,
who will?

Each American where s/he stands,
within whatever limits hirs consciousness encloses,
must act with honest love and the best intelligence s/he has.

The walled gardens wherein we thought to build our treasure,
setting apart small courts of security and beauty,
have turned to sickness and to ashes.

By shutting out need,
by shutting out "ugliness"
by shutting out terror,
we have shut out life
and turn
within the great wealth of our goods
to look death in the face.

If we are to live, we must enter life again,
must plunge within the tide and gamble with our lives.

Who told us life should be full of ease, and happy?
Who told us we could build for ourselves alone
and shut out the siblings who are part of us?

We must tear down the walls; we must build anew.
In the shifting sands of this our chaos
we must build again.

Where shall we stand?
On what great rock can we place our feet?

   (I come from paths of frenzy and excited pressure — the
rush, rush, rush of things which must be done — and stand out
under the stars. The darkness and the night breeze look at my
uproar and it ceases. Why this troubling over little things? Why
the frenzy for an hour here, a hundred dollars there? Mortal I
stand, and know my need for bread and clothes, the shelter
from the cold of winter. But what beyond this follows me where
I stand, related to the universe? Does it matter for the heater in
the bathroom, and if the coffee pot will disgrace me with my
guests?)

We know the earth; we have smelled it through the grass.
We know the flip of birds through the blue sky
and the turning of young leaves.
These things will stand beneath us.
These things will stand firm.
They go beyond the madness of humankind.
They make a pattern of fierce beauty which sustains us.

   (But in the city, what then? In the great buildings and the
endless concrete, how shall I live? In the warehouse where there
is no sign of God's creation except the grain of wooden frame
left on concrete slabs, how shall I know where to stand?)

The eyes of women and of men,
the eyes of human beings which look, and know, and offer love.

Most beautiful of all,
most tragic and most beautiful,
the eyes of human beings.

They look,
they look out from within each self,
and those who have seen and known,
who know their mortality and the struggle —
the agony, the joy and the despair,
the style of tough humor
which makes possible continued life —
these offer love, without pretense,
as one poor traveler to another.

> It is very hard for strong, rich people to know this love.
> They fool themselves too easily;
> they think they control life;
> they think they have built by themselves.

> Sometimes I think that even the Church does not know,
> and this is truly strange,
> remembering Jesus on the cross.
> I think perhaps they think too much
> about Christ in glory at the right hand of God
> and have forgotten
> the look of human blood on a tree.

Some true foundations there are:
the earth itself,
the earth and the trees and the stars.
These things remain.
And within and beyond all these, adding a new chorus to the
universe,
the love of human beings, one for another.
Warm hands of neighbors reach out and grasp our own.

On these things we must build.
Upon these foundations we must build a new house.

WORKING AS A WELFARE CASEWORKER

The more I became involved in East Bayshore, the more engrossing it became and the more I felt able to contribute. In 1968 I checked out the possibilities of becoming a Welfare caseworker. San Mateo County had not yet converted to a system of having eligibility workers as distinct from social workers, and it was still possible to become a social worker by having any kind of B.A. college degree (mine was from 1939, in Literature and Languages!) and by passing a Civil Service exam. The Civil Service exam was very thorough and did in fact test effectively for the types of skills which were needed. I passed it, applied at the South San Mateo Office of the San Mateo County Social Services Division of the Department of Public Health and Welfare, was accepted and went to work in August of 1986. By that time Forrest had just graduated from Haverford College, Ruth had completed one year's work with VISTA in Upper Michigan and had been accepted at Antioch College for the fall. Meredith, then fifteen years old, was the only child still at home, so I felt free to experiment.

It was a good thing I didn't have any heavy household tasks when I got home from work. The job turned out to eat up all the time I could give it, and still left me with great chunks of responsibilities which regulations said I should be handling, but which I couldn't. Before I really started work I had had a momentary fear that Welfare bureaucracy might be so extreme that I would be pushing paper without dealing directly with any of the problems I knew were there. I needn't have concerned myself about that side of things!

On my first day of work I was shown to my desk and to my caseload in the drawer, folders for about seventy families. Looking through them I found three of the families I already knew from St. Mark's Chapel. When I told my supervisor about this, she agreed with me that it would be better not to have folks I knew personally, and reassigned them to other workers. In exchange, though, she assigned me three other families, complete strangers.

There was no organized orientation, training, or even a small pamphlet to serve as a guide. The workers at desks in front and behind me were good and helpful for particular questions, and of course my supervisor was available if I couldn't work it out. It was probably fortunate that the crisis which erupted that first afternoon from my caseload was of sufficient proportions that the supervisor really needed to handle it herself anyway.

The father in one of my families, who had been absent, came into the office to report that his wife had taken off with the Welfare check, and that he was currently trying to take care of their four children in a house without either gas or electricity. As I said, I was very glad to find myself acting basically as a spectator while Paula Beck, my supervisor, swung into action with the gas and electric companies and figured out how to provide some kind of substitute, temporary money for the family without letting the mother off the hook on the matter of the misappropriated Welfare check. It was obvious that this job was going to be exciting, and not any kind of bed of ease.

In some ways the work was easier at first because I took instructions at face value. When I was told that a family could not have a benefit they had requested, I simply told them so. It was only gradually I discovered that there was in our office a great fat notebook of regulations for the AFDC program (Aid to Families with Dependent Children). If I hunted up the appropriate place and could figure out a good rationale for a particular request, I might be able to write up a special request that Paula would okay, and that in fact I might be able to swing it. No guarantee, of course, and it always took some extra work and ingenuity, but those inner-office rulings were not really hard and fast. I developed the practice of never giving a client a solid answer, no matter how sensible and useful a request appeared to me. If it looked possible, I'd tell my client that I'd give it a try and let her know. I can remember several times when a client had a special request about getting something that really could make a difference in her family's life — something to help a kid at school, or to help her get to a training program regularly — and I'd go back to the office and check over the AFDC regulations and write up the most appealing request I could, and maybe Paula would okay it and I could phone my client with the happy news. If Paula turned it down I made sure I phoned the client just as promptly. It was better not to leave the question hanging. If the word was no, the client would be disappointed of course, but the amazing thing was that almost always a client would thank me for my effort, really thank me, without any overtones of bitterness or sarcasm. It would have been so easy for them to resent me, who went home to my easy life each day at 5:00 P.M., but they didn't. It was enough to break my heart.

Did I play favorites with my special efforts? Of course I did. There was no way I could make a standard thing of those special efforts, not with seventy families. They had to be few and far between. So it was for the women whom I'd come to know as loving mothers struggling in almost superhuman ways to make life good for their children that I'd make my own almost superhuman efforts. Mostly, too, Paula wanted to help the families as much as I did, and the original AFDC regulations had been written with the honest desire of providing real help to families. It was just that the opposite desire to save public money and to run a neat, efficient office operation had imposed a whole tangle of stingy restrictive rules.

The real trouble was that the whole thing had become a miserable quagmire of uncertainty. Toward the end of my Welfare experience, a group of us workers were trying to pull together information about Welfare regulations so we could make life easier for all the people and agencies affected by them. We discovered that we could not get our superiors to put into writing, even for us, what really were the correct interpretations of any number of questionable dilemmas.

Special requests, of course, were a very small part of the work. The main thing was getting out the correct Welfare check twice a month. A corps of budget clerks were responsible for the calculation of each family's budget and for getting out the checks, but we social workers were ultimately responsible and had to understand what was going on. We were, in fact, the sole authorities for each of our family's semi-monthly checks. A decision by the social worker could be appealed to a supervisor by the client, but it was a risky thing to do, and most time-consuming.

It took me quite a while to figure out what really was going on. The first step was a "cost schedule" which laid out for each family — depending on how many people of what ages and sexes — the amounts to be allowed for food, clothing, personal

needs, recreation, transportation, household items and intermit-
tent needs, education and incidentals, utilities and housing. As
an indication of how meager these allowances were, the monthly
housing allowance for a family of four in 1969 was $130,
transportation (in an area virtually without any public transportation) was $9.60 and education and incidentals was $2.80. If the
family had any income, that was subtracted from the total
allowances and that amount became the grant for the month.
However, oddly enough, if the family had no income they did
not receive the amount so carefully laid out as to what they
needed in subsistence money. The actual grant was usually
about $100 less per month than the state had recognized that
they needed. I finally figured out what was happening. Back in
1957 (twelve years before) the California State Legislature had
decided they were spending too much on the state share of
Welfare grants and put a ceiling on what they would contribute.
They froze the state level of contribution at the 1957 level. The
figures on the cost schedule were carefully increased each year,
but the actual grant was not. There was no law that said a
county could not use its own money to make up the difference
for a poor family, but I think it was only Marin County, just
north of San Francisco, that actually did that. Some counties kept
an option of county money for special cases, but San Mateo
County simply assured its social workers and the clients that
they could not provide any money beyond the state maximums.

An interesting bit of side information, which I unearthed for
myself, was that the recipients of Old Age Assistance, Aid to the
Blind, and Aid to the Disabled had not been shackled in the
same manner as the AFDC recipients. During the twelve years
since the maximums were applied, Old Age grants had been
raised by $99.50, grants to the blind by $83.50, and to the
disabled by $71 per month. And remember, these are single
recipients, not whole families. Apparently there is a special
antipathy toward (or fear of) families who need help to raise
their children.

As I said, it took me a while to grasp the significance of the
figures our budget clerks were using. At first it seemed just part
of my learning process in becoming a Welfare caseworker: single
parent with one child $148 per month; parent with two children
$172; with three children $221; with four children $263. Howev-

er, after a while of talking to clients who were trying to live on those checks, and having to admit that they really couldn't make ends meet on those amounts, I began trying to stir up the public about the situation. I went out to talk to church groups and wrote letters to the editor of our local paper. I developed a number of good charts and explanations about how the grant was figured, and highlighted how miserably unrealistic the money amounts were for actual living conditions. Women's fellowships at the various churches were the people most willing to listen to me. I was often told after a presentation what an interesting program it was, and sometimes was given a collection which I could give to one of the emergency help groups, but there seemed to be very little feeling of personal responsibility for any of it. People were interested but only as spectators. I did not have the key to making them see that these conditions were the responsibility of all of us citizens.

In January 1970 I had a real opportunity to cast the light of publicity on the ugly inequities of what the state maximums were doing to AFDC recipients. All of us county employees received a cost of living increase in our paychecks. Without doing any study of what items were which, I just subtracted my old amount from the new one and came out with the figure of $28.20. I made out a check for this amount and sent it to the San Mateo County Board of Supervisors, with a letter explaining that I really could not in good conscience accept this money when the people whose needs I was supposed to be serving had not had a cost of living increase in twelve years. I laid out for the commissioners some of the specific hardships I saw, and included my best condensed explanation of how a grant was figured. I had done it more just as a matter of personal integrity than as a strategy, but one good reporter at the Board meeting picked up on it, approved having a photographer come out to the Welfare office to take my picture, and soon I appeared in most of the neighboring newspapers, with good write-ups of my complaints. Most exhilarating! East Bayshore folks were quite uplifted and pleased by the story, although some of them focused on the angle that it showed Welfare workers really weren't worth the money they were paid.

There was considerable reaction from within the San Mateo Public Health and Welfare Department, too. I got a letter from

Dr. Chope, the head of the whole thing, telling me he thought my action was an exercise in futility and questioning my rights as a social worker to go outside the proper channels. To balance that, Paula Beck, my supervisor, sent me a copy of the letter she'd sent to Dr. Chope in response, defending my rights as a private citizen and also asking him some pointed questions about his relation with the Public Health and Welfare Commission, which was supposed to be a completely independent citizens' advisory group. From the head of that commission (to whom I'd sent a copy of my letter) I received a letter outlining their recognition of the problems I'd been pointing out and their own efforts to get the state to change their policy on maximums.

All in all it looked as though I had opened up a most lively can of good worms. My fellow social workers were mostly sympathetic, but no one was willing to join me in sending back *their* cost of living increases, although I got some offers of partial contributions. I tried to interest the man who had been trying to organize a branch of the Public Service Workers Union in our office, but he reacted in extreme disagreement. He told me I was downgrading the worth of us social workers and not doing any good anyhow.

At any rate, the Board of Supervisors sent back my check with a brief note that they did not want to accept it. They assured me, however, that my letter and fact sheets had been distributed to every member of the board. So, what was I to do next? At the time I did not fully appreciate just how golden was this opportunity I had stumbled into. The situation was a perfect one for a Ghandian type *satyagraha* ("truth force") action. Sacrificing my own cost of living increase was exactly appropriate for my efforts to obtain cost of living increases for my clients. It focused attention directly on the real institutional problem, and it was addressed to people who did in fact have the power to remedy it.

Looking back on it, I can see a number of possible next steps I could have taken. I could have at least asked for the chance to appear in person before the Commission. I could have continued the same idea by sending the $28.20 back again, along with a second month's $28.20 and whatever additional contributions I could drum up from other social workers. Of course they might just have accepted the money that time and tried to tuck it away in the county's General Fund. But that part of it wasn't really my concern. I should have let the truth of the situation carry me along with it, and just responded to whatever developed. Who knows? Could it have eventually raised enough fuss to have developed a real awareness in the public, expanded the area of publicity, made a real dent in public acceptance of the status quo for Welfare recipients? At least, I wish I had pushed the central idea very much harder than I did. Instead I beguiled myself into branching off into another line of action.

I don't know why I thought the publicity could be carried along with me, but I did. I let that good reporter know that I was sending my $28.20, now duplicated with a second month, to two of the emergency aid agencies in East Bayshore. There were a couple of small news items to that effect in several of the papers, but of course it didn't have anywhere near the impact of the cost-of-living story. It was back again into the area of good people helping out "those less fortunate." It had lost its focus and chance to target the underlying societal cause.

I am very glad I managed at least the first charge in that *satyagraha* action. It gave me a brief feel for how powerful that style of approach can be, even though I fumbled it before it might have taken off.

Having failed my best opportunity, I was at least inventive about what I did with the recurring $28.20. The first bank they'd ever had right in the neighborhood was opening in East Bayshore. I talked to the manager (an Afro-American man) about helping me start an account for issuing checks to Food Stamp recipients who couldn't manage the cash required in those days for one purchase of Food Stamps. The bank was the issuing agency anyway, so recipients would all have their identification and vouchers right with them. The idea was that we would loan money for one purchase of Food Stamps to anyone who had their identification, no questions asked. If they paid back the loan they could borrow again indefinitely, or rather so long as we had funds. A very simple system. We were just riding along with the Social Services system of determining and documenting eligibility, and filling in one small but important gap. The worst that could happen would be that we were contributing one batch of food, far beyond the cash value contributed, to someone who was in fact needy, but who had no intention of paying back. We weren't adding to anyone's dependency, or raising unrealistic expectations, or training anyone to cheat. In fact, the straight-forward response to a request — no need to concoct a sob story — was one of the best features of our system.

Over a period of several years we found out that about one fifth of the people who used the Meet the Need funds did pay back their loans. A handful of them developed regular systems of using the fund as a most useful extension of their meager budgets at the time of lowest ebb.

It was a good idea, easy to explain and attractive to many people. A number of the social workers from our office contributed on a fairly regular basis, and we started off the fund with a handsome $500 check from a woman who responded to a sympathetic editorial in the *Palo Alto Times*. If we had run out of money, it would just have been a matter of telling some hopeful applicant that there was no more money available right then. We hadn't made any promises beyond our capacity.

I set up a small board of directors, and a lawyer from Legal Services helped us get non-profit standing, but there wasn't much real work involved, except for the secretary/treasurer. We'd meet in the handsome board room of the bank, sit in their good armchairs, get the report from our treasurer and talk for a while about affairs in the community. When regulations changed so that Food Stamps were issued without need for a cash purchase, the Meet the Need fund just naturally dissolved.

About this time, too, changes were taking place in the San Mateo County Social Services division. "Conversion" was coming. Most the other counties in California had already changed to a system of having "eligibility workers" do the financial part of the caseworker job and saving real "social workers" for things like developing child-care plans for selected children and counseling stressed-out mothers on how to cope.

It became apparent that eligibility workers would be treated as not much more than glorified clerks. They would be paid less than we former all-purpose social workers were, and they would be loaded with 150 to 200 families each. There would be no chance at all to consult the big green book of regulations for possible exceptions to the restrictive rules. I figured that 80% of my time as a caseworker had been spent on some aspect of the financial needs of my families. That was what seemed to me to be their greatest need. There was no way, though, that I could handle the kind of job that eligibility work appeared to be. On the other hand, my superiors would have helped me become a full-fledged social worker (one was expected to work toward a masters degree in Social Work) but that didn't appeal to me either. I didn't see how I could feel comfortable providing professional advice to some poor woman who was rightly worried about paying rent and getting food on the table. The long and the short of it was that I turned in my resignation and left Social Services in November 1970. I remember that I kept on going into the office, unpaid, for almost three weeks after I resigned so that I could bring my case records up to date. I was that far behind!

Carrying a Welfare caseload provided the kind of experience I don't think I could have gotten any other way. I wouldn't have believed it from anyone else. There is a great documentary called *Welfare* by Fred Wiseman which seems to me to catch the reality of life in a Welfare office, but I doubt if I would have caught everything going on if I hadn't already been there.

While I was still an active caseworker, Ronald Reagan, then governor of California, was stirring up a great ballyhoo about Welfare reform. I certainly knew the need for reform, but as I focused on his much publicized efforts, I found myself having to decide that he was either totally misinformed and willfully blind, or else that he was a liar. Too bad!

I think President Nixon and President Carter both talked seriously about Welfare reform and probably meant it. I remember being encouraged when word came through the newspapers that Carter's plans were going to be delayed because he had found it was a more difficult and complicated thing than he had realized. I have spent some serious time myself trying to figure out how we might be able to change the system for the better. I can see a number of minor patchwork changes that would be improvements, but for real reform, I'm afraid it would take a major transformation of our whole society. How do we develop a potent body of citizens who really care about the welfare of their fellows enough to safeguard other people's well-being as vigorously as they do their own?

Because I was still working around in the neighborhood after I left the Welfare office, I used to run into former clients.

I was pleased to find that they greeted me with friendliness and concern about what I was doing now. The relationship between social worker and client is definitely an artificial one, with most unfortunate overtones of power and control. It was reassuring for me to find out that I had apparently maintained a human personhood in spite of that.

Without my own Welfare check, I had to pay attention to subsistence finances again. There was a good part-time job that came my way almost like a gift from God. It was a technical writing/data analysis position with a small company that was developing a protein purified from beef liver to be used as a medicine. Again, interesting work and filled with new learning experiences. From that period I picked up a set of salary figures which I have used as a concrete example of the arbitrary value of money. From a board of directors meeting, we employees got a glimpse of the executive salaries in our little company. Our two chiefs were each getting over $100,000 per year with special bonuses and stock holdings on top of fat salaries. I, who had a really good flexible time arrangement and my own pleasant desk, was making $400 per month for half-time work. At the same time, a competent, dedicated woman I knew in East Bayshore was putting her full time into work with young people. She was the sort of person who did not cut off her concern by any time clock, so I knew she was available for troubled youngsters at any time. However, the position was described as being 7/8 time, so she didn't have to be given medical benefits or even vacation time. She showed me her paycheck stub: $375 for the full month! Of all the work represented by those salary figures, I suspect that her work was the most valuable for our whole society and that her skills were at least as high as any of the more academic or scientific skills represented by us better paid folks.

Let me put in here another observation about money which grew from my comparison of the rich and the poor. There are really three kinds of money: (1) the money which grows. This is what rich people have. They have enough excess that it can be put out to interest, or be invested or used to attract more money in any number of ways; (2) the money which stays the same. This is the money which comes to the thrifty wage earner or lower-level professional person. This covers hirs needs but doesn't go very much beyond. It is mostly used up in each successive pay period or may gradually accumulate a useful nest egg for special purposes; (3) the money which devours. This is the money which comes to a wage earner or Welfare recipient, but which does not cover hirs needs, actual or sometimes imagined. This money leads into debt of one kind or another: the loan from friend or neighbor, the installment due on the car or the furniture, the bills run up at the grocery store, the past due utility bills. All of this has to be paid back with interest and throws its victims into a nightmare of juggling one urgency against another, of using all kinds of subterfuges to keep a household afloat for another day, week, or month. The constant hassling that this money-which-devours causes its owners is one of the real curses of poverty in this country.

At any rate, money is a miserably poor way to judge the value of anything, especially human beings.

THE ECUMENICAL HUNGER PROGRAM

In the summer of 1984 I returned on a visit to California. There I was treated to a great celebration of Founder's Day at the Ecumenical Hunger Program (EHP), which had grown to be a well-established agency bridging at least some of the gaps between West Bayshore and East Bayshore. I was honored as the founder, and was surrounded by a host of good friends who delighted in remembering the days when the whole thing got started. Nevida Preston Butler, now the executive director, had been the Red Cross representative for East Bayshore. A warm, vigorous and competent woman, she had felt sad about being restricted in her giving to only those cases that fitted Red Cross eligibility. When one of the other emergency help people brought her along to our small food giveaway distribution, she asked if she could take back with her some powdered milk, canned tuna and biscuit flour to put at the back of her filing cabinet so at least she'd have something to give to a family when she had to tell them no for their main request.

That was typical of our history. It started from what looked like ground zero, like that volcano in Mexico that grew up from a flat bean field. It wasn't really, of course, ground zero, any more than the underpinnings of that bean field had been lying there really quiet.

I think that every poor community develops neighborhood "helping people", the ones you go to when you run out of food or have a family problem you just can't handle. Every little church in East Bayshore had its own missionary society with a small fund which was constantly running out and being replenished. A few of the helping people grew into noticeable agencies. Mrs. Onedia Branch, wife of the minister of the largest Baptist church, had developed a regular storehouse with used clothing and a large refrigerator. Rev. Mrs. Ruth Lankford (the same one whose church I attended) was the representative for the Salvation Army in south San Mateo County. Jessie Kennedy, who worked with the Welfare agency, had developed a beautiful working relationship with Ellen Chang of the First Baptist Church of Palo Alto, who kept her own church updated on the current needs for baby furniture and other household items, for special transportation, for jobs, or even for housing. Ellen made sure that Jessie came over to speak often enough that the Palo Altans stayed aware of the needs in East Bayshore and knew they could really help. All these folks had been "keeping on keeping on" for years, trying to pick up some of the slack left by the Welfare Department.

It was in 1974, when one of the early Ethiopian famines came on television and made the whole country at least marginally aware of hunger in the world. The churches responded, with many talks from pulpits and small local projects undertaken. The director of the Northern California Ecumenical Council had organized a Hunger Commission with a coalition of Heifer Project, Church World Service and whatever other world organizations were around at the time. He was also trying to find funding for a staff person to develop a food distribution network of local resources for local needs. The government, in fact, had offered money for finding local sources of surplus food and ways to distribute it. One such center, the Food Bank, was just beginning in San Jose, about twenty-five miles south of us.

What got me into hunger action was that the Congregational Foundation in my own church offered me a $100 per month consulting fee to explore and recommend to the church ways they could help relieve hunger in East Bayshore. I suppose I might have seen the opportunities and gone ahead just on my own, but I must say it was really a great incentive to be given a specific commission and a bit of money. It made me feel "under orders".

It turned out that I was in a really good position to touch the various elements in our Mid-Peninsula community and bring them together. Besides my earlier work back and forth across Bayshore, I was currently the chairwoman for ecumenical action of our local Church Women United (CWU) group. For years they had been getting women from both sides of Bayshore together, for worship and some common projects. The steering committee liked the idea of setting up our annual meeting with a theme of "Hunger — What Can I do?". We asked Rev. Hodges, director of the Northern California Ecumenical Council, to be our main speaker and gave Mrs. Branch (a past president of CWU) a chance to speak about her emergency help program. Because the same women who came to CWU meetings from East Bayshore churches were the same ones who ran the missionary societies, we had a great wealth of resource people to talk about local needs.

We set up the meeting for action. We prepared pledge and contribution sheets for each church, and also asked them to give us names of representatives for a food planning group to meet again in three weeks. Besides that, the steering committee agreed that we could have the women preparing lunch see how much profit they could make from our usual fee of $1.50 per person, so long as lunch was nourishing and attractive. I had already cleared it with our women's fellowship of the Congregational church, and Eugenia Buss and her crew rose to the challenge magnificently. When they calculated expenses, they found they had produced seventy-nine good lunches for $35 (cupcakes for dessert had been donated). We were able to announce before the meeting was over that we had $83.50, plus a $10 donation as the start of a local fund for combating hunger, both worldwide and local. Certainly tiny, but nevertheless something real and in our hands. Everyone seemed to be feeling good.

In the whole history of the EHP, things fell into place almost of their own accord. It was as though our community had been just waiting for something to focus our resources on, so we could begin to use them where they were needed. I didn't even need to do any recruiting of volunteers. For instance, Pat LaForge of our church simply told me she wanted to help with this, and help she certainly did right from the start. She served as our first treasurer and later on took over the whole operation when I was suddenly placed in the hospital with a detached retina.

When we held our meeting of the food planning group, eleven churches from both sides of Bayshore were represented by good active people who brought in a total of $179 in pledges and contributions. We decided to divide our money, sending half periodically to the Northern California Ecumenical Hunger Commission for worldwide distribution and keeping half at home to see what we could do with it. We sent off a check for worldwide hunger immediately (with our first $93.50, the half came to $136.25!), but decided to consult further with the Food Closet people before we spent local money. There was good consensus among the Food Closets about what staples were most useful, so about three months later we held our first food giveaway. We'd contacted a little food cooperative in Menlo Park which would let us buy rice and beans and flour and powdered milk in bulk at wholesale prices. It turned out, too, that they had fresh local produce which they'd been having to throw out after the long weekend when they weren't open. They were glad to have us pick it up Friday noon.

We checked the grocery ads for the best "loss leader" prices and bought enough of each for easy division among the five Food Closets we'd been working with. In fact, the purchase of super-special values from local food markets became a regular part of our food gathering. It was Jeannette Rust who became our purchaser, and managed to convince grocery clerks that it was perfectly proper for her to carry out cases of their very best sale items. That first time, though, we probably gave out something like twenty cans of tuna, ten one-pound jars of peanut butter, some canned vegetables, the rice and beans and then whatever carrots and potatoes and greens the Briarpatch Co-op had that week. We all met at the Ravenswood Recreation Building in East Palo Alto. The director of that district, Alma Oliver, was in a central position in the community and often heard about families who needed food (and other help). She had a fairly large refrigerator available and was glad to be part of our effort.

Some of the Food Closet people would be in the midst of one crisis or another and would just stop briefly to pick up their share. Others would have the time to stop and talk a bit. They were cheery get-togethers. In fact, the giving away of even small amounts of extra food brought a whole new spirit into the emergency food business. Before we started, each helping person tended to guard her own particular sources of food quite jealously and also tried to hold back some of her food in reserve in case some other needy person might come along later for help.

The availability of extra staples opened things up a bit, but what really changed the tone was having large quantities of perishable foods given to us. I remember a time when a food market offered us seventy-two half-gallons of milk that had just reached their expiration dates. We phoned all the Food Closets we could reach to come and take as many cartons as they could handle, and then I drove around with one knowledgeable community helper to point out the homes where a recent disaster or a continuing need made her sure that they could use at least one or two of the cartons of milk.

There was the time the Briarpatch Co-op had a large number of good small artichokes. Alma cooked them and carried them around all hot and delicious to show neighbors how to eat them. There was a real Santa Claus atmosphere about our operations. It is hard, in fact, to find a more pleasant occupation than taking good food to folks who need it and will use it joyfully. We were not part of the established Welfare system, so no one felt we were obliged to feed them. Besides, our food came to us sporadically and by the grace of God, so it would have been only the most foolhardy who might have come to depend on us. We were in a great position!

If even our local bounties made us feel like a cornucopia, that was nothing compared to what happened when we became part of the network of the San Jose Food Bank. With federal money backing them, that agency had formed just shortly before the EHP, with the aim of obtaining surplus foods from local farmers and other food producers and distributing it to needy people through the agencies already doing that. Their first director was an energetic, free-wheeling young man who traveled all over our rich agricultural area stirring up possibilities and arrangements. He would have had even more loose ends following his progress than he did if he had not had a supreme-ly competent and unflappable secretary at his home office. We could always phone her to find out what was going on.

I remember that the first time they phoned me to see if we could use some part of the twelve tons of ripe pears they had harvested, I thought fast about our capacity at the time and said that if they could come by our way (we were at the far north end of their territory) we could use three medium-sized boxes. They didn't bother to make the trip that time, but it wasn't too long before our little network had expanded so that during the pear season they were sending us a weekly delivery of six or eight "lug" boxes of the type the pickers used in the orchards.

Part of their operation used volunteer pickers to harvest food after the commercial picking was finished, and we seemed to have a good pool of workers to draw from. The first time we agreed to bring a work crew for them, I thought we had six or eight people all ready to go. I got together good lunch materials and plenty of drinks so that it would be a good experience for everyone. When I arrived at the Ravenswood Recreation Department at 5:30 A.M. that morning, though, there were only two people: Alma Oliver and Ollie Wright, a really excellent man whom I was meeting for the first time. Well, three of us was better than none, so we took off for San Jose. There we joined the Food Bank truck and two of their staff workers. We were set to harvest plums from a most attractive eleven-acre orchard in the hills. The owner had bought the place with the idea that selling the plums would help pay for it, but after struggling through the process of paying a contractor the year before and coming out with a profit of only a little over thirty dollars total, he had phoned the Food Bank to come and get them for free.

The trees were loaded with absolutely gorgeous Santa Rosa plums, ripe, juicy and sweet. The five of us set to, each on our own tree, eating as many of the plums as we couldn't resist. We did pick thirty-seven lug boxes of the lovely fruit and the Food Bank hauled them off to their walk-in refrigerator that afternoon and then brought five lug boxes back to us later when we had our Food Closet people there all ready to pick them up and take them around to the folks they knew. It had been a great day, fun in itself and productive for needy people not just in our own community but for a host of people in Santa Clara County.

That was another good thing about having our East Bayshore people helping harvest food. The Food Bank was really supposed to be covering only Santa Clara County, but they couldn't very well make an issue of it when San Mateo County folks had helped get the food. The EHP kept our address at the Congregational church in Santa Clara County partly because it made our tie-in with the Food Bank easier. Really, with the style of networking that was developing, our ability to distribute the food was almost as valuable to them as their ability to get it was to us.

Making use of perishable food is quite a different operation from giving out staple, non-perishable foods when they're needed. There have to be enough people to swing into action on short notice and to stay with the job until it's completed. It does, though, open up opportunities for getting really good nutritious food, and it develops a great camaraderie among those people who pitch in.

The perishable foods also made life more varied and interesting for the volunteers who came each week to the First Congregational church to get the food ready for the Food Closet people. They could count on bagging up rice and beans and powdered milk and so on, but they never knew ahead of time what fruits and vegetables they might be called on to clean up and make presentable. Green beans, plums, pears, or apples to sort over as they went into medium-sized containers so we could send back the lug boxes, melons to check and maybe make up some bags of good but partial pieces. Once there were several great blocks of frozen raw tuna fish that came to us on the Food Bank truck. Ellen got Ollie to help her wrestle them into manageable sized pieces, and we got most of them out that day. Several of them had to stay behind in the church's refrigerator, though, and by the time we got them out, even the ice cubes smelled of fish. We knew without being told that that was the end for our long-suffering women's fellowship group, so we managed to get our own refrigerator, which the church was glad to set up in a back room for us.

No one knew much ahead of time what challenges we might be facing. Bags of potatoes or onions which had developed a few bad members were probably the most disagreeable, but we always had a few volunteers willing to tackle even them, and they were never the only things we had. In fact, although some of the produce we distributed was admittedly rather limp and sad-looking, some of it was absolutely the most handsome and nutritious that could be found anywhere. Above us in the hills, in Portola Valley, there was a man (I've forgotten his name) who was working full-time at developing an organic gardening method which he claimed was even better than the French Intensive. He may have been right. His vibrant Swiss chard stood four feet tall, and his carrots and corn and kohlrabi were magnificent to behold.

Janet Refvem from our group told him about our food efforts and he was delighted to give us his vegetables. He said he didn't want to be bothered with marketing, and he hated to just put it all back into the soil. Almost every distribution day a pick-up truck from Portola Valley, driven by Janet or her husband Tom or the gardener himself, would arrive at our church parking lot to unload whatever vegetables were at their peak just then. It certainly added to the overall feeling that there was an almost unlimited bounty available around us if we could just tap it.

Adding to the upbeat quality of life with EHP was the fact that most our volunteers were people who'd grown sick and tired of talking about problems like hunger and poverty, and they were delighted to be able to get their hands onto something tangible. I suspect, too, that our food operations answered what may be an almost instinctive urge by good housewives to salvage any food that they can. One way and another our gatherings were quite jolly and companionable, leaving participants feeling worthwhile and fulfilled.

One problem I discovered when our food distributions grew beyond a tiny size was that I myself am miserably incompetent when it comes to organizing a group of people into effective work groups. I panic and can't figure out which operation should be placed where, or how many people can be properly used for a specific task. Fortunately that was no real problem for our group. Ellen Chang just naturally took over the role of informal straw boss and would get things set up and steer volunteers around when they came in. If she couldn't make it some days, Pat LaForge or another of the good natural organizers would keep things going. I basically just stood around and floated from one group to another, being pleasant and friendly.

I remember once when I was talking with one of the good volunteers I apologized for my inability to organize things better and she told me, with great conviction, " Miriam, don't worry about it. It's probably one of the best things we have going for us. This is a great idea and you've got us all together. We can see you can't handle it by yourself, so we all have to pitch in. It makes us feel really needed." There's no question that I take great pleasure in being honored as the founder of a worthwhile agency which is still doing its good work, but the truth of the matter is that there were many, many people besides me who gave the early EHP its life and movement.

There was (and still is) a real need in our community which we had come to recognize. We had found that we could gather increasing amounts of food to meet that need. The Ecumenical

> *My LORD GOD, I have no idea where I am going. I do not see the road ahead of me. I cannot know for certain where it will end. Nor do I really know myself, and the fact that I think that I am following your will does not mean that I am actually doing so. But I believe that the desire to please you does in fact please you. And I hope I have that desire in all that I am doing. I hope that I will never do anything apart from that desire. And I know that if I do this you will lead me by the right road though I may know nothing about it. Therefore will I trust you always though I may seem to be lost and in the shadow of death. I will not fear, for you are ever with me, and you will never leave me to face my perils alone.*
>
> — Thomas Merton
> *Thoughts in Solitude*

Hunger Program grew and grew and grew. I knew it was becoming more than I could handle, and so did our board of directors. We'd had a really good board since the first time we had one, about a year after the kickoff luncheon of the CWU. I know Ellen Chang and Pat LaForge and Fr. Chris Sandholt of the East Palo Alto Catholic church were on our first board. Alma Oliver had not wanted even to have a board. As I remember it, Jessie Kennedy felt all right about our having a board, but she didn't want to be on it — she didn't like meetings. It was probably just as well. So much of her time was spent at a breakneck speed, trying to rescue one family or another from a crisis situation, that she probably wouldn't have been able to come to many meetings anyway. Etta Mae Smith of the C.M.E. church in East Menlo Park was the Food Closet person who attended board meetings most faithfully, and Nevida Butler came whenever she could. They kept us tuned into the realities we were facing.

During the course of our growth and transitions, we added Byron Bland, campus minister at Stanford University, Don Mason, minister of the Covenant Presbyterian church, and Joe Haletky, music director for one of the Palo Alto Lutheran churches. Joe was also treasurer for the Downtown Palo Alto

Food Closet, which had been born after our food distributions started. He volunteered to take over our treasurer tasks, too, for which Pat was duly grateful. It was Joe who brought in copies of that lovely prayer by Thomas Merton (printed here) which speaks of not really knowing where I'm going, but trusting that God will lead me by the right road anyway. It was a good prayer for our board. They steered the EHP through some troubled times as we moved from being a small, rather slipshod group into the larger, more efficient agency it became.

At any rate, we did have enough money to offer a stipend-type salary to a second staff person, and were lucky enough to get Lindi Ramsden. She was a recent graduate of Stanford, a highly competent and open person, eager to try new things. The first major thing she had to do was to reorganize our storeroom so that it would meet Public Health requirements. Along with that, of course, she tightened up our weekly food distribution systems. It was great that she was not a cold, efficiency-expert type of person. She was instead a friendly, upbeat sort, with a generous spirit. Everyone liked her.

Where she made the biggest impact, though, was in persuading me and the board that we should apply for getting CETA workers. The two of us worked together on putting the request together, but just at the last minute — the afternoon before the deadline, in fact — we discovered that we would have to refocus our entire presentation in order to have any chance at all. For me that would have been the end of it, at least for that year, but not for Lindi. She spent almost the entire night rewriting the whole request and submitted it in time. We were given approval to have three CETA workers, with salaries paid by the federal government. It was a giant step into the big time!

It was certainly a period of transition for me, too. I found myself thinking of Jesus' words about not putting new wine into old wineskins. I could almost feel my old seams giving way. If I can rightfully lay a claim to being the founder of the EHP, Lindi was certainly the architect and builder for an expanded edifice.

There came a time when an unexpected opportunity in another direction opened up for Lindi (I think she's now an ordained minister in the Unitarian church) and she left us before we were quite ready. The board and I hung in with it and chose a new director. Then I left town, assuring myself that things were really on a safe and secure track. Well basically they were, because of the board, but there were those troubled times I mentioned earlier, until Nevida Butler agreed to leave her position with the Red Cross and take over as director. The rest of the history of the EHP is in other hands than mine.

I think everyone trying to supply temporary needs is sure to hear about "putting a band-aid on a cancer" and to be questioned about what good we're really doing. So, what good had we indeed been doing with all that activity? Were East Bayshore families any less hungry and poor than when we started? Well, yes they were, by a day or a week or so. It's an important thing to provide food for growing children to grow on, even if it's something that has to be done time and again. And then there was the growth of knowledge and understanding among the women and men from the two sides of Bayshore, black and white and hispanic. We all had a chance to learn of each other's problems and ideas and enthusiasms. Because we affluent ones were working with the helping people of East Bayshore rather than giving the food directly to the people who needed it, we avoided the risk of falling into the Lady Bountiful vs. grateful peasantry syndrome. Instead, we were all working together for the benefit of the needy ones, and we comfortable people from West Bayshore were able to see the enduring commitment and understanding and compassion that kept the helping people going. Many good relationships formed among us, many expansions of hearts and minds.

GRANDMA HOPE IN SOUTH GEORGIA
September, 1991

There aren't many "Live-in Grandmas" these days, but that is what I've been calling myself for these last seven or eight years (since about 1983). My younger daughter Meredith had moved to Lake Park, Georgia with a good young man named Jim Tatch whom she'd met in Oregon. He'd come to her brother Forrest's wedding in California so we'd all met him and liked him, but the idea of their deciding to settle in south Georgia was quite startling. However, Meredith has always been able to convince us that she knows what she's doing, so there certainly was no great outcry of any sort.

I had visited them twice: first time in the early spring, with lovely weather and azaleas and red bud trees blooming. That was just a visit to visit. The second time was more serious and exciting: Meredith had given birth to Jasmine Hope Tatch, their first child and my first grandchild. That is a real occasion for any mother/grandmother, being there to help with the beginnings of a new life. It didn't really matter that south Georgia was at the peak of its hot, humid summer. That's easy to put up with at such a time. At least it gave me some notion of the realities of life there.

It was when Jasmine was about two years old that Meredith and Jim issued me a sincere invitation to come live near them. I had arrived at a kind of dead end in California, or maybe it was just a freedom from commitments. My mother had died (peacefully and well at age 87) and Forrest and his wife Sally were competently embarked on the first stages of raising their young one, Shawna Rose Nixon. They were glad to have Grandma Miriam around, but I wasn't really needed. At any rate, I decided it would be a good move for me to take off for Georgia. I'd been distributing my household treasures to my grown family for a couple years, so there wasn't much left to ship to Georgia. I arranged a final pick-up truckload of things Ruth wanted, went to Oregon for a visit with her and Greg and had them take me to the airport for the transcontinental flight to Valdosta, Georgia. That's ten years ago this month.

It's been a real change from the west coast in many ways, but not that much in other ways. Flora and fauna may be a bit different, but their essential beauty and inter-relatedness remain the same. People may speak with a different accent and have some different customs, but their essential beauty and inter-relatedness are also the same.

What has it meant — and what does it still mean — to be a live-in Grandma? Well it's not exactly easy, and not without real confusions and buffetings from life, but I think that we've all managed pretty well and that it's a good way for me to spend the days of my life. And it has been very much the days, as in "daily". I've become more and more aware of the daily quality of living: the getting up each morning and being there as the kids go out to catch the school bus, the straightening up of the kitchen with the new round of dishes, the gathering of laundry and sending it through the washer.

It took me awhile to be able to adjust my ways to those of the Tatch family. The first couple of years I had my own little place and continued my accustomed style of being my own boss and choosing my own comings and goings, but gradually I became aware of the fact that what I welcomed most in my life were opportunities to help in the growth of the children. When Jim and Meredith moved into a sprawling house with six bedrooms I consulted with them about moving in with them and becoming more fully part of their family. It was Meredith who said she didn't think we could theorize about that sort of thing very effectively, so why didn't we just go ahead and try it. Jasmine must have been about three and a half and Charles hadn't yet reached his first birthday. There was certainly plenty of plain old work to keeping the household going, so I knew I was being useful. It wasn't just that, though. There is something about the potential of the growing child, the unexpected responsiveness and growing skill of the young one that is fascinating and meaningful for me. It was a sort of second chance at those earlier years of helping my own children grow, more like a kind of echo than a repeat. I am no longer on the front line of decision making and responsibility. I have to stand back and stay out of the way sometimes. And a very good thing that is, too. Even when I first came to Georgia I no longer had the sustained energy that child-rearing requires. There are times that require the very best, steadiest, wisest maneuvering that you can manage, and if they happen at a time when you're really frazzled out physically and mentally, heaven help both you and the child. Thank God for the resiliency and recovery capabilities of children!

Anyway, I have been very glad that it's Meredith and Jim who are steering the course for Jasmine and Charles and Andrew. I try to add what I can to their growth and their sense of well-being, and I guard against letting my energy level get so low that I can't respond with some degree of love and decency to a need they may have from me. These things do come to a kind of natural balance, though. The kids are all pleasantly perceptive, and they know they can't expect any great athletic participation or even just staying out in the hot sun from me.

We have two Grandmas in the family. Jim's mother Edna lives about four miles away in the same house where Jim grew up. She's a few years older than I am, but we're at about the same level of recognizing our limitations.

I had hoped that I'd be better at managing old age than I really am. I've watched and applauded some of those inspiring TV specials about older people who radiate vitality and interest in their chosen fields and who parachute from airplanes or develop new styles of painting or raise tropical plants. I'm glad they're out there and doing such vibrant things with their living, but I'm just not up to it. It isn't only my stiff back and hips in the morning and my eyes not working right. What's even more disturbing is that I have already begun to lose words in my head. I reach for one that I take for granted will be there and it's just not there. I remember when my mother was mentioning the same problem, but she was into her eighties by that time, and I'm just seventy-three. Well, there it is. Some of us just go to pieces faster than others, I guess.

I think that that keen awareness of things which has always been so important to me, which has seemed to be almost an essential duty of my living, is still with me, at least part of the time, but I'm not at all sure. I don't feel as though I can trust my perceptions of reality as surely as I once did. I remember an essay by Robert Louis Stevenson in which he commented that it's a fallacy for older people to try to put down the young by telling them "Yes, I thought that way once, too, but now that I've lived longer I can see things more clearly." There may be greater wisdom by longer life, but there may also be a loss of perception. I haven't been able to find that essay again, but I'll claim it as my own idea now. Old age does not necessarily bring greater discernment about life. Those perceptions I had in the flush of youth may have hit closer to central realities than anything I'd come up with now.

My doctor assures me my basic health is good, but I do sometimes wonder what will happen to our family when my current aches and pains and uncertain vision go farther into incapacity. In my lighter moments I play with the idea that the burden of an ailing Grandma may be just what this family needs to develop character and patience and compassion. Could be, but in any event, there doesn't seem to be any way to avoid completely the possibility of being a burden on people I don't want to burden. We'll have to ride along and see how it goes. I just hope that if my mind goes, I'm left with an amiable disposition.

Even though my grandchildren and family are my top priority, I've kept up some concerns beyond the family. One night I read in the *Valdosta Daily Times* that some local citizens were meeting to form a Food Bank for the community. It was like a bell for an old fire horse. I went down there and met a number of interesting people from this new community. Ethel Greer, an older Afro-American woman was the respected inspiration and goad for action. There was a young man from Legal Services, Sister Ellen Roach from the Catholic church, David Boyd from the local War on Poverty agency, and a handful of others. A pleasant group, about equally black and white. They certainly knew much more about their community than I did, and it was a good way to get an idea of what kinds of things were going on.

The atmosphere was relaxed and not at all urgent. My overall impression was that there really wasn't very much going on in the Valdosta area. I heard about agencies and civic groups and government programs in which many of them were involved, but they all sounded more static than dynamic, as though they were settled into established patterns of action. There didn't seem to be any of the expectations and tensions which had made the California Mid-Peninsula such a fertile field for the growth of the Ecumenical Hunger Program.

Dynamic or not, the group worked away at it in their own

style and developed a Unity Food Bank which is still operating to increase the food supply for the established agencies, and so on to the needy.

My biggest bonus from working with the group was discovering the Wednesday evening Bible Class which Mr. David Boyd had been leading for years at the Bethel C.M.E. church in Valdosta. After he invited me to come, I began going there, and it was such a treasure house of personal experiences and Christian insights that I became a regular participant for some six years. It was both a spiritual well of living water and a continuing contact with the black community here.

I never knew for sure what direction a particular meeting would take. We talked about current politics and the local drug scene as well as exploring religious points of view. Mr. Boyd encouraged all of us to express our ideas, and because he worked closely with the local socio-economic problems, he often had provocative news stories or personal experiences to lay before us. He used to let me bring in my special concerns, too, and there were several times when I got the whole class to sign on to a letter about social issues that I was ready to mail to our state or national congresspeople. They sometimes teased me about my excitement over successive burning issues, but they did listen and gave me good, common-sense feedback.

It was more than verbal feedback that they gave me on the occasion when I told them about what had been going on with a local ecumenical effort to start the Community Soup Kitchen. The steering committee was ready to begin offering meals, but they hadn't been able to find a place where they could set it up. Several of the larger churches had been closely involved with the preliminary work, but none of them could free up a kitchen and hall for the community. They all had internal groups who were using the facilities and didn't see how they could make room for the Soup Kitchen. After I'd alerted our Bible Study group about the need, they and Mr. Boyd carried it on to their whole church and got general approval, so that they issued an official invitation to the Community Soup Kitchen to use their one and only kitchen and fellowship room for starting the feeding operations. Eventually the kitchen and hall proved too small for the Soup Kitchen and they moved into a large old school facility which was managed by the War on Poverty agency, but I have the feeling that the generosity of the Bethel C.M.E. folks made a really decisive difference by opening up a good path at the time when the initial enthusiasm for the project had reached its natural time for fruition.

What kept me going back with eagerness to Bethel C.M.E. week after week, though, was not just the chance for a forum on social concerns, but the warm and enlightening style of Christian fellowship that I found there. People seemed genuinely glad to see me each time and encouraged me with warm hugs both before and after our meetings. We sang songs together, a good variety of hymns and then gospel songs, some of which I had not heard before. I was so taken with one of them that I managed to get a tape recording of Mrs. Mary Whitfield leading our group in singing *Another Day that the Lord Has Kept Me*. "He has kept me from all evil, and my mind is stayed on Jesus. Another day that the Lord has kept me." It's a very simple song, but it carries the voice of people who have been struggling for a long time just to survive and who know how much they need Jesus. With my current day-to-day style of living I've been gaining some wisdom about just how much I need Jesus, too, and it's a good song to have on hand.

And then there were those very special times when, by talking together about our understandings of some Bible passages, we'd come to a broadened or deepened understanding that no one of us could have arrived at alone, and that illuminated things for all of us. Someone would offer an idea, maybe not quite fully formed. Someone else would add to it, or maybe object to just one piece of it. We'd share variations on the idea, and maybe a story to illustrate it. When everyone who wanted to had finished adding their bit, Mr. Boyd might sum up the whole idea, and then ask the next person to go on to the next passage. I remember several times when a passage that had special meanings for me would make me speak up about it, often when my idea was still groping and tentative. Bless those good folks! Someone always caught at least a corner of the idea and gave it more body from their own experiences and understandings. It was the same kind of sharing I'd experienced with the Bible Study group out in California. Not an intellectual effort to pursue logical theology, but a willingness to talk about one's whole experience in trying to follow the ways of Jesus. Whatever might come up in those Wednesday evenings, it always strengthened my spirit to be accepted into fellowship with people who were so sincerely trying, with honesty and humility, to live good, faithful Christian lives.

Grandma Hope in Georgia, 1988.
Children nos. 1, 3, and 5 (l. to r) are my grandchildren: Andrew, Jasmine and Charles. Children nos. 2 and 4 are Christina and Bruce McDonald from across the road.

FROM TRIDENT TO LIFE

It wasn't until I read the U.S. Bishops' pastoral letter, *The Challenge of Peace*, in about 1984 that I began to realize that I should be doing something about our world's relentless progress toward war, and the dangers of nuclear weapons. There certainly had been plenty of peace actions around me in California, but I'd been quite content to let my work with hunger and poverty justify me in letting other folks carry on the work in that area. Issues of war and peace had seemed too huge and complicated for me to want to get involved. The Peace Pastoral (which I read in the Easy Reading version published by Pax Christi, the Catholic peace group) tied the straggling ends and complications into a broad but logically organized whole, and issued a live and urgent call to action. At least that was how I read it. A short while later, when I had been accepted into the communion of the Catholic Church and got acquainted with our local parish, I had to realize that most of the parishioners had been immunized against the words of the bishops, so that the pastoral letter had had almost no impact. Nevertheless, the words of these thoughtful and authoritative men did galvanize me into action.

I tried to organize a local peace group. Again, it was the Bethel C.M.E. church that provided the setting and supportive organization for a public forum entitled, "What Should Christians Do to Promote Peace in Our Nuclear Age?". Everyone seemed to feel it was a good, lively meeting. There were about seventy people, both black and white, and some twenty people signed the sheet with their addresses and phone numbers, indicating that they'd be interested in being part of a Valdosta peace group.

The forum had taken place on Nov. 11, and unfortunately the decision was made to wait until after the Christmas holidays to get started. We never did pick up again that little surge of momentum which might have helped us get the group off the ground. As far as I know, our area is still without anything which could be called a peace group.

By now, though, I had made contact with both the Fellowship of Reconciliation and Pax Christi, and I heard about an annual action at the Kings Bay Naval Submarine Base, which is the east coast home of the Trident submarine, within driving distance of Valdosta, at the southernmost part of Georgia's coast.

For some three or four years, right after Christmas, peace groups in the southeast part of our country had been coming together at Kings Bay to commemorate the Feast of the Holy Innocents with vigiling, protest marches and, sometimes, with trespass on the base. The idea is to draw attention to the parallel between King Herod's slaughter of boy babies in Bethlehem to preserve his power and our country's preparation to slaughter millions of people with the nuclear warheads of the Trident submarine. Everything I heard about the actions sounded worshipful and serious. Everything I began to read about the Trident submarine sounded truly monstrous and insanely destructive. I wanted to go.

People in the peace movement are very good about sharing resources with each other. They helped me arrange a ride. Judy and Jack Cumbee, coming from Alabama, were going to pick up some people from Koinonia Christian Community in Americus, Georgia and then they would pick me up at a way point just an hour's drive from Valdosta. Everything went smoothly and we were on our way to St. Marys, Georgia. It was a great way for me to get acquainted with some interesting and lively people and to find out a bit about Kings Bay and the peace movement in this part of the country. St. Marys had been just a small resort town on the coast, but signs of federally funded growth were everywhere, a military boom town. Our driver knew the way well to Crooked River State Park, where all the comfortable cabins had been reserved ahead of time, and were filled with peace people. Simple cabins, but well-equipped they were, with double beds and couches and each a kitchen with utensils. Central heat, too. No real hardship here.

Headquarters were set up at one of the central, larger cabins. That year (1985) Martina and John X. Linnehan were coordinators for the event. Since I was not attached to any one group, they let me sit around at the registration desk and watch the action as people came in and passed back and forth. A festive air, joyful greetings of friends, exchanges of news from people who didn't see each other very often. It was a real overview for me of the peace activists of the Southeast, families as well as single men and women, young and old. There was certainly plenty of disjointed activity as people figured out where to sleep, and who else was here, but everything was well under control in a relaxed sort of way.

One minor event reassured me even further about the high caliber of this gathering. Two men introduced themselves as being from No Business as Usual, a group I had heard about in California. It was a group well known for stirring up provocative, media-catching actions, a group one could easily believe had ties to the Communist party. Martina treated them in friendly fashion, but took them inside for a long talk. She told us she'd explained to them our long-established rules of total non-violence and respect for the local authorities. However she did it, it obviously worked. The next day on our march, they walked along just like the rest of us, not even carrying a sign.

The evening candlelight vigil at the entrance to the base moved along well, about 150 people with lighted candles in glass containers joining together in a simple and moving religious-oriented liturgy. The next day we gathered again for a 2½-mile walk along the main road to the base, with signs and some singing. I was unhappily surprised to find that the walk was becoming too much for me, so I was glad to get into the relief van which cruised by us and to get driven to the entrance. Dorothy Smith, a quiet woman already over eighty, was having no trouble at all and walked steadily along, keeping up easily. And I'd been feeling protective toward her, and trying to watch out that she was all right!

At the end of the march we held a commissioning service at the entrance to the base to provide a send-off for the small group of people who were planning to walk up to and over the forbidden line at the base. Again I found it a reverent and inspiring service. I stood behind Fr. Bob Cushing, a young parish priest from our diocese who had decided he needed to do this action of "divine obedience" (an action meant to demonstrate the importance of a peace activist's focus on obedience to God even when there is a conflict with civil law. The term is used to emphasize the existence of high law, and to avoid the civil disobedience being seen as merely an objection to the civil authority involved). Those of us who were staying behind in support placed our hands on the shoulders of the more active participants during the words of the commissioning, and then sang together at a safe distance while they walked up to the entrance, stepped over and were arrested. They were all back with us at the evening meal, having been given letters of disbarment, forbidding them to come back on the base without special permission from the commanding officer. There was real celebration to have them back with us, a truly festive mood, but it was not frivolous. Dorothy Smith told me she had felt torn with guilt for not walking up with them when they went.

During the next year I read a good deal about the Trident. It is truly a monstrous machine of destruction. When it's fully armed it carries 24 missiles, each one of which has 8 nuclear warheads capable of being aimed individually at separate targets, traveling up to 4,000 miles and landing with an accuracy determined in feet rather than miles. Each warhead has at least 20 times the explosive force of the bomb that flattened Hiroshima. What we have, then, in one submarine is the capability to strike simultaneously 192 areas on our planet with a destruction which is quite beyond any real calculation. And our government has been pouring billions of dollars into building not just one or two of these monsters, but a projected fleet of 18 (earlier there was talk of 24). It must be a measure of the insanity of our society that grown men, chosen by the electorate to lead our country, have been discussing quite calmly and without serious objection the specifics of making and launching these submarines.

At any rate, when announcements of the 1986 Feast of the Holy Innocents arrived in the mail, with dates given for a weekend of training for people interested in civil disobedience, I was eager to go and arranged transportation again. This was my introduction to consensus decision making and to the building of an "affinity group" (a group of people who take the time to develop mutual understanding and trust among themselves, so that they can be effective in acting together and also in supporting each other through hardships after the action, if that proves necessary). There were close to twenty of us, some seasoned veterans of past actions at Kings Bay or at other sites around the country, several of us considering civil disobedience for the first time. Peg McIntire and Marilyn Elsen, who had trespassed the year before, came along to act as support people and share their experiences. Bob Cushing acted as facilitator, but the meetings were very much shared among all participants. We each talked about where we were personally in feeling we had to express some kind of resistance to our government's militarism and willingness to destroy millions of people. Several in the group expressed a feeling of answering the Spirit's call to divine obedience, even if it entailed civil disobedience. The tone of our meetings was, in fact, deeply religious. Father Bob is, after all, a priest, Anne Dougherty and Marilyn Elsen are active Catholic sisters. Judy Scheckel had been a Sister for years before she left her order. Tim Murphy was a seminarian and John Frank had been (and still is) an active lay leader in the Catholic church. Beyond that, Martina and John Linnehan, who were around taking care of the logistics of the weekend and sometimes sitting in with us, had both been members of religious orders earlier in their lives.

It wasn't heavy-handed religiosity at all, and to me it felt good and strengthening, but Dorothy Smith, who was really eager to take part in a resistance action, felt the need several times to make sure she wasn't misrepresenting herself and where she stood on things. She explained that she doesn't believe in God, but that she cares deeply about people and all living things. She said she agreed fully with the basic thrust of what we were trying to do, but it wasn't at all a religious call for her. Was it really all right for her to become part of our group? I think we all felt she was an especially gentle and deeply-rooted spirit in her own right, so we reassured her and tried to welcome her thoroughly. She did, in fact, decide to become a member of the core group which walked onto the base.

We talked about the principles of non-violence which is, of course, much more than the refusal to use physical violence. I would summarize it as self-awareness and clarity of purpose, and an essential bedrock recognition and respect for each other person, not only our companions but also the human beings in authority whose orders we would be refusing to obey.

We worked together on a Statement of Purpose, which we would use as a press release and present to the base authorities before we crossed the line. We considered scenarios for an action which would have meaning. The idea which carried the day was to carry roses to the base as a sign of life and love, to counteract the style of death and destruction we perceived in the submarine base. Also Bob Cushing agreed to try to negotiate with the base commander some location outside the base gate where we could plant a couple rose bushes. It was suggested that those of us who decided to trespass should write a personal letter to the base commander explaining why we were doing what we were planning to do. Throughout the action, every effort was made to communicate to the authorities what we were planning to do and why. This had been the practice since the first Feast of the Holy Innocents, and it not only minimized the danger of unexpected overreactions, but also had developed some friendly connections.

By the end of the weekend, I felt I knew a great deal more about the peace movement than I had before, at least in this southeast part of our country, and I had developed a great respect for the amount of careful, responsible work that went into a resistance action. I felt comfortable about courting arrest with this group of people.

However, there came an intrusion into our comfortable feeling of security. This was the year of the Great Peace March, that surge of people which had started out with great ballyhoo and handsome tents from California, had temporarily broken down in the desert, but had reorganized itself and marched across the whole continent to arrive at Washington, D.C. and then on to appearances on Donahue and other television shows. At least some remnants of them were planning to continue their march to the Kings Bay base and then on down to Cape Canaveral in Florida. Some of them had expressed a wish to join in our Feast of the Holy Innocents action. What were we going to do about that? Here were these outsiders whom we didn't know, about to push into our neat little, carefully planned event. I'm parochial and fearful enough that I could feel the protective defenses rising up in my own spirit. But on the other hand it seemed quite churlish to refuse entry to these people who had proved themselves to be sturdy proponents of peaceful, non-violent action.

We had a long meeting just among ourselves first. It was especially hard for Father Bob, who had been doing a lot of bridge building with local authorities and felt personally responsible for seeing that nothing out of line happened. We talked a bit about having them set up their own separate action, but that quickly showed itself as unrealistic. Judy Scheckel was a great help in opening up our courage because she had been in many different types of resistance actions around the country and knew some of the Peace March people personally, but yet had become a safe part of our little home group. We finally agreed that we had to invite them to join us.

Then we ran into another serious hurdle. Several of them felt, as a matter of principle, that they needed to be completely non-cooperating when they were arrested. That means that instead of walking along with an arresting officer, one goes totally limp and has to be carried away in some manner. We listened carefully as they explained their thinking and feelings on this matter. My best summary of the rationale goes like this: total non-cooperation is just the next step in civil resistance. When you arrive at the point of refusing an order from a proper authority, you have already decided to act on your own authority and have refused the orders from a source you no longer respect. Why, then, should you allow your body to cooperate readily in their plans for how they handle you? You don't really want to cooperate at all in any of their actions.

We asked a lot of questions and talked around back and forth. There were five people who felt strongly that they needed to carry out non-cooperation fully. Most of us, including me, were beginning to understand their approach to things, even though we ourselves were not ready to take on that kind of extra problem. On the other hand, no one felt strongly that there was something really wrong with going limp after arrest. We decided that we should support those five in acting on their consciences. Fr. Bob agreed to warn the base authorities that some of the protesters might go limp and to suggest that they have stretchers available to carry them.

We felt at least minimally acquainted with the newcomers by the time we broke up our meeting and joined the larger group. There had been ten new people added to our ranks, and a total group of twenty from our affinity group who were planning to trespass on the base. We were ten women and ten men, six from the state of Georgia, four from Florida, one from North Carolina, and then one each from the states of Washington, Massachusetts and Vermont, with six whose homes I do not know. Another interesting breakdown was that there were at least ten Catholics among us and only three who I knew were not Catholic.

The commissioning service seemed especially sharp and

clear that year, and then we were walking toward the open gate of the base. The first group of three people, abreast and each carrying a long-stemmed white rose stepped over the line and were arrested and taken off out of our sight. The next group, four this time, crossed the entrance and were arrested in their turn. This time three of them went limp and slid down toward the ground. Base personnel did have stretchers there and they were carried off. However, shortly after they disappeared, one of the uniformed men came out to the gate office and the gate was clanged shut solidly and locked.

Our two liaison people, Robert McGlasson, a pro-bono attorney, and Rev. A.B. Short, a Baptist minister who was a veteran of these actions at the base, went up to confer. When they came back they reported that the non-cooperators had continued their limpness right on to the steps of the base bus in which the guards were planning to carry them over to another building for processing. Considerable irritation had ensued, with someone deciding that the gate should be closed until they began to move under their own power. The authorities wanted us to petition them to abandon their non-cooperation so we could get our action moving again. We conferred, but decided that our earlier agreement had been to support them in their determination of conscience, so that we should not put any extra pressure on them to give in.

Our negotiators reported our decision and continued talking to the base guards, while we formed a circle in the road and sang peace songs together. It was a cold day and we needed to keep our bodies moving as well as our spirits sustained. It was a long time we spent outside the locked gate, certainly over an hour. I found myself thinking how completely impregnable the base looked, with its bricks and iron gate and the uniformed men standing at ease but capable behind the ironwork. I had to realize, too, how ridiculous our little band of thirteen people shuffling around and singing songs must look. Oddly enough, though, I found that I was supremely glad to be there, that it felt like the right thing to be doing. It seemed very important to be filling a small niche as a human, vulnerable counterpoint to that impersonal mass of destructive power.

As it began to get darker and colder, our friends brought some blankets to us, and there seemed to be no objection to our settling down on the curb close to the gate. We sat there talking.

Some of the younger people were preparing themselves to spend the night. Dorothy Smith agreed with me that we really didn't want to, but we'd just have to wait and take it as it came. Finally A.B. Short came over and said they'd reached an agreement. They would open the gate for us as only two people at a time came up, but if any more people went limp, they'd close the gate for good. We got together again to make our plans. There were still two non-cooperators among us, who hadn't changed their minds or their consciences. We decided, without objections, that we wouldn't be shortchanging them if we left them to the last group. Since there were thirteen of us, that last group would just naturally have to be three people. That plan was okayed by base personnel. We paired up and began to move forward again. My partner Tim Murphy and I had earlier agreed we'd like to kneel for prayer before we were arrested, but it was a very quick decision to abandon that idea for fear it would look too much like going limp. We walked up as impressively as we could with our white roses in our hands and were arrested gently and respectfully, he by a man and I by a woman guard, and then taken to wait in the base bus until our whole group was assembled.

The final group of three did not make it. We got the report a little later that they had walked through the gate in good order, two of them had gone limp and been placed on stretch-

Storming the Bastion of Power.

Miriam Hope and Tim Murphy crossing the line at Kings Bay Naval Submarine Base. Photo by Ben Goggins.

ers, but then the stretchers had been carried outside the gate and the gate closed finally. All in all, I felt that both sides in this encounter had behaved with decorum and with proper respect for fellow human beings. I did manage to get one of the women guards to accept my white rose as a gift.

Processing took place in a huge recreation building. We were guarded at all times, but the atmosphere was certainly polite and relaxed. We were, after all, no real threat to them. They took our data and pictures and read each one of us a debarment letter, forbidding reentry onto the base without the commanding officer's express permission. When they asked me to sign that I understood the meaning of the letter, I went ahead and did so. Some people refused, but I didn't see any reason not to. We had to wait while they took a bit of extra time with Bob Cushing, who had received his first letter of debarment at last year's action, and so was charged more strongly this time and would have a court hearing. Finally they put us all back on the bus and drove us off the base. Our peace folks came and picked us up and took us back to Crooked River State Park. What a fine group of people our peace companions were! How excellent the simple food they offered us!

The next morning, when we were breaking up camp and saying our good-byes, I found John Frank surrounded by his four children. He and his wife Pat are equally peace activists, and they had worked it out that after John had his free time for the entrance onto the base, Pat would be free to go along with the Peace Walkers on their trip down to Cape Canaveral. As John looked around at the tangle of kids, he said to me, "Now the really difficult work of peacemaking begins!" It was a good comment to carry along with me as I headed back to my own daily efforts to help develop harmony in what are often confusing pieces of household living.

Our Feast of the Holy Innocents witness of 1986 was not a particularly important resistance action as such things go, but it has been important for me. It was highly instructive, spiritually satisfying and has brought me into closer community with a group of excellent people. It has also been a milestone for me in accepting personal responsibility for what my government is doing and in redefining my relationship with that government.

A TRIP TO NICARAGUA

In 1987 I took a trip to Nicaragua with Witness for Peace. I had been reading about Nicaragua and Central America and when a newsletter from Witness for Peace gave the schedule for their short-term delegation trips and urged us to recruit people from our own communities to go on them, I realized that I really wanted to go myself. I wrote to ask whether my old age disabilities and limitations would make me a liability, and received a good letter from Gail Phares about other older people who had been real assets on their delegations. Gail herself, who is one of the founders of Witness for Peace and deeply knowledgeable about the whole area, was leading a mid-South delegation from November 17 to December 1, which fit in well with my family's plans. I applied, was accepted and began trying to revive what little Spanish I had and to add more to it.

It was a magnificent trip. It was my first time outside the continental United States, so there were many new things to take in: the lush tropical foliage and birds, the Spanish language all around and the primitive and often impoverished styles of living. I found that primitive living in itself didn't feel foreign to me. My old days of primitive camping in Oregon and California came back and I realized that this would be just an extension of that close-to-nature way, except that one stayed permanently in the single place, with other people around. When we were staying with a *campesino* family in the mountain village of El Serrano, I fully appreciated their good well right at the front of the house, with its sound cover and the smooth-working pulley which helped them draw water. My host Adolfo was obviously a good craftsman and general husbandman. There was, though, a group of crudely made shacks in one area of Managua which were certainly poor by almost any definition.

Our days were full, though not hectic. We interviewed a good variety of influential people and learned about the economy of Nicaragua, the past history, the women's movement, the relief and development efforts of The Council of Evangelical Churches of Nicaragua (CEPAD), an ecumenical agency of protestant churches, the legal system, hospitals and the new peace commissions which had been formed throughout the country (this was the time when the peace efforts of the

Esquipulas agreement were being most vigorously pursued, and there was still hope). There was, in fact, a full spectrum of opinion about the value of the revolution and the Sandinistas. Cardinal Obando's office was at the extreme end of complete opposition to the Sandinistas. The young priest who was taking the cardinal's place during an absence told us that the people were worse off now than they had been under Somoza. When we asked him about the Christian Base Communities in Nicaragua, those groups of people who have become the foundations of the poor people's church in third world countries, he said that they had become tools of Sandinista propaganda. But after we spent several days living and worshiping with such a group, we had a wholly different impression. Most the people we talked with had some reservations about the Sandinistas, but they were quite fully part of what they called *el proceso*, the process of change. They were putting great, committed efforts into working with it. There was an atmosphere of hope and expectation, along with a recognition of how much hard work and sacrifice would be needed.

The only official Sandinista with whom we talked, the Commandante of Region V in Nueva Guinea, didn't bother with any political discussion, but told us about the nature of his region and its problems, what he was trying to do with those problems, things that had failed, but also some that had worked. The most outspoken, full-hearted support for the revolution and its Sandinista government came from a young Brazilian nun who had been sent to Nicaragua with five other sisters of her order, because her order wanted very much to be part of what they saw as a God-inspired effort toward social change which could benefit the people of all Latin America. Sr. Lourdes saw the struggle in Biblical terms. She said that we were now in a desert time, but had full confidence that good would prevail. "The Lord has a thousand ways to save his people," she assured us. I have remembered her voice many times since.

The folks we stayed with in Juigalpa, members of a Christian Base Community, weren't what anyone would call influential, but they were certainly lovely to be with. The night we arrived they welcomed us with a great burst of music in one of their private homes. We sat around a large, smooth dirt floor with religious pictures and symbols around the walls, and open windows filled with children who couldn't crowd inside. We sang songs together and listened to special groups. We expressed greetings and good wishes back and forth and prayed together. Afterwards we went off two by two with our host families to their homes. The next night we came back to a different home for one of their regular meetings. In many ways it was like a Bible study meeting in our U.S. churches. The main difference, I think, was that these folks were themselves "the poor" and were living in the midst of the poor and needy and of problems that needed help right now. Jesus' words do have a different impact when ministering to the sick and the poor is done right next door. Many of these folks had served as the core group for the literacy and immunization programs begun in the communities by the Sandinistas and they felt that these programs had helped them follow Jesus' teachings. Maybe that was why Cardinal Obando was considering them propagandists for the Sandinistas, but I would have called it good personal experience instead of propaganda.

After their meeting we walked over to the small parish church where the French-born priest was fully in accord with the efforts of the people. That was where I had my first chance to hear and join in with the songs of the *missa campesina*, a collection of most stirring and revolutionary songs which were, nevertheless, altogether appropriate for a church worship service.

On my desk here at home I keep a photo of Nubia Deltrano whom I met in Juigalpa. She was (and I hope still is) a beautiful example of one of those "helping people" I've seen in action in other poor communities. Before the revolution she had worked for a small medical clinic run by the Catholic Church. After the revolution, the Sandinistas had incorporated that clinic into their network of medical centers. They had given Nubia several months further training at the Juigalpa Hospital and provided her with a certificate. She was very pleased to be working there, even though she said shortages of supplies made things difficult. She obviously went beyond office hours in her work.

On the evening when a group of us were preparing to walk to the Base Community meeting, a small girl came by and gave Nubia a message from her grandmother, asking if she could get a shot that evening. Nubia picked up her equipment and stopped off at that house on the way. After the church service,

I noticed her talking quite intently and privately with a young woman. It certainly looked like some form of counseling for a problem too difficult to be borne alone.

It is good to have Nubia's picture near at hand. It keeps alive my memories of Nicaragua and of the people there. That trip was an important experience in my life and I'm very glad I had it.

It's one thing, though, to have an exciting trip with new sights and sounds and to rejoice in the kinship with endearing people. It's quite another to come home and begin to pitch in on the effort to turn around my own country's policy. Because it was my own country which armed the contras whose victims I had seen in the Juigalpa Hospital and whose destructive actions I had witnessed in the countryside. It was my country's embargo which idled machinery for lack of parts and denied medical supplies to the struggling clinics. It was my country which acted as the main obstacle to a vigorous effort to change one small country's government so that it worked for the health and well-being of all its people.

I wrote an extensive letter about my trip and experiences and sent it to friends, family and acquaintances. I talked to as many groups as I could, showing slides and answering questions. I continued writing letters to my representative and senators and to the local papers, hoping they might have a bit more impact because of my personal experience.

The talk with slide show really went quite well. People listened and asked questions. They were often knowledgeable about the pattern of poverty and oppression in Central America. But there were also many who had trouble seeing our country as being anything less noble than the defender of democracy and the poor throughout the world. I hope the talks had some influence. However, I found very little feeling of responsibility or urgency about whatever our country might be doing. I felt as though I were running up against not a brick wall, but rather a sticky morass of longtime ignorance and complacency. I'm afraid we have lost the feel for active participation as citizens.

We like to think we have freedom and full information in this country, but too many of us are content to sit back and listen to news commentators talking as though they understand even the most horrible developments, as though everything is under control. We hear only a centrist position from both Republicans and Democrats and see only what is the current hot item of world excitement. Since Violeta Chamorro won the election, Nicaragua has almost completely disappeared from the news. I do continue to get newsletters from several sources and have been able to follow major changes and confrontations and problems. The struggle is still going on and many solidarity groups from our country continue to provide what resources they can to help grassroots efforts which now face cutbacks or even direct opposition from the current government. Our U.S. government has failed miserably in providing the economic aid that Violeta Chamorro expected to help her improve the economy. We are apparently now using that as pressure to undermine her efforts to keep working ties with the Sandinistas and to preserve some of the gains of the revolution. I don't have enough information to have an accurate picture of what's going on, but things have certainly not improved for most Nicaraguans and our own country is still trying to enforce its own agenda.

The trouble is, it's not just Nicaragua. In El Salvador, Guatemala and Honduras, too, our government has been backing the ruling elites, while the people suffer. In Panama we backed Noriega for years before we finally decided he was a dictator and drug runner and had to be removed by an invasion. Our hands are not clean, either, in the Middle East nor in Africa. Start reading beyond the superficialities of the media and one begins to see that our foreign policy has had a shameful history of manipulating other countries for what our leaders see as our own self-interests. Not what I would see as our ultimate self-interest, like building a world of neighbors who can trust each other and work together for greater freedom and security for all people, but a world we ourselves control — that seems to be their vision.

It's a somewhat different moral problem from our nuclear stockpiling. At least when we're building our great overkill of weapons we must realize, at some level, that we're planning our own suicide at the same time that we're planning the deaths of millions of other people. There's a grim sort of justice about it. If we're caught in a nuclear explosion, intentional or accidental, or if we poison ourselves with the by-products, it is our own evil coming back to us.

On the other hand, when we engineer brutalities in weaker countries outside our own boundaries, are we thinking to get away free and innocent? We sit comfortably behind the walls of fortress U.S.A. and send money and arms and specialized training to stifle attempts by downtrodden people to change their conditions, without even dirtying our own hands. It seems altogether vile and cowardly. I find myself thinking of a quotation from somewhere which says "God is not mocked." I wonder if our drugs and crime and violence and general ugly confusions are not related in some intimate way with our willingness to bring death and terror onto poor people whose faces we do not want to see.

THE METANOIA COMMUNITY

In 1985 and 1986, while I was making my two brief excursions into protest actions at Kings Bay, the network of peace people in the Southeast continued to work at developing a more solid expression of our vision for an alternative style of meeting the problems our society faces now. Right after the 1985 Feast of the Holy Innocents, the core group met for evaluation and focused on the need for a permanent peace presence in St. Marys. They knew we did not want to act just as "outsiders" who descended on the town once a year to cause trouble and then disappeared again. We had to show the same commitment to peacemaking as the Navy showed to war making if we hoped to be taken seriously by the local folks. Martina and John X. Linnehan, who were at the time members of the Immanuel House community in St. Petersburg, Florida, but who had previously been successful in real estate, volunteered to scout around for a possible site for a permanent faith and resistance community to locate in St. Marys. They did, in fact, find a parcel of land on the railroad spur that leads into the Kings Bay Naval Submarine Base, and began the process of buying it.

Location on the tracks was important so that the new community could be a link in the continental network of train watchers who monitor shipments of missile propellants and nuclear warheads across the country. Starting from the Pantex Plant in Amarillo, Texas, which is the final assembly plant for all U.S. nuclear weapons, peace activists across the country have been alerting each other — and hopefully their own communities — about the movements of trains carrying the deadly cargo to deployment sites around the country. They have been doing this for years. Now that the Navy was building up the Kings Bay Naval Submarine Base for a whole fleet of Trident submarines, the Department of Energy and the Department of Defense would be focusing on shipments into Kings Bay.

By the time in 1986 when I came back for my second Feast of the Holy Innocents and my own adventure with trespass, the purchase of land was almost complete. Martina and John X. were purposely keeping a low profile at the protest so that there should be no obstacle in the way of their becoming landholders in St. Marys.

Besides the long-term plans for permanent residence, another plan for closer identification with the St. Marys community was introduced that year into our activities. Herb Walters of the Rural Southern Voice for Peace (in North Carolina) organized a "Listening Project." Peace people went out into the community, just knocking on doors and talking with residents about how they felt about the submarine base in their town and the transport, storage and deployment of nuclear weapons on the huge Trident submarines which would be home-ported at Kings Bay. It was not an effort to persuade anyone of our own fears and opposition, but really to listen to the variety of voices and attitudes there. Herb had developed a good list of basic questions, and they were tabulated later and reported back to the community.

The piece of land on the tracks was not that inspiring to look at. It was altogether wild, supporting nothing but a dense clump of Georgia slash pines and the Spanish bayonet plants which have such tough, sharp points that they are often recommended for planting under windows if one wants to repel burglars. Nevertheless, Martina and John X. agreed to take on the task of founding the new community. A steering committee for the Kings Bay Project was formed to help them. The original members were: John Benish, Glenmarians for Peace, Sautee, Georgia; Elizabeth Cheatham, Morganton, Georgia; Joe Cohen, Decatur, Georgia; Judy Cumbee, Vine and Fig Tree, Lanett, Alabama; Fr. Bob Cushing, Pax Christi, Warner Robins, Georgia; Shelley and Jim Douglass, Ground Zero Community, Bangor, Washington (site of the first Trident base); Tom Egan and Ed Perrin, Pax Christi, Tampa, Florida; Ron Foust, Koinonia Partners, Americus, Georgia; Patricia and John Frank, Pax Christi, St. Leo, Florida; Mark Reeve, Clergy and Laity Concerned, Decatur, Georgia; Rev. Max Rice, Jubilee Partners, Comer, Georgia; Rev. A.B. Short, Community of Hospitality, Decatur, Georgia; and Herb Walters, Rural Southern Voice for Peace, Burnsville, North Carolina.

Besides the valuable contributions of varied background experiences and know-how, the committee provided a solid, accountable entity for contributions from individuals and from Koinonia Partners and from the Glenmary Society. Over 500 peace folks contributed money for construction and operation.

Koinonia Partners extended the new community a line of credit to purchase initial materials (they later graciously converted that to a grant) and the Glenmary Society made a substantial grant that made it possible to complete the construction.

It was Bob Geyer, working at that time as an accountant for Habitat for Humanity at their headquarters in Americus, Georgia, who offered to draw up plans. He did this over his kitchen table with John X. and Martina. Bob did architectural work as a hobby, and he and his family used their vacation time that summer to supervise and work on the "peace house", as it was called at that time.

Construction on the house began in July of 1987, with completely volunteer help. Special mention must be made of Tom Gagnon of Cobbtown, Georgia, an accomplished handyman who came and lived with the Linnehans for four months. Tom supervised the work crews who came on weekends, and then did substantial work on the house during the week. On a few occasions, he had to redo the well-meaning but less than professional work of the volunteers. It was the likes of Bob, Tom and many others from the southeast peace movement who made the dream become a reality. It wasn't quite as efficient or well-funded as the Navy's construction on the base, but the commitment was equal, or we like to think, deeper.

On August 9, 1987, close to a hundred peace people from around the Southeast came for an old-fashioned wall raising. On that day the Community was officially named "Metanoia", the Greek word used by John the Baptist (Mt. 3:2) and by Jesus (Mt. 4:17) which is usually translated "repent" but which also means "change of heart," "turn around and go in a new direction" or "live in a new way." It seemed to the group that the word expressed the transformations that must happen if the human family is going to survive Trident and the nuclear age.

By the 1987 Feast of the Holy Innocents, the house was 97 percent finished. In fact, over 100 people (including me) were served supper from the new kitchen on that occasion. Today, as the Linnehans live at the comfortable and practical community house with its large main room, functional kitchen, six bedrooms — all without air conditioning but with fans, three porches, high ceilings and solar panels — the only explanation they have for its accomplishment is to call it "the Miracle House by the tracks." "It happened because it was supposed to happen!" they maintain.

Martina and John X. have entered into the life of St. Marys, getting acquainted with neighbors, joining the small Catholic church, going to City Council meetings, all without disguising in any way their peace purposes, but without forcing their views on people. I especially enjoyed the photos and story of a Fourth of July float they entered in the city parade. They were told they'd have to take the very last place, but they concocted a most jolly-looking Peace Conversion Machine into which they fed toy weapons and warships while taking out schools and hospitals from the other end. They said they did get a bit of applause from some of the spectators. They (and a few other peace activists who've joined the core community for shorter or longer periods of time) have brought us consciously into a broader area of peacemaking which goes far beyond protests. It has given us the incentive to work at building up communities which work at peacemaking day by day, small encounter by small encounter.

My own participation in the peace movement has been of an opportunistic, fly-by-night type. If I receive news of an action near at hand that fits into my family's plans and my level of energy, I am delighted to seize the opportunity to join in, and have done so with some intensity. But I know very well that the real work of the peace movement is elsewhere. I just contribute small tidbits as I can. That I should be reporting here, in considerable detail, these minor actions in which I myself took part, may well seem badly out of proportion, as though I were not aware of the broad, multiform mass of vital activities which make up the life of peace groups across our whole country.

There may be, however, some benefit in my leading the reader into my own personal experiences. Our popular media have so sadly undervalued the peace movement, making it seem to be a marginal, shallow-rooted phenomenon, that there are many misconceptions about it. In this troubled time, when more and more people are beginning to realize how badly we need an alternative vision to our self-serving power struggles, it's a shame that we should be distracted from taking seriously the work of committed peacemakers. I hope that by reporting my own experiences within the framework of the peace movement,

I may give the reader some feel for how a peace action moves along on the inside.

Some time in 1988 word began to circulate that the first nuclear Trident II submarine, the U.S.S. *Tennessee*, would arrive at the Kings Bay Naval Submarine Base some time around the end of the year to be outfitted with its lethal weapons. The Metanoia Community, of course, had to develop plans to meet it. I was lucky enough to be able to sit in on some of the early discussions. Again I was impressed by the creative good sense and commitment of the Metanoia people. There was to be no attempt at any kind of sabotage. They would check ideas with environmental experts. They wanted to be sure that all people who took part in an action would be told ahead of time what would be done, and why.

With the energy those meetings gave me I was thinking of trying to carry along with them, finding some way to get back and forth to St. Marys and seeing how I could join in on whatever they decided to do. Unfortunately, I had a long session with some kind of cold-like sickness, and found myself in the aftermath painfully crippled with "miseries" in my back and shoulders and arms. I finally consulted my doctor who tried out various painkillers but had no real cure. I found out that most my contemporaries had been fighting the same kinds of problems for years, almost taking them for granted. "Welcome to the club!" One factor, though, which did seem real was that stressful living tended to tie up muscles, which could cause the kinds of symptoms I was having. It seemed I'd better give up trying to keep pace with these energetic peace people and just follow the action from a distance, through their good newsletters.

It wasn't until January 1989 that the U.S.S. *Tennessee* finally pushed its way up Cumberland Sound and into the St. Marys River and docked in Kings Bay. If I'd had to depend on the *Valdosta Daily Times* for information I would hardly have known anything was going on, in spite of the large number of dignitaries who'd been invited for the occasion. The *Florida Times-Union*, though, gave it front page coverage, with long-range views of the huge submarine and a close-up view of Anne Hall of Seattle, Washington being arrested, rather forcibly, by two police officers. The story of the protests, with eight arrests at the Base gate, was carried front-page, with a photo of the protesters on the beach at Fort Clinch State Park, pictures of the crew members on the deck of the *Tennessee*, Navy dignitaries and Senator Sam Nunn on page six. It was good coverage, with much technical information and enough details of the protests and arrests to give me an idea of what had been going on.

The group at the Peace Camp on the Fort Clinch side of Cumberland Sound had conducted their funeral and mourning services without any complications, but at the entrance to the base, the Navy had apparently sent a helicopter over the protesters, circling them seventeen times and altogether drowning out their speeches and songs. At first they simply sat down in the roadway, but in some kind of transition there was a reported attempt to climb over the base fence, and a chaotic melee ensued with Georgia State troopers. I probably wouldn't have known more about it if I'd been there.

At any rate, eight of the peace folks were in the Camden County jail, and the *Tennessee* was docked in Kings Bay. Of course, no one had been really thinking we were going to stop the progress of the *Tennessee*, but a lot of work had gone into trying to make the protest peaceful and a chance for some kind of dialogue. At least we had been there as a counterbalance to the congratulations and celebrations of U.S. military might.

There were two large-scale events planned for later in 1989: Pax Christi USA decided to have a National Action on May 5 and 6 at Kings Bay and the Fellowship of Reconciliation planned a Conference and then Action in October. It was Pax Christi that drew my close attention. I'd been a member for years and we had a small Pax Christi group at St. John's Catholic Church in Valdosta. We usually did something on May 3, which is the anniversary of the U.S. Catholic Bishops' *Challenge of Peace* (the same document that had inspired me into peace action), but this time it was going to be a major national action, right at Kings Bay, and the plans included an action of peaceful divine obedience. Peace people from all over the nation would be coming. It seemed important that we Georgia peace activists should be represented as strongly as possible. Our own Bishop Raymond Lessard had agreed to preside at the Mass which was to be the main event outside the gates of Kings Bay. It was an event I certainly wanted to enter into.

I got out my ban and bar letter from the 1986 trespass, thought over the $500 fine and six months in jail maximum it ordered, and decided I could handle that all right if need be. As I've said, I feel useful and needed in my family, but I'm certainly not essential. Retired folks are often really in a good position for risking arrest. Besides I knew that the whole thing would be carefully planned and conducted in a worshipful way. When other people are willing to do the hard work of organizing a meaningful action, I'm delighted to be able to participate. I arranged to be picked up by Lora and Bill Shane of Warner Robins, Georgia and was promised a return ride with Anne Richter and Sheila O'Brien of Tallahassee, Florida. All systems go!

It was a great gathering. Folks from California to Maine, with plenty of points in between, were sharing experiences and ideas. When announcements were made about people willing to risk arrest, the leaders explained that there were two different actions planned: one which would violate local and county ordinances about blocking the road in front of the base; the other which would violate federal ordinances about trespass on the base itself. Well, my disagreement wasn't with the locals, but with our federal government, so I went with the smaller group considering federal disobedience. There certainly wasn't the pleasant leisure we'd had in 1986 to get acquainted and work through differences or doubts, but then I had already worked through the basic questions, and most the others seemed to have had more experience with protests than I had.

Our federal group was to go first for simple trespass over a yellow tape at the base entrance, and then the other folks would move into their action of blocking the road. It had already been pretty well worked out with the local authorities that that group would be picked up and cited, but then released. We federal trespassers would probably not be detained long this same day, but would have to return to Brunswick (about a forty-minute drive from St. Marys) for a hearing and whatever at a later time. No one seemed troubled by this, although many of them would have to be coming quite a distance from Michigan or Washington, D.C. or New Orleans. There were just three of us from Georgia, and the other two were both farther away than me. At any rate we organized ourselves into smaller groups for the trespass. I was incorporated into the Pax Christi Michigan group along with Carol Carson from Memphis, Tennessee (the two of us would walk together). There was a group of quite young folks from a Catholic Worker house in Washington, D.C., and then a contingent from New Orleans, most of whom worked with a social service agency sponsored by the Catholic church.

After the Mass, which included an inspiring homily by Bishop Gumbleton, we all walked up the sidewalk toward the base entrance, two by two, stepped over the yellow line and were arrested. They had us sit in a large bus while they took us in in groups for processing. All calm, orderly and respectful. As we'd expected they didn't detain us long, but we were ordered to come for a hearing in Brunswick June 12.

While we sat in our bus, the group who had planned to block the roadway moved out across the road with signs and banners and knelt for prayer. When they refused to move after being officially ordered to do so, they were arrested, put on school buses and driven to a nearby middle school where they were given citations for obstructing traffic, and then released. There were 48 people involved in that action, and 20 of us. The total 68 protesters made that the largest protest to date at Kings Bay. The *Florida Times-Union* carried a detailed news story the next day, so I was able to fill in what I had missed while we were sequestered in the bus. The action itself had not been for me nearly so interesting or dramatic as my first venture. This time the learning and the formation of community would come after the action rather than before.

For me a major reward of taking part in the peace movement has been all the lovely people I have met and shared a bit of life with. On my trip back to Metanoia and then on to the hearing at Brunswick, Jody Miller-Shearer gave me a ride from a pick-up point near Valdosta but not out of his way. It was a most pleasant interlude. He and his wife had been serving as volunteers with a social service program of the Mennonite Church. They lived in a small community group in New Orleans with other minimally-paid Mennonites, and coordinated their efforts closely with a Catholic organization working on the same community problems. I prodded him with questions to find out more about this whole area of volunteer service from a church base, and felt quite rewarded by inspiring but down-to-earth information. Jody told me the kinds of constraints on his time that he was facing, and knew he would have to plead "no contest" and pay whatever fine was levied.

When we got to Metanoia House and the warm welcome there, we found that 15 of us from the original 20 trespassers had made it. It was a great time for sharing experiences with each other about the courts and our various dilemmas. Helen Casey, an active member of Pax Christi Michigan, was only a bit younger than me, white-haired and vigorous. She had taken part in many protests in her area of the country. She usually pleaded "not guilty" and rode out the court actions, but this time she felt she needed to get home again. Her husband had been ill, and traveling back to Georgia for subsequent court appearances would be too much. She said she felt a bit guilty about doing it, but she was planning to plead "no contest." Jody and the other people from New Orleans had work to do there which they wanted to get back to. Likewise Matt Goodheart and Heather Quain were involved in community service work in Michigan and needed to get back. Heather was the youngest and least experienced of our group. She had not yet reached twenty years, a quiet and seemingly self-effacing girl. It must have been a very courageous decision for her to join the protest group.

Chuck Walker from Georgia was also on his first experience of civil disobedience. He said at first that he thought he'd just plead "guilty" and let it go at that, but we all encouraged him to make it "no contest." The effect is the same but you don't have to admit you were doing anything wrong. It's better for the other people with you. When he'd come to the Kings Bay Action he'd been living and working at the Koinonia Christian community in Americus, Georgia, but was now at Jubilee Partners in Comer, another Christian community closely allied to Koinonia which works at helping Central American and other refugees.

Jonathan Kirkendull and Sue Frankel, who were members of a Catholic Worker community in Washington D.C. and Jack Marth from New York were set to plead "no contest", except that they had no idea where they were going to get money if they were fined, because they'd been living in voluntary poverty. Carol Carson, my partner at the trespass, was really struggling over her decision. She had a tough situation at home because her husband was definitely against her action, and their teenage kids were caught in the middle. Besides she was trying to keep two part-time jobs that she liked but which had rather unusual schedules. She really wanted to push the protest further, but finally decided (after sleeping on it overnight) to go with "no contest" so she could get back home.

Sanderson Beck, probably in his late thirties but looking younger, was a relative newcomer to Georgia, having spent most of his life in California. He had been actively involved in the protests on the train tracks out of the Concord Naval Weapons Station which shipped armaments to the contras in Nicaragua. This was the same location where Brian Willson had been run over by a train and lost his legs. Since that time peace people had kept up a constant vigil, stopping trains at least temporarily as they came out of the Station.

Sanderson told us he'd been arrested forty-four times in the last several years but was usually just released. He had once managed to get a trial by jury, which had acquitted him. He had also taken peace treks across the country, visiting peace communities as he went, and had published several books on nonviolence and other peace ideas. He was planning to plead "not guilty" and ask for a trial before the district judge. He would have liked to have a jury trial, but since our charges were only misdemeanors rather than felonies, we didn't have the right to one.

I was closer to the Brunswick area for court appearances than anyone else and my grandmotherly duties at home were not that urgent. Besides I didn't like the idea of just appearing and paying a chunk of money to the government. I decided to plead "not guilty" too, and ask to be tried by the judge. I figured the worst I could do would be to make a fool of myself at the trial. It was reassuring to have Sanderson there, so that I'd know when to say what at the hearing.

Martina and John Linnehan had been very careful to keep the focus on us and our decision making, but they had, of course, a great reservoir of experience right in our same area. Martina had completed a 45-day stay in the Camden County jail after her arrest in January at the melee during the arrival of the U.S.S. *Tennessee.*

She told us about their rules: almost no personal belongings permitted and a generally chilly temperature, for which Metanoia had a long-sleeved, white sweatshirt available on loan for anyone who might be going to jail next. I heard piecemeal, not from Martina herself, about how successful she'd been at developing good contacts at the jail, helping organize their library and working out a plan to involve the local school board in providing GED classes at the jail. She was currently working on the school board end of that deal.

Besides the Linnehans we had the added presence of Karol Schulkin from Ground Zero, a sister community in Bangor, Washington, at the west coast home of the Trident submarines. Karol had been sent to Metanoia with her home community's blessing to act as a safety back-up person in case a set of arrests on Good Friday should decimate the Metanoia core group. They had planned what they thought was a perfectly safe Good Friday service in an area where several earlier services had been held without incident.

John X. had informed local authorities of their plans and received no objections. However, when they were well into their simple ceremony, the nine people assembled were accosted by an officer from the base with a bullhorn telling them they were in violation of the law and to vacate the area within five minutes. They were arrested as they were heading for their cars.

Security guards actually ran after some of them for arrests. It was primarily the core group of Metanoia who were at the service: John X. and Martina Linnehan, Donna Harden, Janet Horman, Robert Randall, Sherrie Alderman and Bill and Lillian Corrigan from Atlanta. Their trial was scheduled for June 19, just one week after our hearing. If things went badly at the trial and many of them were jailed, it would be very hard indeed to continue work at Metanoia House. So the Ground Zero community had "lent" Karol to us. Not only was she an inspiring, warm, competent person, but she had experiences from Ground Zero's brushes with the law, which were considerably more extensive than Metanoia's.

At any rate, on the morning of June 12 we all filed into a courtroom at the Camden County courthouse for our hearing. We were told that we would each come up individually to answer questions and register our pleas before Magistrate Graham who was presiding. I hope it was only chance which determined that Heather was to be the first one. We gave her what supportive gestures and signs we could before she left the safety of our pews. She walked up quite calm and self-possessed to go through the process. She answered the questions about name, age and so on quietly but firmly. It turned out that she was still living with her parents because of a physical disability which keeps her from being able to work at a regular job. She was giving serious amounts of volunteer time to a service agency which worked with the poor. When the magistrate asked her how she pleaded to the charge of unlawful trespass, she said "no contest" and he then sentenced her to a $200 fine, one year's probation and 50 hours of community service. She said something about how she had no money, but he apparently paid no attention to her and called up the next person.

That scenario was repeated with each of the other 12 people who pleaded "no contest". Several of them raised objections about the fine, citing their work as volunteers, with no more than minimal stipends. No arguments changed his sentences.

When Sanderson Beck and I came to the point of registering our "not guilty" pleas he sent us back to our seats to deal with later. We were then directed to the Probation Department to fill out the necessary forms and information. While we were there it became apparent that the question of the fines was not finished. Jack Marth, Sue Frankel, Janet LeBoeuf and Chuck Walker felt so strongly about it that they refused to sign an agreement that they would pay the fine, and Heather was still deeply troubled about it. Word of the problem was apparently passed on to the magistrate and he told those objecting to the fines to come back for further hearings in the afternoon, before he dealt with Sanderson and me.

He started the session by telling us that we had put him in a very difficult situation. We were obviously people of good intent, but we had been breaking the law, and he had to follow the law in sentencing us. He asked if everyone realized that refusal to pay the fine could mean no probation at all and up to six months in jail. He asked for further explanations of refusals.

Janet LeBoeuf, a thoroughly respectable-looking and attractive woman in young middle age, talked about how her religious faith taught her that she needed to use all her resources, including money, for good things, not evil. Paying money into the military machine of our government was completely against her religious principles. Jack Marth said he wouldn't mind giving money to some useful community purpose, but he had been working with poor people and seeing their needs and he refused to put his money into our government and its military spending.

At this point some of the Probation officers contributed the idea that fines went into a local service fund, not into the general U.S. Treasury. No one, however, had any solid information about just where it did go. We seemed to have come to an impasse.

Magistrate Graham called Heather up in front of him again and reviewed her case more fully. Finally he forgave her fine and reduced her hours of community service to 30. I think it was Jonathan Kirkendull who had pleaded a recent series of medical problems and expenses, to whom he granted an extension of time in which to pay the fine and complete the community service. There seemed to be nothing further forthcoming in any easing of the sentences.

Then Janet LeBoeuf asked for permission to speak, and asked if they could possibly serve some time in jail instead of paying the fines. Magistrate Graham agreed to this, and gave them each five days in jail and increased the hours of community service to 100. The four who had adamantly refused to pay fines went off, in the custody of marshals, to the Glynn County jail in Brunswick. I felt they were glad to exchange their time in jail for the necessity of paying $200.

For Sanderson and me it was just a matter of establishing that we wanted to be tried by the federal judge rather than the magistrate and being given the chance to ask for a court-appointed attorney. Sanderson said he didn't want one, and I knew that my assets were too great for me to be eligible. We all went back to Metanoia House to prepare for returning home.

We had all taken part in a serious adventure. The original trespass had been made with varying amounts of soul searching. Our discussions at Metanoia had been lively and revealing of each one of us. We had been required to stand up before a magistrate and state ourselves. And we had all come through with dignity and self-respect. The farewell hugs we exchanged were warm and earnest, and our good wishes to each other were most sincere. As I said before, a major bonus of taking part in the peace movement is the comradeship of admirable people.

Almost everyone needed to go to the airport in Jacksonville for a flight home. Matt Goodheart, though, was driving back to Michigan, taking Heather along with him. Because he wasn't pressured for time he offered to give me and Sanderson a ride home, going out of his way to bring me back all the way to Lake Park. We stopped for lunch at our Tatch family home, giving Meredith a chance to meet everyone.

I had picked up a good packet of information about court procedures and what types of defense are usual, and the data about an intriguing book which Helen Casey had brought with her: *Defending Civil Resistance Under International Law*. It was a special edition for pro-se protesters and was obviously filled with useful things at a lay person's level. I had devoured as much of it as I could at Metanoia, and ordered my own copy as soon as I got home. Sanderson promised to bring me the tape of his trial at which he had been acquitted. We were both intent on getting back for the trial of the Good Friday Eight which would be taking place in a week's time before Judge Anthony Alaimo, the same judge who would be presiding at our own trial. This would be the first time that peace protesters had come before Judge Alaimo. Other actions had been at the state level, in state courts rather than federal.

By the time of the Good Friday trial, I had read enough about courtroom procedures to be able to follow it fairly well. Several of the Good Friday Eight had retained Attorney David Buffington of Brunswick to represent them, and Attorney Bill Sheppard with his assistant Matt Farmer (also an attorney but new at it) of Jacksonville were acting on behalf of Donna Harden. The others represented themselves.

The trial turned out to hinge on legal technicalities: just how clear and distinct the boundaries of the base had been, and whether the defendants had used reasonable haste in leaving. The District Attorney had obtained aerial views which were supposed to show the area in question and the boundaries of the base. They apparently didn't. Judge Alaimo studied them, asked questions and then complained that they really didn't show much of anything. The base commander was put on the stand and tried to explain how the boundaries were marked.

It turned out, under questioning by Bill Sheppard, that the system of marking boundaries had been changed since the arrests were made, and in fact that new regulations were now in effect. Sheppard verified with the commander the fact that another group, the United Methodists, had used the same area for a religious service earlier in the year without any concern on the part of base Security. During the course of cross-examination a picture emerged (at least for me) of the base commander having seen the core group of Metanoia all together right next to the base and having taken action rather suddenly without much of any consultation with the regular security group.

At the conclusion of the prosecution's presentation, John Linnehan, acting on his own behalf, asked for dismissal of the charges. Judge Alaimo called for a ten-minute recess. When he returned he said that he did not at all subscribe to the defendants' behavior, and that they should have been able to leave in the five minutes allowed them. However, the government's evidence as to where base property began was really unclear. He announced a directed verdict of acquittal. There was certainly general rejoicing among us peace people. I had liked what I saw of Judge Alaimo. He seemed ready to take a direct hand in the questioning, in pursuit of the facts rather than any concern with his own dignity or technical proprieties.

In our group of celebrants outside the courthouse, I was able to talk with Bill Sheppard briefly, and when I told him my situation he invited me to come talk with him in Jacksonville before my trial. Later at Metanoia House I had a good chance to talk in a leisurely fashion with Matt Farmer, who had done most of the leg work in preparing the case. Sanderson lent me the tape of his successful trial, and all in all, I felt much better prepared to begin figuring out what I could do at my own trial.

I had received my copy of *Defending Civil Resistance*, read enough of it to realize what a dense jungle of jurisprudence I was attempting to enter, had composed a statement that I liked and laid out three parts of a "necessity" defense that seemed natural to me before I called Bill Sheppard's law office. Bill Sheppard himself was very busy and seemed likely to remain so, but Matt Farmer invited me to have lunch with him in Jacksonville. He said he was impressed by the work I had done, and especially liked my statement and the fact that I was very clear about my basic intent to attack the evils of the Trident rather than to get myself off the hook.

He warned me that the "necessity" defense (basically that one did a minor illegal act in order to prevent a much greater evil) had been used by the Operation Rescue people and hadn't been very successful. He suggested the First Amendment freedom of expression right as a possibility. I asked him about international law as a basis. He thought that was something that would be really developed in the future, but that most judges now would simply rule it as irrelevant. All in all, he was inclined to think I might be better off acting on my own, without an attorney, because judges tended to be more lenient with an unskilled lay person.

I asked him if there was any way to know just when the trial would be. At the hearing we'd been told that it would be not less than thirty days nor more than three months before the trial. He suggested I could call the District Attorney and ask. That would be within normal procedures.

Even on the ride home from Jacksonville on the bus, I had pretty much decided I wanted to try for the justification by international law. It might be a long shot, but that was the ultimate direction that really made sense to me. I knew I couldn't handle that by myself. I really would need a lawyer, and Matt had told me that their office was too busy with other cases and wouldn't be able to handle mine. I called the New York office of the Lawyers' Committee on Nuclear Policy, who were the publishers of my good book, *Defending Civil Resistance*. David Birman, the director at the time, was very helpful and agreed to send me names of their lawyer members who worked in my area. He did, in fact, send me five possibilities within two days. Unfortunately I had followed Matt's suggestion about finding out about a trial date. Of course it might have been coincidence, but about three days after I asked about it, I got a notice that my and Sanderson's trial was scheduled for July 11, just six days away, with a weekend in the middle. What a scramble that was! I called Matt Farmer and found that he was out of town for an indefinite period. I called David Birman who urged me to ask for a "continuance" which would give me additional time. All I had to do was to ask for it just as the trial got started. I found myself thinking of those folks who are suddenly called on to pilot a plane by themselves and have to rely on instructions from a stranger at the airport. Of course it wasn't really that bad. All I had to do was give up my dreams of glory and go back to the outline of my "necessity" defense and remember that the worst I could do would be to make a fool of myself.

Meredith and the kids drove me to Metanoia for the trial. What a pleasure that was! The good folks at Metanoia made us all welcome and enjoyed having the kids playing up and down their staircase. Meredith had a real chance to meet the people I'd been talking about.

The next morning John Linnehan took Sanderson and me to the courthouse early so we could view the videotape they had made of our trespass, and I entered my Exhibits No. 1, No. 2, No. 3 and No. 4 at the office of the Clerk of Court. We went on into the courtroom where Sanderson and I sat by ourselves at the big central table. Friends and supporters, my family and his wife sat behind us, with reporters and government witnesses.

District Attorney Miriam Banks had been helpful to all of us at our hearing, and she was helpful and friendly again at the trial. I had told her I wanted to ask for a continuance, and she made sure I had the appropriate space at the beginning of the proceedings to ask Judge Alaimo for a continuance. I had devised what I thought was a good approach. I told him I felt that my presentation of this case was important because I was speaking not just for myself but for all the millions of people threatened by the Trident who had no chance at all to speak about it. I said further that I had come to appreciate what a specialized discipline of precedents and tradition the law was and that I wanted to have time to find a lawyer.

He turned down my request rather briskly, saying that thirty days was certainly time enough to have found a lawyer (July 11 was really only 29 days rather than the required 30, but that didn't seem worth quibbling over). The prosecution began presenting its case. When they prepared to show the video, I asked if the kids could come up where they could see it, and Miriam Banks helped with arranging things. I felt the kids were adding a pleasant family atmosphere to the proceedings. They certainly didn't hurt my cause. I didn't see any point in denying that I had trespassed earlier and that I knew what I was doing both times. I made no attempt to cross-examine witnesses from the base. Sanderson, however, did ask a number of questions about whether anyone had permitted him to ask for a visitor's pass, and whether the sounds of the bullhorn and recordings had drowned out his chance to say what he wanted to say. When Sanderson tried to question the witnesses as to whether they knew they were working to make a submarine which could kill millions of people, Judge Alaimo cut him off, saying it was irrelevant and to go on to the next question. The Judge did, however, agree to let him make an "offer of proof" about the relevancy of international law. First, though, Attorney Banks asked me about my 1986 trespass and the letter of disbarment. I simply affirmed that I had indeed been on the base without permission and that I understood the penalties laid out in the ban and bar letter.

Sanderson's offer of proof covered the elements of the necessity defense, the terrible destructiveness of the Trident and the fact that international law forbids the use of nuclear weapons. He also described how hard he had tried in other ways to stop the criminal actions of our government. When Sanderson wanted to list the violations of international law, Judge Alaimo refused to let him and declared his offer of proof irrelevant. At that point Sanderson offered him a number of books: Robert Aldridge's *First Strike* and three of Sanderson's own books on peace and non-violence. He also made sure that the clerk of the court had recorded his objection to the judge's ruling.

I must say that Judge Alaimo treated Sanderson with full respect throughout the trial. He always addressed him as "Dr. Beck" without any trace of sarcasm. Sanderson does, in fact, have a Ph.D. degree in Philosophy from the World University in Ojai, California. At any rate, Sanderson began his official testimony in very much the same vein as his earlier comments. He covered the Nuremberg Principles and the complicity of our government as well as the workers on the base in the crime of preparing nuclear weapons of mass destruction. He said his purpose in being on the base was not at all illegal, but simply to inform the people there of the criminal nature of what they were doing so they could make their own choice. Judge Alaimo questioned him from time to time during his presentation, and then finally asked Attorney Banks if she wanted to cross-examine. Sanderson objected that he wasn't really finished with his defense, but the judge effectively cut him off. Attorney Banks asked Sanderson a number of questions including what other opportunities he had had to talk with personnel on the base, whether he had tried to get his message to Congress, and how long he had lived in Georgia.

Now it was time for my own defense. Judge Alaimo assured me that I didn't have to say anything at all unless I wanted to. I told him I had prepared a bare-bones defense and wanted to give it. First, in accordance with the procedures I had been reading about, I outlined what I was setting out to prove: that I had crossed the line at the base in an effort to stop a very real danger; that the danger was not only immense in terms of nuclear destruction, but that it was altogether imminent in terms of money being used up extravagantly when it was desperately needed for our social problems; as a final part of my defense I planned to show that my religious convictions had led me to this action.

I had made a crude chart showing the comparative power and destructiveness of the bomb that destroyed Hiroshima in relation to the Trident submarine with its Trident II missiles. I had almost completed my discussion of the numbers on this chart when Judge Alaimo said I didn't need to go further. He agreed that the Trident was the most destructive weapon yet devised by man. I rounded off my talk about the Trident and offered in further evidence a good report from the Center for Defense Information entitled, *Trident: A First Strike Weapon.* Judge Alaimo accepted it without question. I didn't have anything tangible with me to talk about how desperately our social services needed money for serious problems in our society while we were pouring money into the Trident. Again, the Judge said he would accept the idea that I felt too much money was being spent on defense and not enough on social problems. I was willing to settle for that.

When I began to talk about my religious beliefs, he said "I think you're testifying. Maybe you'd better come up into the witness stand here." Quite friendly and informal. I talked about my meeting with God in the Oregon mountains and how I had ever since tried to tune myself to that Being, and that this action of mine felt totally in tune. I went on to say that just by myself I wouldn't be so thoroughly sure, but I had joined the Catholic church some four years before, and their teachings also strengthened me in my decision to cross the line. My own bishop had presided at the Mass which preceded our going into the base. It turned out that Judge Alaimo was himself Catholic, and he expressed surprise that Bishop Lessard had presided at the Mass. "Did Bishop Lessard cross the line?" he asked, and of course I had to admit that he hadn't especially blessed the civil disobedience. I submitted two more exhibits: the sympathetic news story from our diocesan paper, *The Southern Cross*, showing several bishops with their robes conducting the solemn Mass, and the official text of the bishop's pastoral letter, with a bookmark in an appropriate place and yellow highlighting on the phrases about saying no to nuclear weapons. Judge Alaimo did use this occasion to ask questions which clarified that the platform erected outside the base, which the prosecution had spoken of as a platform from which people could express their views, was in fact the central location for a solemn Mass, with no idea of a public forum.

I felt I'd done the best I could and stopped. I don't remember Miriam Banks asking me any questions in cross-examination. After a ten-minute recess we came back for our final statements. Sanderson again went first and spoke extensively. After he'd been talking quite a while, Judge Alaimo interrupted to ask him how much longer he thought he needed. Sanderson said about ten more minutes, and the Judge accepted that, but he did watch the clock. When I stood up at the speaker's stand with my concise statement, I was glad it was concise, just for the contrast, and I began to read:

I walked onto the Kings Bay Naval Submarine Base May 6 to try to stop the death of our planet Earth.

Let me take just a minute to be personal and tell you how it is with me: I am coming toward the end of my life and have felt the need to think about my own death and to prepare myself for it. This has not been a sad or disagreeable process. I've been aware for a long time that I would be dying sooner or later, and I've been blessed with a feeling of being in the hands of a loving God. At present anyway, I think I'm accepting the idea of my own death quite gracefully.

But there is another death facing me which I do not at all want to accept, which I feel I must fight against.

That is the death of our whole society and of the Earth itself. I cannot avoid hearing of terrible things going on which seem to be leading to our destruction in one way or another. I am not speaking just of the nuclear weapons which we continue to stockpile, but of a whole climate of violence, hatred, greed and careless exploitation: drugs, the destruction of the rain forests, pollution of air, soil and water, the greenhouse effect, death squads and imperial oppressions, lies and manipulation by our public officials. There seems to be a whole convergence of disasters eating away at our human life on Earth.

Sometimes it seems that we have been trapped in a machine of great gears turning into each other by laws of their own, beyond any human control. And yet this is not really impersonal or inevitable. Every gear is composed of individual human beings who perform their tasks in obedience — conscious or unconscious — to the dictates of the great conglomerate which surges through them. Human beings have built these socio-economic organisms. They could not run without human consent. Surely it must be possible to gain conscious control of them and turn them toward life again.

Now let me come back to the Trident submarine at Kings Bay Naval Submarine Base here in Georgia. The Trident submarine is for me not just an evil in itself, but an embodiment of all that's wrong in our world. With this machine of massive destruction we are preparing to work the deaths of millions of human beings who share the same air and water with us, but who live in other nations whose leaders we consider to be our enemies. Just why are we preparing for this vile action? When I cut through the talk of preserving our freedoms and our "way of life," I have been forced more and more surely to the conviction that it is our possessions and the comforts of our living that we are really trying to protect. When we realize that we, who make up only 6% of the world's population, control almost half of its entire resources, we react with a paranoid obsession that we must protect our privileged position with all the firepower we can develop and deploy. Never mind that we have already enough warheads to incinerate all the Soviet Union. If there's danger that they are building more, we feel we must match them, level by level, type by type. Again we face that seemingly impervious machine with its gears of corporate profit and unreasoning fear.

There is no way to know whether human beings can in fact take control of the gears of destruction, but those of us who are awake must at least try. The international decisions made at Nuremberg about the war crimes committed by individual German citizens in the name of their Nazi state made it clear that the individual citizen remains responsible for the criminal actions of his or her government or public officials. The building of this fleet of Trident submarines appears to my best insights to be a criminal action. Therefore I must do what I can to stop it. When I stepped over the line at the Kings Bay submarine base, I was saying as loudly as I could "Stop this evil madness!".

We must not give up hope. All of us — each in his or her own role in life — must wake up, and turn our thoughts and actions from the path of death and destruction to the path of life and loving helpfulness.

I do believe it was impressive. I could hear the silence deepening around me as I spoke, and Meredith told me later that the reporter from the *Florida Times-Union* had tears in her eyes when I finished.

Judge Alaimo, though, did not even need a recess. He declared us guilty without any doubt. He said we were obviously people with good intentions, but we had broken the law and that could not be permitted.

He instructed Sanderson and me to go to the Probation office for a pre-sentencing investigation, and then that we would be getting a date for our sentencing in the mail. At that point, Sanderson created an interesting diversion. He told the Judge he wanted to be sentenced right then, that he had already given great quantities of information to the Probation Department, that he would not accept either probation or a fine, and that he would not promise to return to Brunswick for the sentencing. Judge Alaimo seemed startled, asked Sanderson several times if he really meant he was refusing to pledge his return for sentencing, and then had him escorted out of the courtroom by two marshals who were taking him to the Glynn County jail. His wife Karolyn left the courtroom to follow them over to the jail, and the rest of us moved out more gradually to gather for lunch at a pleasant park-like area near the courthouse.

Martina and Karol had put together an excellent picnic lunch and we stood around, or sat on blankets or found a good tree trunk to lean against (I always need a back rest and some help in getting up again). Everyone was feeling basically good about the trial. They all said Sanderson and I had done a wonderful job, and were pleased that the atmosphere had been human and respectful, and that we'd been able to talk about the real issues of the Trident, rather than just technicalities. (It has been a recurring pattern in many trials of peace activists across the country that the judge rules any consideration of moral reasons for their actions as irrelevant and so inadmissible.) Karolyn Beck came along fairly soon to join us, and reported on Sanderson's admission to the jail. She said he'd really wanted to just start serving his jail sentence instead of waiting around and then arguing the terms of his sentence. He figured at the time of the sentencing the judge would just make it "time served".

At any rate the food was good, the companionship was lovely, the grass and trees and sun were beautiful, Jasmine, Charles and Andrew were enjoying a good picnic and Meredith had a little more time for mutual enjoyment with these good people. All in all it was a good completion of a memorable morning. We went back for my interview with Probation, then said good-bye to the folks heading back to Metanoia and to Karolyn who was returning to the jail briefly and then on home to north Georgia, and Meredith and the kids and I drove off to our own home in Lake Park. Just how much and what the three grandkids received from that trip no one else will probably ever know, but I hope most of it was on the side of good things about life and people.

The next morning's copy of the *Florida Times-Union* had a good story about the trial, with a quote from my statement boxed in for special emphasis and attributed to "Miriam Hope, Peace Activist." The *Valdosta Daily Times* had absolutely no mention of anything about the trial. I had kept them informed, hoping that since I was a local citizen there might be some interest, but no.

While I was at Metanoia I had asked about appeals. Karol said that they'd had bad experiences with an appeal at the Ground Zero Community. The appeal had been denied and it had left a precedent which had been used against protesters several times since. It seemed best to let well enough alone and just wait for my sentence.

It wasn't until the end of summer that I got a notice that my sentencing was set for the sixth of September. That was my seventy-first birthday. The Metanoia folks keep track of these things, too, and I received in the mail a magnificent birthday greeting with individual messages of love and encouragement from a host of people at the Southern Life Community gathering. None of the slick Hallmark style either. About three feet by three feet with a hand-drawn birthday cake and candles and the messages all around. At one time and another I had added my little message to such a group letter. It was great to be the recipient. I have, of course, tucked it away with my mementos.

Sanderson had been all this time in jail. I got word, both from him and from Metanoia, that he had finally asked for and been given a court-appointed attorney, and that they were preparing an appeal of our case. I wrote to him that I thought we would be serving the peace community better to let well enough alone; that we had been only the first in what would be a succession of later protesters that fall. But it was, of course, his decision, and he continued with the appeal.

It turned out that I wasn't sentenced on my birthday. The sentencing was postponed to Sept. 15. Elaine Roberts, coordinator of the Tallahassee Peace coalition made a special trip to pick me up in Valdosta and go on to Metanoia. She said that she hadn't yet spent a night at the house since it was completed, and besides she wanted her school-age daughter to have a chance to see what was going on. An excellent arrangement for me!

Again the stay at Metanoia was pleasant and valuable. Martina helped me get things together that might be accepted at the jail, if I went there. I had brought along a case for my glasses and a small container to hold my teeth at night. In addition, following the white-only rules of the jail, I had brought a pair of white cotton socks. Martina brought out the long-sleeved white T-shirt (no pockets) which several other people had worn to try to stay warm in the jail. She suggested I put on a second pair of white cotton underpants so I would have a change. I put in my small unopened bottle of aspirin with the official prescription my doctor had written for me earlier at my request so that I could continue to hold my arthritis at bay. All this went into a paper bag with my name written clearly on it. If I did go off to jail at the end of the sentencing, Elaine would carry my purse and information back to Meredith. The Metanoia people would come to visit and keep contact. How bleak things would have looked if I'd been on my own!

That evening I got a call from New Orleans. Janet LeBoeuf wanted to give me her support and told me she'd been on a juice-only fast in prayerful preparation for my sentencing. She wanted to share, in whatever way she could, with my experience. In case I did end up in jail, as she had for her five days, she asked me to give her greetings to the women in the jail. She gave me the names of two of them especially who would probably still be there. As I said before, good people!

Judge Alaimo opened the sentencing in a very cordial manner. "Good afternoon, Ms. Hope," he said to me. So I said, "Good afternoon, Judge Alaimo".

I was not at all prepared for what came next. I didn't understand it then and I still don't understand it. He began talking about how he really wouldn't mind giving me another chance at a trial, this time with a lawyer. Not that he wanted to give me any more chances at a platform for my views, but anyway. I thought I ought to say something, so I said I did think I could have made a better defense if I'd had more time, that I really would have liked to bring up the matter of international law. He came back quickly and sharply on that one, that it would have been a waste of time. International law was irrelevant; it certainly didn't have anything to do with my stepping over a line. "That's right," I said, "but it has a great deal to do with the nature of the Trident submarine." He didn't respond to that. I don't remember what he did say after that, but it wasn't enough to jolt me into focusing with an open mind on a possibly new set of circumstances. Had he just been thinking about Sanderson's appeal and taken it for granted I was part of that, too, or was there something more? If he really was offering me a second trial, I plain muffed it. I would have liked to have had another go at the real issues of the Trident, with a good lawyer steering things. In that first trial we had been talking directly about the real issues, not just picayune technicalities, and it would have been good to do some more of that.

But I was tense and I was tired. The sentencing before mine had run a long time. I had even been afraid my sentencing was going to be put off until late afternoon. I was just holding myself together until I could begin reading my statement. I wish I'd had the presence of mind to have asked him to spell out what he really did mean and to follow that on out, wherever it led. Instead, I'm afraid I rather cut him short and urged him to proceed to the sentencing. If there was a special opportunity there, I missed it.

Well, it happened as it happened. Mostly I feel good about the way I lived through my bit of courtroom drama. So I read off my statement:

> Your honor, you have found me guilty of trespassing on a U.S. Navy installation. You may even have wondered how I could possibly consider myself not guilty. But I'm sure you know that the meaning of events depends on their total setting and on the angle from which one perceives them. I would like you to understand my actions. Will you please at this time join me briefly in looking at the events of May 6 from a broad angle of past history and our current worldwide human situation?

> You were probably only a youngster* at the time when we dropped the atomic bomb on Hiroshima and then later the second one on Nagasaki. But you were old enough to remember the wonder and awe and dread that enveloped the whole world as the details of that devastation came into our news media. We talked about the death of worlds, and this new weapon that was so terrible that surely no one would ever use it again.

---

*In truth, I discovered in 1990 from a news story in the *Florida Times-Union* that Judge Alaimo had served on a bomber in World War II, had been shot down, and held in a German prisoner of war camp for almost two years. At the time of my sentencing he was good enough not to interrupt me for corrections.

But 44 years have passed, and what was once un-thinkable has become commonplace, an integral part of our national policy. Our leaders now talk of "counter-force" and of "prevailing" in an extended nuclear war. It has become part of the educated person's vocabulary to understand kilotons and megatons, and to accept the idea that we must have a reliable source of tritium so that we can trigger our nuclear weapons. We call it "defense," but it isn't really defense. It is as though we had carefully devised a system to protect our house from burglars. But if a burglar comes, the only choice that system offers us is to blow up the entire neighborhood, our own house included. We have, indeed, fallen into a vast insanity.

I find it terribly hard to know these things and to watch the world around me going on with business as usual. Work and recreation continue without any apparent awareness of the actuality of nuclear danger. The surface calm of our so-called "good life" is not broken. Each evening we watch the news on TV and allow Dan Rather or Tom Brokaw to lull us into the feeling that everything is really all right. The experts and officials talk and talk about the complications of our various dilemmas, and we let ourselves believe that what they are saying does in fact make honest sense, that surely they know what they are doing.

When I heard about plans for a national gathering of Pax Christi at Kings Bay, I knew that I should be there to join with others in worshiping God and praying near this base where the Trident submarine is being prepared for its heavy-laden trips out into and under the oceans.

Now the Catholic Mass is, for those of us who participate in it, a soul-stirring and vital experience, but it doesn't really do much toward breaking the surface of our worldly business as usual. In his homily at that Mass, Bishop Gumbleton talked about the failure of the Church during the holocaust to say some kind of "No!" to the appalling evil of that time. He spoke of workers in a Nazi crematorium, throwing dead bodies into the furnaces, who could hear their village church bells calling them to the regular worship services. The Church failed to tell them that their work was in conflict with their sharing in the body and the blood of Jesus Christ. Bishop Gumbleton urged us, as members of the Church, to be a stronger voice of protest against the appalling evils of our own time.

Granted that setting aside a simple barricade and walking over a yellow tape is far from being an ideal protest against the evils of the Trident submarine, it is at least something, a small disruption to business as usual. I hope, your honor, that you may understand better now just why the public Mass and worship service by themselves did not satisfy for me the need to register my protests as effectively as I could.

I do believe strongly in the value of as much understanding as possible between opponents. And I want you to know it's not a one-way street with me. I try to listen to what other people say and to lend myself to differing viewpoints. One objection I've read and heard cut strongly into my assumptions, so that I've had to think about it seriously and work through it for myself. I'd like to share that with you, too.

Some opponents of our protest against the Trident submarines say that we are attacking the very thing that protects our rights of free protest. As I said, I've thought about that, and I don't think it's true. What really protects our freedom to protest is the Constitution of the United States and the integrity of the courts (thank you). The real dangers to freedom do not come from the Soviet Union or from any outside force. They come from within our own country — from the decay and increasing lifelessness of our systems for elections, from a lack of accountability by public officials, from a submissive media controlled by monied power and used for massive manipulations. They come from the willing ignorance and apathy of our citizenry, too many of whom have given up even the effort to participate in decision making by our government. We are in greater danger of losing our freedoms through lack of use than through the arrival of foreign soldiers on our soil.

On the other hand, we certainly don't want foreign

soldiers on our soil, either, and I'm willing to accept the idea that we probably need some weapons for real defense, but a fleet of twenty Trident submarines is not the kind of weapon that we need. The only thing that Trident submarines protect is the power of our leaders to dictate to all the other countries of the world exactly how they shall behave for the perceived self-interest of the U.S., under threat of annihilation. That is not a power that protects my freedom — or anyone else's. What it does do is drag us all into complicity for a terrible crime against all humanity. On May 6, I knowingly committed the minor crime of trespass with the intent of turning my country away from the much greater crimes of international blackmail, or, if that fails, the total destruction of all human society.

If by my trespass on the base I have been able to interrupt even briefly the turning of those great gears of destruction which trap us all in blind acceptance of a wrongful national policy — if I have provided a little free space in which a few more people can open their eyes and see just what it is that we are really doing — then I am well content.

On the matter of sentencing, I want you to know that I cannot in good conscience pay a fine to our government. Part of my protest is against the excessive national resources that go into military preparations, so that there is no money left to try to treat the terrible wounds that afflict the human fabric of our country. I would, however, be perfectly glad to give equivalent amounts of money to efforts for social improvement. I have listed three organizations, with their addresses, to whom I would be especially pleased to give money. One of these is a residential drug rehabilitation program; one feeds people; and the third builds houses for people who need them. They are the kinds of efforts I wish our government was putting its energies into, the efforts which build true strength that really leads to peace.

Finally, I want to thank you, Judge Alaimo, for the way you conducted my trial. I feel it was open and pleasantly human. I understand and applaud your concern for the integrity of the law and your fear of lawlessness. Along that line, I have brought with me today two articles which explore the question of the lawlessness of the use, or even the threat to use, nuclear weapons. One is a statement of the Lawyers' Committee on Nuclear Policy. The other is a speech by Dr. Francis Boyle of the University of Illinois Law School. He delivered it to the annual meeting of the American Society of Criminology this past November. I am not suggesting that you should try to read them now, or that they should affect in any way the sentence you give me, but I do hope you will be willing to read them thoughtfully at your leisure.

As I mentioned each of the things I was presenting to him, I carried them up to the judge's bench and handed them to him. Then I went back to my place to wait for the statement by the prosecution. It was not Miriam Banks this time, but a young man from the Navy, Lt. McAbee. He gave me a pleasant surprise when he started his statement. He told the judge that this was the first time he'd been involved in a case like this and that he felt, after listening to me, that maybe the peace protesters did care as much about our country and its well-being as the Navy personnel, that perhaps we were all aiming at the same goals, but just taking different routes. He said it appeared that I had no recognition of how many evils and dangers there were in the world, for which our country needed its defenses. He offered in rebuttal to my charges of blackmail by our government that surely that couldn't be true because we were having so much difficulty getting foreign nations to do what we wanted them to. There were a couple points at which I almost spoke up, but decided this was not the time.

After Lt. McAbee finished, the judge made his final statement and ruling. He said he thought I was trying to expiate some kind of guilt by bringing down suffering on myself. (I didn't have a response to that because I didn't know whether he might have been partly right.) "The scenario is not complete without the sentence, is it?" he said to me. He imposed the maximum sentence of my 1986 ban and bar letter: six months in jail and a fine of $500. However, "the imposition of the sentence is suspended and the defendant is placed on probation for a term of three years. The defendant shall contribute 500 hours of voluntary community service to a civic or non-profit organization as approved by the probation officer." I asked him specifically about payment of the fine. He said he would leave that to the discretion of the probation officer. If I could work it out with him within 30 days, it would be acceptable to the court for me to pay the fine to a non-profit agency instead of to the government. I was free to go.

I phoned Meredith to let her know, briefly, what had gone on and that I'd be home that evening, and then we went out again for a picnic lunch at the park-like area. It was very pleasant again and we found some things to feel good about: Lt. McAbee's recognition of peace protesters as possibly lovers of our country, and the basic fact that I could now return the Metanoia sweatshirt without spending time in jail. The precedent of paying a fine to a charitable agency instead of to the government seemed like a good one for us generally. But there was no doubt that the sentence was a stiff one. It augured no good for Sanderson, still in jail, unsentenced. It had been obvious that Judge Alaimo did not want to send an old lady like me to jail, but Sanderson was neither old nor a lady, and besides his approach to authority was much less conciliatory than mine. There was a pall over our gathering.

In fact, Sanderson was brought in for his sentencing four days later. He was given time to deliver a long and emotional statement, but was then sentenced to the full maximum of six months in jail and a $500 fine. He was later transferred to a federal prison in California, and finally released in January of 1990.

Whatever divinity it is that shapes my ends, it seems always to have been kindly disposed towards me. My probation officer in Valdosta, Nicholas Carroll, turned out to be a relaxed, kindly man. He checked out the Wholeway House, a residential drug treatment center recently opened in our downtown area, and agreed with me that it would be a good place to put my $500.

Finally there was something the *Valdosta Daily Times* was interested in. They gave me a color picture on the front page, standing by the Wholeway House sign on the front lawn, with a story about my earlier action and my refusal to pay more money to the government. A number of people at St. John's Catholic Church saw it and were quite sympathetic (the folks who thought I was an idiot or subversive probably just didn't say anything). At Bethel C.M.E. Church, Mr. Boyd had made copies for everyone and we spent most of that session talking about nuclear weapons and militarism and defense and true peace. Mr. Boyd thought I had really gone too far in my protest and that I was lucky not to have had a heavier sentence, but he was glad to have me back again and that we could talk about it.

At least I had completed one important part of my sentence, and with some benefit. Nick Carroll set me up with a packet of monthly report forms and some work sheets for recording my community service hours. First, though, I had to ask his permission to go to Jacksonville, Florida for the gathering of the Fellowship of Reconciliation. They were having a convention first, focused on Ghandi and his vision, and then were planning to go to St. Marys and the Kings Bay Naval Submarine Base for a vigil and protest with acts of divine obedience. I had decided I didn't want to go back there quite so soon, partly to make sure I was really on solid footing with the Probation Department, so I assured Mr. Carroll I wouldn't be getting into any trouble and he sent me a fine official permission slip for the Jacksonville area, with dates.

The convention was a good, inspiring one, with a magnificent display of large photos of Ghandi's life and actions. Just as for the Pax Christi event, there were peace people from all over the nation. I saw Karol Schulkin again, with some more Ground Zero folks. I met several people I had known in California and we exchanged news. Chuck Walker was there from our own adventure. He said he had just completed his hours of community service. Martina and John Linnehan were there, of course, helping prepare people for the civil resistance action. I was expecting to see — and did — many of the From Trident to Life regulars: Peg McIntire, Robert Randall, Joe Cohen, John Benish. I'm sure there were others, but I have forgotten exactly who all I kept running into.

I was especially interested in the plans for civil resistance. I was called on to talk about my experiences with the trial and Judge Alaimo, and put in a plug for the Lawyers' Committee on

Nuclear Policy and the importance of international law for what we were doing. The stiff sentence I had been given might have scared off potential protesters, but there was in fact a sizable group of people (20 odd?) who gathered for closer consideration of how willing they were to risk arrest. I was not disappointed in finding again that this group of people had sturdy souls they were willing to bare to each other in figuring out how to be most effective in fighting the evil we perceived in the Trident system. I was especially interested in Jim Crabtree from Kansas City. He was not only a calm and apparently mature and experienced man but he was also a practicing attorney. How great it would be to have that expertise right within our ranks!

They were well into their discussion, but far from done, when the time came for me to catch my bus home. I watched the newspaper eagerly for news of the demonstration. Nine people had been arrested crossing the line onto the base. Among them were Jim Crabtree and also — surprisingly — Peg McIntire. Peg is about eight years older than me, but marvelously active. She was in that first group of activists whom I helped send off toward the Kings Bay gate the first year I went to the Feast of the Holy Innocents. She was one of the close support people for our own affinity group the next year. She had walked on down to Cape Canaveral with the Peace Marchers for demonstrations there and had spent two days in jail that time. I had spotted her on TV news stories several times since. She had certainly done her full share of being arrested, and would be at special risk because of her earlier arrest right there at Kings Bay.

I got over to Metanoia for their hearing, enjoying again the special hospitality and companionship of the place. I wanted especially to find out more about Jim Crabtree and to encourage him to ask for a trial before Judge Alaimo. Jim and his wife, Maril, were members of a small community group in Kansas City who had been experimenting with living a non-violent lifestyle. He had been asked and had served as the attorney to defend a few peace protesters in court. He said he hadn't wanted to jeopardize their interests by trying out any radical style of court behavior, but if he was defending just himself he would like to try out a non-confrontational, absolutely non-violent style of defense. It sounded fascinating, and I gave him all the information I could think of about my own experiences with the court and Judge Alaimo.

The hearing in the morning went along quite smoothly. Magistrate Graham allowed all who pleaded "no contest" to pay their fines ($250 this time) to a variety of charitable organizations. He also ordered them to serve 50 hours community service. Because of her previous arrests Peg McIntire had to pay a $300 fine and do 70 hours of community service. Sandra Sampson entered a "not guilty" plea, but waived her right to a judge and agreed to be tried by Magistrate Graham. Jim Crabtree, as he had planned, declined to enter a plea for himself, so the magistrate entered a "not guilty" plea for him, and since he did not waive his right to a trial by the judge, the magistrate told him he would be tried before Judge Alaimo. Paying a fine to a charitable organization instead of to the government seemed to be established as a sound precedent, and Jim Crabtree was on the way to what promised to be a most illuminating trial before Judge Alaimo. I felt very good about that hearing and was eagerly anticipating my return trip to watch Jim's trial.

It was not to be. On the day before I'd arranged for someone from Metanoia to pick me up at the Jacksonville bus station John Linnehan phoned that the charges against Jim Crabtree had been dropped and there would be no trial. No one knew anything about just why. Miriam Banks had reached Jim in Kansas City to tell him as he was almost heading out for his trip to the airport. He said he felt as Daniel would have if he'd been all geared up to meet the lions and then they hadn't showed up. Jim assured us that the government always has the right to dismiss charges without any need for explanations. He had no idea about it at all, and asked us if we ever heard anything about it to let him know. Jim had been talking to people at the courthouse and on the base in an unusually open way. Was there something about his unorthodox approach that scared them? Was it possible that Sanderson and I had somehow softened up Judge Alaimo so much that he thought he couldn't face another peace protester? That seems most unlikely. We will probably never know. It is, of course, something of a victory in itself to have charges dropped, but I wish that trial had taken place: Jim Crabtree might have broken new ground.

Before the missed trial I had got started on my 500 hours of community service. At first I did a bit of shopping around with several agencies, but it wasn't long before I found an ideal location and stayed with it. Mrs. Juanita Miller, the same woman who had founded Wholeway House where I donated my fine, was also the moving force in a grassroots effort of long standing in our community. Camp Relitso had been started about twelve years earlier when a core group of black parents had been able to buy from the school board the whole complex of a black school which had been abandoned when schools in Valdosta were integrated. Juanita assured me they could certainly use any volunteer hours I could give them, so I went out to talk to her and see their place. What struck my eye especially was a large room with a sign saying "Library" over the door and great numbers of shelves filled with books. When I looked more closely, though, it appeared that the organization of the books was only spotty. Juanita agreed that the only way to find books was, in fact, to browse around. There had been a couple of retired school librarians who had at first offered to take charge of the books which local schools and individuals had contributed, but the task had proved too large and confusing for them (there are certainly well over 5,000 books there). If I had had less than 500 hours to put in, I might have hesitated, too. As it was it seemed to be an almost ideal job for me. Camp Relitso was closer to home than downtown Valdosta where the other agencies are located, I could work along on my own with my own schedule of days and hours, and besides there turned out to be all kinds of amazing treasures to find among the scattered books. I consulted with our local library, mastered the basic essentials of the Dewey decimal system and plugged away at it. By the first summer, when the big old building came alive with kids, I had been able to get shelves labeled in a sensible way, and had a chart of the organization of the Camp Relitso Library. By going in myself three days a week for a couple of hours I maintained a bit of guidance for the teenage volunteers who actually ran the library. Gluing in pockets on books which didn't have them and typing up library cards to go in them turned out to be excellent tasks for the teenagers, too. I was proud of my community service, and I'll have to admit I wouldn't even have thought of doing it if I hadn't been ordered to.

* * *

People have sometimes asked me if my protest was really worth it. Would I do it again? Well, of course I would. It gave me a whole succession of interesting and instructive experiences and let me develop special companionships with people to whom I'm glad to feel related. But beyond that, and even if I'd been subjected to more hardships than I ran into, I'm very glad I seized the opportunity to express some of my deeply-held beliefs right out in the world of action. It's not really all that easy to find a time and a place where a word of truth can be uttered clearly and unequivocally. Most of the time our actions are cloudy and muddled, restricted by qualifications and the need to hedge on bets. I think that at Kings Bay the evils of our time and the hard work of many, many peace activists came together in such a way that I could step into a special niche to add my voice to a strong word of truth.

I don't think there's many of us peace activists who fool ourselves into thinking it's an easy task we've undertaken or that we can expect to turn our country around any time soon by what we're doing. And yet, when we talk with like-minded people, when we find that many plain people, the general public, have many of the same questions and fears that we do and listen to us with considerable sympathy, and when we read and hear competent, influential, intelligent people also recognizing the insanity of the arms race and our militarization, we do begin to hope that we are making some impact on the direction our country is taking. And then comes along Operation Desert Storm, and President George Bush proves able to whistle up 500,000 military personnel and the weapons of destruction that they operate out onto the Arabian desert, and we watch with the rest of the country the "smart" bombs hitting their targets all clean and neat, and General Norman Schwartzkopf not only immensely competent but also human and compassionate. What are we to think? Was there really some good value in our having all those weapons ready to go? Is this way of power and violence leading us to a better world?

Well no, gradually more of the reality of the thing comes out. We begin to see pictures of the Iraqi women and children burned in what they thought was a shelter. We see the tangled lines of cars and trucks strafed along the road from Kuwait as they tried to flee. We watch the thick smoke coming up from oil fires in Kuwait, we see Iraqi children suffering in their mothers' arms or in inadequate hospital beds. It was not a clean war. There is no such thing. Our original insights were accurate enough. It was just that we had let ourselves forget how immensely powerful the status quo is. It provided us on a massive scale with the same perspective of armed impregnability versus small human efforts which I had seen outside the gates of Kings Bay while thirteen of us circled around in the road singing songs.

So, should we decide that there's nothing we can do, and live our lives individually, leaving the big decisions to the people who've been chosen to lead us? No, we can't do that. There's no way we can give up on it, while we're alive.

I think it helps immeasurably to have some kind of trust in the Mystery of the universe, to have some way to keep contact with God. Things are always happening beyond our control, and they are not always bad. The forces of death are indeed powerful, but the forces of life keep springing up in fantastic and unimaginable new ways. The United Nations does appear to have been strengthened, the Berlin Wall is down, great masses of people in Eastern Europe have taken power into their own hands. George Bush has announced deep cuts in weaponry. We know that the final answers are not in. There is always the chance that we can influence, in some way, the direction things take.

I will have to admit that I'm not terribly optimistic myself about our human race's chances for survival. I remember telling John Linnehan once about my last-ditch thinking on the subject. There is the chance that by some set of miracles, by the grace of God, we may find our way to transformation and a whole new way of life. If there is such a way out, every effort we can make to find that way out is infinitely worth it. On the other hand, we may not be able to, and will end in some kind of maelstrom of destruction, fast-moving or slow.

But if there is not a way out, then at least it would be good if our human race could go out with some "style," some modicum of grace and dignity. In either case the demands on us and our little lives are the same. We are called on to live our lives the very best way we know how, with love, and courage and integrity.

TO MY COMPANIONS IN THE STRUGGLE

Before the floods come, give me once your hand.
We cannot stand here doing nothing;
We must make some statement, some attempt.

That which endures is the full-of-grace,
The complete, the pure — even though it be
No bigger than the tip of grass pushing upward.

The ant, moving across an endless stretch of patio,
Moves in harmony and meaning.
It does not matter if I step and kill its progress;
What there is has been in its own sphere true.
There is nothing which can destroy the reality
Of its having been.

Do not despair.
The agony of life tosses in its turmoil
Strange, glorious songs which sing themselves in beauty.
We cannot harness them.
We cannot tie them down to build a house.
They bless our working hands and then pass on,
Leaving the sound of joy within our hearts.

SECTION FIVE

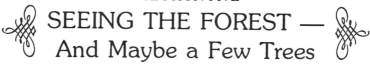 SEEING THE FOREST —
And Maybe a Few Trees

I

Void but not void, the living stillness — IS — without beginning and without end, the pulsing heartbeat that we feel around us: the blade of grass, millionfold but each one each, pushing up to light and life and dying once again; the ant, the microbe, the worm, the tiny spider floating through clear mountain air on hirs long string spun from hirs own body. Fertile, profligate, crowding into being, pushing, shoving, devouring, giving way, this yeasty stuff of life goes on and makes whole landscapes for the eye of Man to cherish — and for the eye of Man to never see, or to brush over blind without perception.

The eye to see, to hold, to draw within — consciousness, the response. We do not know. We do not know how much each other thing is conscious, too. We cannot tell of bird or dog, or even plant or worm or rock. We do not know, for sure, if fellow human being feels in hirs heart and mind the same response to all the things of life, the same response of "Yea! Here, and here and here they stand, forming stir within my being, taking part in what I am."

The I and Thou of Martin Buber says it well in one great document of meaning, and in our daily life we speak and reach across, and know another lives within hirs separate moving flesh, behind hirs separate eyes, and know, or guess, or leap to faith s/he feels much of the same things we do. Sometimes there seems to be even a whole consciousness of Man — or tribe, or group, or section of the earth — grown together in one past tradition and past effort moving through the present.

The viewer is part of the view, the seer of the scene, and I who sit upon a chair, typing by my front room window, must stop and look at weeds within my lawn, and think of daily needs and how we must keep moving, not just look around and feel, but find our way to life within this mass of moving entities, within this conscious-unconscious field of present mortal being.

We have lost our way and turn inward, troubled and diseased. Fever grows within our great piled prisons of the city, where concrete shuts out human beings from all the green and growth of plants and fields, where need feeds on itself and tears and devours what could give it strength in other places and in other times. We cling to each other for support, suffocating in the soft warmth of flesh held close, of hugs and protestations of affection. We fear each other on the streets, and watch askance at strangers moving in their own enclosure. There is no way to go, no movement toward a growth or future. We look around and see again and again the death built from our own designs, the wheels turning one into another in perfect answer to their own necessity, and what we thought were gears controlled by men, turn on in greater speed, beyond the reach of brakes in any one man's hands.

How do we live? How do we move as earth turns before the sun and day gives way to day? How do we get from morning waking to the dark bed at night? Many do not need to ask, and these are perhaps the blessed, who tend small children, growing, and put food on the table and make joyful pattern for the family; who spend their strength in work of mind or body to provide food, shelter and real needs which build a place of safety for a well-loved group. But beyond this, what? When fat excess makes sloth and whining discontent; when work is meaningless, or grates against the better parts of feeling that we call ourselves, putting on a smooth, inhuman armor so that customers will spend their money without a hitch, or clients move along and never break the surface of the regulated forms, what then? When daily, working life has not been fully joined, and the young look out and see no forward place that can be gained, and see no hope for building something worth their time, what then?

Shreds and patches, tatters.

We cannot think the things we do can save us from the tumbling chaos building on our past mistakes. There may be a way to turn the wheels, to stop the gears, and find within ourselves new growth, new strength, as small green grass blades move up through cracks in the concrete to stand triumphant where no green blade should be. But then again there may not be. And cheery, blind assurance that turns its eyes away from possibility of defeat and cannot dare to take the full measure of the dreadful things that face us, is not tough enough to answer to our need in this present time.

Honesty first and some real tie-in, solid foot on earth, to actuality. There is nothing gained, or won, or kept without these. But what is actual? What is real?

We do not live here by ourselves. Win, draw or lose, the stars stand in their spheres, the earth turns, and the great expanse of wilderness cries "Fraud!" to the idea that Man is the measure of all things. True, it seems we can destroy the earth, kill other life besides our own with poisons and stupidity, but have we changed those laws we found, are we now taking charge of the sprouting of the seeds in vacant lots, of the birth of baby whales in ocean depths? The laws stand. The laws stand, willy-nilly; and other forms of life surround us, give us air and food, and place to stand where we could get some restful pause and view of Man within a larger framework, where we could see Man as "the naked ape", the two-legged animal standing fearful with hirs machine-made lightning bolt uneasy in hirs hand, master and slave of hirs own ingenious tinkering — but not, praise God, of the whole universe.

II

Way back there in the Garden of Eden
Way back there when Man became Man —
Way back there in the Garden of Eden,
What was the name of that fruit?

"The fruit of the tree of the knowledge of good and evil."

Adam looked at this one and s/he said "This is good";
S/he looked at that and s/he said "It's bad".
"This is a weed, and that's a flower —
I'll plan this thing with my own rule of thumb.
I'll lay out rows and set up fences;
My own little plot will be just as I please.

The thistles are evil and the dandelions worthless.
What was God thinking of, anyway at all?"

The tiger, burning bright, s/he walked the jungle.
S/he walked the jungle and found what was hirs.
S/he knew what would feed and what didn't matter;
S/he slid through the jungle as the jungle was.

> *But Man!*
> > *Whump!*
> > *Hack!*
> *S/he cut it here;*
> *S/he slashed it there!*
> *S/he brought it up short*
> *With a rule and a square.*

S/he wanted it tidy; wanted it "balanced";
Wanted it fitted to hirs own little frame.
Couldn't stand naked, out in the open;
Couldn't stand naked, be as s/he was.
Had to get clothes on, be someone special,
Had to be different from just what s/he was.

Well actually, of course, s/he probably didn't have much choice. The tiger had those claws and teeth and the running, leaping power, and everyone else worked out some special style — or disappeared — and God wasn't really there yet to walk in the cool of the evening (was, but wasn't, I suspect — at least not that way) and Adam did what s/he found s/he could do some time when the fruit wasn't as handy as it had been, or some four-legged animal got in hirs way. Before s/he knew it s/he was well on the way to a different way of living, a different style that had people grouped together and figuring out rules of their own for their own piece of the earth. S/he probably didn't think much beyond one piece of meat or fruit at a time until s/he was already a long way down the road, and there s/he was — and here we are.

III

Intricate and vast is the reality of human life on this planet Earth. Within our American industrialized metropolitan areas and their well-groomed or frowzily discouraged suburbs, within small scattered farmhouses and shacks, within the busy, affluent towns of Switzerland and the gray, depressed areas of less fortunate Europe, within small villages of Africa and Mexico, within the refugee camps of Cambodia and Lebanon, in prisons and in hospitals, we human beings wake to the sun — or to an alarm clock call — and come to consciousness again and live another day, each from the center of hirs own awareness. The demographic tables and charts, the news analysts, the careful studies of social movements, of anthropology and of psychology do not express it all, and cannot. For the living reality lies multiform, in each billionfold consciousness.

Each one views the world from hirs own center, and meets the needs and challenges that come within the sphere of hirs effective realm. There is no way to bridge the gap of separateness, to stand completely in another's shoes and see the scenes and feel the feelings that s/he sees and feels. The searching mind, the compassionate spirit can reach across and share a part, but when it comes to bedrock each one sees from hirs own eyes and lives within a world that is both less and more than what a scientist could read.

The young rejoice. They laugh and play. Even in wartime. Even in the camps of the refugees. Even dirty on the streets. But despair can reach even to the young. Hunger cuts the roots for growth, can snuff out life before it's fairly started.

In the fortunate sections of the world, where social structures provide a place for most people to find their niche, the young can keep their joy, at least in part. There they can let it grow into the fuller, calmer satisfactions of mature strengths turned to good accomplishments, of family growing strong and healthy with secure protection, of love and friendship given and received. Small villages living on the edge of need, where hard work by all — and no calamities — can give good chance that all will have enough, seem often to make a stronger network for their people than do the great cities where luxury is available and one can think of security "from the cradle to the grave." It is not, in any case, a matter of needing a high standard of living. What the young person does need is a place in the social fabric, a place to live, to use the growing muscles of hirs body and hirs mind in ways that satisfy. With hardy souls the satisfaction can be just the inner knowledge of a job well done, but most of us need recognition and approval from our fellows, or at least from one or two we trust.

The griefs of those who cannot find a place to live and work within some kind of social structure are desperate and many. We all have seen — at least on TV screens — the faces of the war-blasted refugees. It is not just the starvation and the lack of shelter. It is the uprootedness, the lack of any power, of any chance to use their own strengths and skills to steer their lives. We have seen or felt the anguish of our American unemployed, thrust suddenly into a vacuum in their living. And on our streets and in our mental institutions there are the many who never did find ways to tie their lives and needs into the patterns of the social give and take.

There's a burden of real woe within the world. Even the blessed and fortunate find suffering. Having a decent livelihood and a healthy, growing family does not at all rule out discouragements and betrayals, the feeling that one's life is tasteless, without meaning, the knowledge of failures in relationships one holds most dear, the recognition that those failures build upon each other, making tangled wounds that seem beyond the healing. We have not escaped the pains that earlier humankind noted:

> "Yet man is born unto trouble, as the sparks fly upward."
> "*Sunt lacrimae rerum.* (There are tears in things.)"
> "Fie on't! O fie! 'Tis an unweeded garden, that grows to
> seed; things rank and gross in nature possess it merely."

It has to be a form of inexperience or of blindness not to recognize evil and suffering in the world.

So, what's to do?

If one is caught oneself in the bitter grinding of poverty and injustice there's not much option. Stand and face it for survival, singly or in welcome groups of fellows who try to hold together for some mutual aid, if only just from day to day, or hoping for some real improvement later on. There have been many human spirits grown to greatness this way, even if only in patient acceptance that refuses to grow bitter. But there are many, too, who break under the pounding, and go to suicide or drink or drugs or beating on their wives. It is not easy being at the bottom of the heap.

Or again there's not much choice if one is trapped in the tyranny of sickness and other forms of disability. The old and sick, the crippled and disabled — whether born that way or pounded into it later, whether physically or mentally afflicted — are usually not able to do anything more than meet the needs of each day as it comes.

So is it also for those people, fortunate or otherwise, who are caught in the immediate cataclysms of personal disaster — the sudden death or deadly illness, the tearing apart of a family or relationship that had seemed stable, the breakdown of the psyche. One does the best one can, calls on all resources available, survives from day to day and gets through some way. Maybe one is finally strengthened by new understandings and reasons for gratitude; maybe one is embittered and made fearful, trying to forget the catastrophe, to wall it off and act as though it had not been. Again there's possibility for growth or break-down — or part of each — for the one who lives it through. (Just as an aside, have you ever noticed the reaction of someone who is told "but then, *you've* never suffered!"? There is an immediate defense, an affirmation that one has indeed been through the fire. I think we all recognize that personal suffering is part of life, that life cannot be considered complete without it.)

But what about the people standing at least somewhat apart from the cesspools of social oppression or the private "slings and arrows of outrageous fortune"? What about those people who have some energy and resources beyond their own immediate needs? Is every person's suffering in truth partly our own? Are we bound together by such kinships of spirit and by such interdependence in economics and in politics that we have to feel responsibility for the whole?

I suspect that in practice the commonest response is to ignore whatever unpleasant things lie outside one's own daily round. So long as there are no next-door neighbors, no co-workers, no acquaintances, no relatives who go hungry (not from dieting but from lack of food), the fact of hunger in the world isn't real. There are, of course, degrees of willful blind-ness. With all the coverage on TV and the newspapers it's hard to decide consciously that the reporters are making it all up and to claim there is no hunger out there. But it's easy enough to leave the fact as a painless statistic at the back of the mind, without real substance. If the narrowly focused person watches a spirited documentary long enough for the fact of hunger to become real, it's not that hard for hirm to come to the conclusion s/he should send in a check. Or to give a worldly-wise growl that s/he knows non-profit agencies work on people's pity, and consequently s/he is justified in using most of hirs money for hirmself. Either way it's only a brief crack in the wall of protective ignorance.

Is there anything so much wrong with this way of confining one's sense of reality to the immediate area of daily survival? It may make for an easy conscience, and the freedom to ply oneself and one's nearest and dearest with luxurious goodies. What's the harm?

Well, there is that problem of interrelatedness. Festering sores in a society have a way of spreading out of their segregated plague areas or exploding into violence that can engulf even affluent neighborhoods (though it's usually the same poor, downtrodden victims who get the worst of that punishment, too.) An outbreak of polio may strike your children as well as the ones down the street a way. The ills in one part of society do affect the total society, so it may be seen as enlightened self-interest to work for correcting at least the worst of them.

Now that we are faced with the destructive power of nuclear weapons, there is in fact a new dimension. The interrelatedness of all human beings, of all justice and injustice, of all balance and imbalance, has become apparent. It is not just the deployment of those weapons that must be stopped, but all the aggressive bitterness in our world — the deprivations, the desperate hatreds, the selfish power, the oppressions and injustices. They do concern us all. They may make the difference between life and death, not just individually, but for our whole race of humankind.

It may be hard to see what any one person can do to stop the political march toward the use of nuclear weapons. We must believe that group demonstrations and initiatives have some impact, and adding one more body to those is at least not meaningless. And we should be able to see that the threat of nuclear holocaust does not come just as a separate thing of nuclear warheads stored in readiness. Those nuclear warheads are the peak of the whole climate of distrust, fear, hatred and the grasping for selfish power. Until we can find ways to mitigate that climate, to develop channels of real communication and mutual understanding, we are simply putting off the evil day by some small segment of time.

In simple truth, every person's survival depends on every person's efforts to generate as much good will and compassionate justice as s/he possibly can, both near at home and as far away as s/he has any vision and influence. The person who refuses to look beyond hirs own immediate round of daily activities is coasting as dead weight on a task that means life or death for us all.

Looking at it, too, from a matter of unavoidable personal results, an inescapable harm in the narrow view of life is just that it *is* narrow. The human spirit who confines hirmself to it remains narrow, too. S/he shuts hirmself off from the sharing of other people's experiences, which could make life vastly richer and more varied. S/he remains small and blind when s/he could be growing into generosity of spirit.

The ugliest and most mean-spirited of ways to ignore the suffering of others is to look for ways to explain the suffering as being a result of the victim's incompetence, laziness, or actual wrongdoing. With this kind of defense in hand, the stingy spirit can afford to study the suffering in full detail — and may even offer some grudging help — but s/he has successfully muffled the call to personal responsibility.

There is a form of non-involvement that's hard to fault. There are good, moderate, sane, responsible people who accept thoroughly and with compassion the reality of human suffering but who take a careful measurement of its enormity and decide quite consciously to use their own energies in a balanced blend of limited commitment to others along with the enrichment and enjoyment of their own personal domains. As I say, it's hard to fault that style. There have been many gracious and productive lives built on it. And sometimes there may have been more solid improvements made in other people's living conditions, or in advancements toward nuclear sanity, than what has been achieved by totally committed, passionate crusaders. I myself think that they may be missing out on experiences of special glory, of the most abundant living, but I'm not going to pretend that I know that.

All right, we've now considered several ways of responding to human suffering which leave the responder not totally committed to facing suffering that is not hirs very own. But let's go a higher step, rise above the limitations of self-protection and indolence and ask ourselves the question once again: "What are we to do about the weight of suffering in this world of ours? What are we really to *do* about it?" Forget whatever becomes of us as the doers and look directly at what it is that needs to be done. Still a tough question, isn't it?

It's kind of axiomatic when a group gets talking about wide-scale world problems for someone to say that all our problems would be solved if we could just learn to love one another. It's really not true. At least not automatically or at a single step. Honestly loving each other would simply put us at a place where we could begin to untangle all the mess of evil confusion we have around us. It would simply free our energies from the distrust and self-interest that clog our efforts at solutions.

Quite possibly if we look with absolute clarity and compassion, without any protective blinders, at the suffering in the world we must first suggest that we simply sit and weep. But this cannot last for long. We have 365 days in each of our years, and bodies and minds built for action. It is better to be doing something. And there is no doubt that some improvements can be made.

Human beings *have* made life better for most of us over the years. It is no small thing to have escaped from the fears and sudden death that most wild animals live with. We have large areas in our lives of relative security. We have systems of law that do, in the main, provide steady guidelines for behavior that all must follow, strong as well as weak. The working of that law is often corrupt and less than just, but it is there: the intent is stated, and it can be used to provide protection against the abuses of power. Brutal atrocities are still being committed against individuals and groups, but at least there is a place to bring them to the light, at least there is a common agreement that these things shall not be done, even when an aggressor has the power to do them.

Many diseases and disabilities have been reduced and

brought under control. Our life expectancies are now greatly extended. Childbirth has been made safer, and the lives of children protected, at least partially. Most backbreaking toil that kept men and women tied to drudgery has been replaced with easier work for shorter hours. Means of communication among us have been increased, and vastly extended education has opened that communication to great masses of people. We have not made the best uses of it — how banal and manipulative our media can be! — but it is there and it can be used for good.

And oh, the arts and music! Through the years great beauty seen and recorded for all to share and enjoy. Perceptions that make meaning of our common experiences, even if those perceptions are sad, can bring us strength and hope that may outweigh even the grimmest of the sufferings we face.

Throughout the years, too, human beings have found ways to come together for the comforts and the insights of religion. Again, the best expression of our relations with the transcendent has often been thwarted, turned into narrow, selfish channels, used on the side of bigotry and greed. But the good remains, and can be discovered and made new again by the humble, seeking spirit. We have a rich heritage and great gifts from the long history of humankind.

There are still problems that lend themselves to the direct straight-line approach. There are people still who toil in life-destroying ways, who face injustice from the powerful. The law is thwarted and side-stepped by new and subtle strategies. Sickness and crippling disabilities are not yet overcome. Opening school doors to all has shown us that there is more to education than sitting in a classroom through the years; we have to find new ways to help young minds grow. The symbols and the language of religion need to be attuned again to speak the central word in our own changing times. For each of these things, taken singly, we can see one or another way to attack the problem. We can hope to make some real improvement if we work with competence and learn the ropes of that particular section of our world, and are prepared for long endurance and the sufferings of setbacks and disappointments. Each of these struggles is worth doing and worth doing well, and merits words of praise and inner satisfaction for the ones who do them.

But there has come about a strange reversal of our progress.

The very things that seemed to lead to better living have brought us to new and terrifying dangers. Our increasingly powerful technology has brought us to the threat of nuclear holocaust and to the poisoning of our air, water and soil. The long, hard work which brought working men and women out from drudgery has often left them prey to selfishness and greed, to dissipation of their leisure time, to craving for gaudy things that have no solid worth, to whines of discontent and mutual distrust. Too often our young people seem to count on easy living as their right, to turn away from any work that is long and tedious, to pamper themselves with distractions and with self-gratification close at hand.

It seems as though the thrust of our western technology has passed beyond the place where it was really serving human needs and has run against a dead end of excess, making a whirlpool of contrary forces and meaningless confusions. I think it is the young who have most desperately felt the punishment of this eddying turmoil. Especially the students of the '60s, with no major work at hand except the studying of the scene, cried out against the material excesses and the catastrophes looming from our blind misuse of natural resources and of our economic and political power. A continuing core of activists of many ages look hard at the capitalist system that dominates the inner workings of the advanced western countries and (from outside) the development and even the survival of the third world countries.

They scrutinize its emphasis on private profit and its idea that encouraging the self-interest of the few can create a productive economy that benefits the many. They see that multinational corporations, wielding economic power greater than many national governments, can control the most fertile lands of an undeveloped country and use them for high-profit crops which fatten the luxury of the already fat and leave the poor with only marginal land for growing food. They see how economic control flows almost inevitably into political control, and how seldom self-interest is really enlightened with concern for others. They see how efforts at reform are distorted by the patterns of political/economic power so that benefits intended for the poor are siphoned off to swell the profits and the prestige of people higher up. I think they're right to feel we need a change from our current style of capitalism, and that it is not possible to effect that change without running into serious conflict with the current powers that be.

Most activists that I have known are not taken in by the claims of totalitarian communism. They've developed hard-headed ways to look at politics and to see what's really being done. They aren't much taken in by rhetoric alone, no matter where it comes from. I think they're sound realists, most of them, trying to develop other ways than capitalism to deal with our needs and problems, here on our own soil and from our own best heritage. I think the work they're doing is vitally important or even essential to our survival.

But as I see things, there is a dimension to human life that extends beyond their worldwide view of the economic-political scene. It may ultimately mean that even a more just and compassionate system will not serve to bring us into the kind of human life that we long for. The symptoms of this inadequacy lie in areas like that of the people freed from drudgery who find their leisure time burdensome or even debilitating. Or again in incidents when oppressed groups only recently set free have turned their newfound strength to bullying other groups smaller than themselves. Helping people gain their own security and plenty of food, shelter and the other necessities does not necessarily make them stronger, more generous people. Often, in fact, it seems almost to work the other way. The children and grandchildren of dust bowl farmers have too often picked up the ease and luxury of a new life without developing its opportuni-ties, and in the process they almost invariably lose the tough survival strength of their parents. There is something more involved here than the need to free people from special oppres-sive circumstances or even from an oppressive worldwide system.

Some years ago I had the great good fortune to attend a session of a seminar being taught by Howard Thurman, a man of deep insights, a warm and generous pastor and teacher who taught at Howard University for years. His subject was "The Mystic Experience and Social Activism." Dr. Thurman was then in his seventies, with his teaching style so mellowed that he led us through concentrated and profound ideas as easily as though we had been strolling with him through pleasant meadows. The gist of what he had to say that day — as nearly as I can bring it back on paper — was this:

When we experience direct personal contact with God (the mystic experience) we find ourselves "totally dealt with", no inmost part unrecognized, all the defenses we had built to face the world utterly washed away. We find ourselves altogether naked and vulnerable, open and exposed. But at the same time we are absolutely safe, totally secure, "at home" with one who knows us through and through.

The beauty and deep satisfactions of this encounter can be used as a model for how we would like our relationships to other human beings to become. If we can clear our perceptions of any impact from the role this person plays, from whatever status and whatever power or lack of it s/he wields, if we can go, in fact, beyond all virtues and all faults, we can perhaps enter into the central being of that person. In doing that we offer hirm a confirmation of hirs being within ourselves, and at the same time find a confirmation of our own identity in hirs response.

Relationships at this level offer both participants great wealth and strengthening even in themselves, but also offer the opportunity for supportive work together which is undergirded with full trust and lack of fear, so that full energies can be turned outside against a problem instead of being held back for self-protection.

Our society makes it very difficult to experience this kind of trust. Not only is our time so invaded by outside stimuli and demands that there is little of the time alone which can make possible the experiencing of our own unadorned selves in the security of God, but when we wish to turn this unconditional trust toward our fellow human beings, we find the way beset by fears and competitions, and by oppressive systems that enforce those fears and make competitiveness and the need for self-protection almost necessary for survival.

Dr. Thurman pointed out the extent to which the agents and agencies of injustice have become faceless to us. We no longer see them as being composed of living

human beings, but as realities and powers of their own —
utterly faceless and without human characteristics. He
urged us always to look for the human face behind the
agency action, and on the other side to try to make
ourselves be seen even by the "faceless" agency as living
human beings in our own right. He said that his struggles
of social activism have been aimed not really at improving
conditions in the world just to make them better in and of
themselves, but so that improved conditions might make
possible a climate where trust between fellow human
beings becomes natural.

Here is a view of things that brought seemingly disparate
pieces of my own experience and perceptions into a meaningful
whole. I had never been particularly clear in my mind as to how
— and whether — my need to remain conscious of God was
related to my need to try to improve things in the world. As I
explained in the fourth section of this book, "On Roads Toward
Social Justice," I had become involved in our local poverty area
as an outgrowth of showing my children that the individual
could do something about what seemed wrong in the world
about hirm. Once I was in it, the work was so satisfying that it
simply made sense to stay with it.

With Howard Thurman's perspective, I had a rationale for
how the two things fit together. Besides that, I could understand
more rationally now why I often felt that some kinds of
manipulative strategies used by progressive movements — even
when they did achieve particular goals — were actually counter-
productive for the kinds of change I was aiming toward. With
Dr. Thurman's definition of the ultimate goal as being a climate
for mutual human trust, it became easier to sort out techniques
that were really on target and to select for priority effort those
areas of injustice that most clearly distorted the human spirit.

Well, so much for my personal gains from hearing Howard
Thurman. To bring it back to a more general view of our forest
through the trees, and to the question of what to do about evil
in the world, I think it does add greatly to the effectiveness of
work to improve living conditions if we expand our vision to an

ultimate goal of a climate where trust between human beings is natural. That should keep us aware of the dimensions of the human spirit within the problems of material needs and injustice. It should keep our attention focused on what is actually happening inside our neighbors' heads and hearts rather than simply on how well clothed, housed and fed they can become.

Part of this idea — perhaps even the central part — is easily acceptable by humanists who find no reality in the transcendent. The basic need for trust, for some form of community has been proposed in many forms and from many directions. It's a sound and sensible idea even at the level of earthly good will and sweet reasonableness. Why then do we need the model of a personal relationship to God to love our fellow human beings?

I think the experience of God provides us with a kind of plumb line, an indication of where the true center lies, a way of feeling where we are in relation to *all* the other living beings who center in God also. It is so easy for our human love to be guided by our own personal needs and desires, by our biases and predispositions. A love for one can so easily shut out others. Our love for a victim may easily lead us to fierce hatred for the one who victimized hirm. The closeness of our own loving group may urge us to shut out all "aliens" who could disturb our harmony. When we build without a plumb line, judging the proper position of each new board by what's already there in place, by how that board relates just to the ones closest to it, we are likely to end up with a building all askew.

It is so easy, too, unless we have been stripped ourselves to the essential core of who we are, and have some way to glimpse the inner core of who another is, to be always dealing with false paste-ups on the outer surface. We may find ourselves "performing" to another. The other may be showing us only what s/he thinks we wish to see. We find ourselves on shifting sands. There may be other ways to reach the kind of integrity that's needed, but I know at least that this one way, this keeping touch with God, does do the job.

I feel I need to say something here about the nature of this "divine plumb line." It has to be a freely moving thing that relates always to a vital center. If the experience of God has become rigid in a stated dogma or a code of ethics which is tied down in words to be analyzed, it cannot serve the purpose that I'm speaking of. If it's been nailed down firmly at both ends, it has become part of the rigid structure, as subject to misalignment as any other 2 × 4. That's the problem for too many folks in organized churches. If they've come to tie their faith to rigid forms instead of to a first-hand experience of the living God, they've lost the real life of their religion. It's only as one keeps the contact ever new, returns again and again at each new time and place to·realign one's being with the vital center, that one can claim eventually to own a true tool for integrity.

Maybe I've made a decent case for the idea that having a consciousness of God provides one with a very useful tool for dealing with the pitfalls of loving our fellow human beings. However, any such gain is certainly offset in a utilitarian sense by the higher standards one must accept for what constitutes true love for one's fellows.

In the Sermon on the Mount, Jesus taught a love for enemies as well as friends, noting that if we are to model ourselves on God we must follow hirs example of sending the sun and the rain on the good and the bad alike. In the New English Bible translation, the difficult passage "Be ye therefore perfect" becomes a more meaningful teaching: "There must be no limit to your goodness, as your heavenly Father's goodness knows no bounds."

The idea of sin is no longer much understood outside the walls our secular age has put up around the thought systems of religion. I suspect this may be perfectly natural and right. It is really only when one recognizes God — some transcendent glory other than oneself — that sin becomes real. One can be muddling along "perfectly okay", knowing that human folk are fallible and full of flaws but feeling all right with doing one's best and trying not to hurt others, and there is no sense of sin in one's inadequacies.

It is only when a shaft of divine light falls into one's life — glorious, a new dimension, beyond all one's own capacities — that suddenly one sees how mean, ugly and tattered are the things encrusted around oneself, possibly even the essence of oneself. The recognition of sin doesn't have anything to do with comparisons with one's neighbors, with how much damage one

> ## A SPECIAL KIND OF LOVE
>
> *It is a special kind of love,*
> *the love that tries to be like God's for us.*
> *There is no stopping for right cause,*
> *to see if th'other is worthy of our love.*
> *There is no pulling back for ugliness and sin.*
> *There are no bargains made,*
> *   no conditions set.*
> *The heart is open and is given,*
> *reached out to touch*
> *   the inner being of the other.*
> *And being given is not withdrawn again,*
> *even for danger to oneself,*
> *even for need to take upon oneself*
> *   the burden of another's sin.*

does by evil deeds or with estimations of how much could really be expected of a limited creature like oneself. It is instead the contrast between the infinite glory of God and one's own darkness and disharmony. "What a wretched state I am in!" cried Isaiah* when he found himself in the presence of Yahweh. And so do we today who are given the sight of the Lord.

Our past meannesses, the ugly, stingy ways we have behaved, can now be seen as sin, but the really deadly sins lie ahead of us. It is when we rebel consciously, when we know we are behaving in ways out of tune with the truly best light we have, that we feel the full reality of sin.

Is sin really there all the time, even for people who have not sensed God? I do not know. I am sure it is not in my province to call anyone else's deed a sin without their say-so. And I doubt if anyone who does a discordant deed without the knowledge that it is discordant sins in the same sense as one who knowingly strikes a rebellious note. I know sin's real for

---

*Isaiah 6:5 (Jerusalem Bible)

me, within myself. There were those eight years of my life when I said "No" to God each day. I know the shriveling of the soul, the guilt, the well-earned enmity against the self. It was no illusion. It was no puritanical training from outside myself that shackled an otherwise free soul. And it was my greatest honesty and clearest sight that knew I sinned.

I do think that individual sin is real and that it brings along with it immediate grief, regardless of what happens in the world, but it may well be a thing that each person has to know hirmself before it's really sin. The multitude of sins burdening the souls of those who know them can probably account for much of grief, but I think it leaves untouched the great expanse of amoral selfishness and cruelty and the seemingly inhuman disasters in the world.

I think there is a kind of corporate sin. When our U.S. government dropped the atomic bomb on Hiroshima — and maybe even more so, the second one on Nagasaki — we all took part in an evil that we knew was evil. It does not matter that we were not asked. We profited from the end of the war; we profit every day from our country's security and wealth. In the same kind of way we cannot shed the guilt from the betrayal of the Native American peoples, from the oppression of the black slaves. Even from guilt for the sorry state of things revealed at Watergate, we cannot really claim exemption.

As we are born into our culture and share in its way of life, we pick up not only the good, strong heritage of people and of movements that did go right, but must accept upon our own shoulders, too, the cruelties, the treacheries, the mean deceits that went before. We are part of the whole body, willy-nilly, and will deal more honestly with fierce consequences if we can accept our own share of complicity in the ugly deeds that moved us toward our current disasters.

I have thought, from time to time, that this type of corporate sin could be equated with original sin. I still think it adds a helpful dimension to it, but I now think that that time-honored doctrine of the church has something even larger to say, and it is a thing with which I am not altogether comfortable.

I really have no trouble in my mind disposing of the notion that it was Man's sin that turned a trouble-free earth into the place of conflicts and perilous living that it is today. The patterns of the natural world are as they are, and it leads to all kinds of mental folly to set up a picture of Adam and Eve in the garden being the cause of death and of changing lions from peaceful, grazing animals into the predators they are. Even St. Thomas Aquinas felt free to say that it was not a sign of good sense to believe that wild beasts were at one time tame. Judging by *A New Catechism*, by the bishops of the Netherlands, the Roman Catholic Church is now perfectly capable of doing without a precisely delineated historical dogma on the fall of man, and I'm sure the validity of the central Christian message would shine forth much more brightly without any such unnecessary baggage.

The central part of the original sin idea, though, is not disposed of when we clear away the excesses of a literal reading of the Garden of Eden story. It does seem all too easy for us human beings to fall into narrow, selfish ways, to strike meanly into a potential competitor when we can, to snatch for ourselves the good things of the earth which should be shared. Our failings are so universal, we so much take for granted the being "only human" that it is a natural deduction to think that there is something intrinsic in the human spirit which leads away from good, and toward all forms of wickedness.

As I said, I do not feel quite comfortable with this. The times I have felt most fully myself, when I should have known best what was truly intrinsic to my being, were those times in the presence of God when I was able to be fully tuned to hirs glory and light. In Hirm there is no darkness. In me there was no darkness either, at those times; there seemed to be nothing from my essential being which was not included in the entry into light. Also, in the innocence of small children — and often, too, of humble older people — I have trouble seeing the ugliness of sin.

Actually, my preference is for a notion that there is a kind of automatic alienation from God that occurs when the creature becomes a living thing apart and distinct from the Creator. The IS cannot know Itself by Itself as a single whole. It generates, and generates again, infinite varieties of creatures which have their own inner seeds of growth and motion. With conscious Man, more able to know and reflect the IS than are other forms of life, there comes along with separateness a free will that cannot be altogether a part of the movements of God, and so Man in hirs mortal life finds hirmself always at some remove from the God who is nonetheless the source of hirs being.

For all practical purposes, though, whether it is that we are born into sin or that we pick it up along the way is probably a moot question. We acquire so much horrid baggage with our own selfishness and corporate guilt that by the time we've grown to maturity we all have a great tangle of falsity and complicity in evil around us and in us. George Bernard Shaw remarked "Every man of forty is a scoundrel." I trust he was including women, too, and I think he really gave us more time than most of us need.

Is the recognition of pervasive sin a kind of knowledge with which we can rest easy — "Ah, so that's the way it is. That explains why we have so much difficulty."? In a word, no. Sin is never simply a fact. It is a jangle, a discord, something against the grain that has to be put right. It is only death — bodily or spiritual — which can make one ready to rest easy with sin.

With one's private sins the approach is fairly straightforward. Entry there where the light shines, where God lives, is all that's needed. Hirs grace and glory wipe sin away as the rising sun disperses night. The difficulty lies in preparing oneself so one *can* enter. That's where honest repentance is required and the willingness to relinquish whatever one was trying to gain through the sinful act or thought. One bends the knee and weeps the honest tears of sorrow for the evil done. It may be one will have to make whatever reparations can be made before one even tries to enter there where peace and cleansing reign. It may be God will take you in as soon as knowledge starts in your heart that you will in fact stretch yourself to the fullest to repair the damage done.

You cannot clutch against your breast even one small shred of the false self-glory you tried to drape around yourself. There is no concealment. There is no carrying with you any falseness or any camouflage.

But once your spirit is prepared with humble openness to God and recognition of your sin as sin, the whole way is opened up to you to enter again into wholeness and harmony. "As far as the east is from the west, so far hath he removed our transgressions from us."* Sin is cleared away entirely; it is not there any more. You may have to face whatever ugly gashes you perpetrated in the living world around you. You may have to strive mightily and for a long time to try to transform the damage you have done into something less harmful, but the woeful burden of guilt is lifted from your spirit. The circumstances are not altered — effect will follow cause regardless — but you yourself can enter in renewed, made whole again. Surely forgiveness is a magnificent blessing!

But there are real difficulties when the sin is corporate, or when it is another's. What wonders might have shown forth if the American public, acting as a whole, had been willing to recognize the wrongs committed in Vietnam, had analyzed and studied them, not shifting blame, and then had repented in some kind of modern equivalent of the old Jewish sackcloth and ashes! Well, there were a few calls for something of the sort, and many individuals must have felt our guilt, but it surely did not happen and the thing lies heavy on us all.

Usually there seems to be no way to repent a sin that belongs to a whole group of people and from which one draws the advantages accruing to that group. I suspect that even the Amish with their attempts at isolation cannot really free themselves from a share of corporate American guilt.

Certainly there is no way for one person to repent for the private sin of another human being. One can urge hirm to do hirs own repenting, but if s/he sees no need, one cannot do it for hirm.

When Jesus came into the world he entered upon a course of love that made him a participant in the total beings of many, many individuals. He did not turn aside from them; he did not fend them off. He accepted them altogether, part and parcel. With his amazing love he saw beyond their darkness to their humble hopes, their anguished reaching toward the light, and gathered them into his own spirit.**

But along with their goodness — the strange innocence of those suffering guilty ones whose guilt has been rather forced on

---

*Psalm 103:12

**John 14:20 "... and you in me and I in you."

them by the sickness of the world than by any original malice of their own — he had to take within himself also all their flaws and ugliness and sin. With this burden lying not just "on" him but truly within him, he moved with unyielding integrity against the evils and corruption of his contemporary world. It seems almost by his own will that he orchestrated (or let others orchestrate) a grand confluence of the evils that surrounded him into one great meeting with himself.

On the cross, offering himself and the totality of all the troubled beings whom he loved, he carried the whole awesome reality of his world into the very core of God, transforming it by his agony into such a thing that it could be incorporated entirely into the glory of God, in whom there is no darkness. There is a triumph here which makes the resurrection almost anticlimactic. Or rather, when the crucifixion is understood in this way, the crucifixion/resurrection is seen as being a single movement.

I do not at all pretend to understand the mystery of how this transformation can take place — the vile ugliness of accumulated sin made able to enter into the perfect light and beauty of God — but for me it is the essence of the Christian faith that it does in fact take place. The cross is the way. As far as I can see, it is the *only* way that pervasive sin can be brought into harmony with God, into the essential order of the universe. I do not really think that the crucifixion was a deed done once for all time that ransomed all of us forever from the power of sin.

I think it is a transformation that has to be achieved again and again, in every time and place. We do in fact have to pick up our own crosses and follow Christ. And surely those crosses are something more than just the burdens that life puts on us anyway. They demand from us the same kinds of sacrifice and love that Jesus showed. Just how much he can help us carry the burdens, and how much we cannot avoid shouldering ourselves I do not know. But he is there and he does help, and he will not desert us. Beyond that I know nothing more.

Miriam Hope

ABOUT THE AUTHOR

Born Miriam Hope Collier September 6, 1918 in Salem, Oregon. Mother Ruth Graybill Collier. Father Percy Meredith Collier.

Grew up in Portland, Oregon, with sister Jane Collier Anderson, two years older, and brother Robert Percy Collier, two years younger. Attended Ockley Green Grade School, Jefferson High School and Reed College (B.A. degree 1939).

Suffered psychotic breakdown in San Francisco, spring 1942.

Spent two summers, 1943 and 1944, as lookout for U.S. Forest Service on Coldwater Peak, Spirit Lake Ranger District, State of Washington.

Married Champion N. Nixon May 1945 in San Francisco.
Gave birth to and reared three children:
Glen Forrest Nixon, born July 1946 in San Francisco. (Now married to Sally Cooperrider Nixon, with two children: Shawna Rose Nixon, almost 12 years old and Laura Janelle Nixon, 9 years old)
Ruth Lisbeth Nixon, born January 1949 in San Francisco. (Now Mrs. Greg Powers).
Meredith Ann Nixon, born March 1953 in Palo Alto, California. (Now Mrs. James Tatch, with three children: Jasmine Hope Tatch, 13 years old, Charles Alexander Tatch, 10 years old and Andrew James Tatch, 7 years old).

(continued)

Divorced C.N. Nixon in February 1955.

Worked for Spinco Division, Beckman Instruments, Palo Alto, CA from 1957 to 1968.

Worked for San Mateo County Public Health and Welfare Department in East Palo Alto, CA from 1968 to 1970.

Founded and worked with Ecumenical Hunger Program in Palo Alto, CA from 1975 to 1979.

Married Bernabe Cintas, 1979, in San Jose, CA.

Divorced B. Cintas in 1981.

Had name changed legally to Miriam Hope, 1981.

Moved to Valdosta, GA in 1981.

Currently lives with Meredith and Jim Tatch and their three children in Lake Park, GA.